Markus Nehl
Transnational Black Dialogues

Postcolonial Studies | Volume 28

For my parents

Markus Nehl received his PhD from the Graduate School »Practices of Literature« at the University of Münster. His research interests include African American, Black Diaspora and Postcolonial Studies.

Markus Nehl
Transnational Black Dialogues
Re-Imagining Slavery in the Twenty-First Century

D6

Bibliographic information published by the Deutsche Nationalbibliothek
The Deutsche Nationalbibliothek lists this publication in the Deutsche Nationalbibliografie; detailed bibliographic data are available in the Internet at http://dnb.d-nb.de

© 2016 transcript Verlag, Bielefeld

All rights reserved. No part of this book may be reprinted or reproduced or utilized in any form or by any electronic, mechanical, or other means, now known or hereafter invented, including photocopying and recording, or in any information storage or retrieval system, without permission in writing from the publisher.

Cover layout: Kordula Röckenhaus, Bielefeld
Typeset by Francisco Braganca
Printed in Germany
Print-ISBN 978-3-8376-3666-6
PDF-ISBN 978-3-8394-3666-0

Contents

Acknowledgements | 7

Introduction: Slavery—An "Unmentionable" Past? | 9

1 The Concept of the African Diaspora
   and the Notion of Difference | 39

2 From Human Bondage to Racial Slavery:
   Toni Morrison's *A Mercy* (2008) | 55

3 Rethinking the African Diaspora:
   Saidiya Hartman's *Lose Your Mother* (2007) | 79

4 "Hertseer:" Re-Imagining Cape Slavery in
   Yvette Christiansë's *Unconfessed* (2006) | 109

5 Transnational Diasporic Journeys in
   Lawrence Hill's *The Book of Negroes* (2007) | 135

6 A Vicious Circle of Violence: Revisiting
   Jamaican Slavery in Marlon James's *The Book
   of Night Women* (2009) | 161

Epilogue: The Past of Slavery and
"the Incomplete Project of Freedom" | 191

Works Cited | 197

Acknowledgements

With a focus on twenty-first-century literary negotiations of slavery, this transnational study is a slightly revised and updated version of my PhD thesis submitted to the Faculty of Philology at the Westfälische Wilhelms-Universität (WWU) in Münster in October 2015. No book—and certainly no doctoral dissertation—can be written without the help, advice and encouragement of others. First and foremost, I am deeply indebted to my "Doktormutter" and mentor, Professor Maria I. Diedrich (WWU Münster), who has strongly supported my project from the beginning through all of its various stages. Without her invaluable input, inspiring guidance and constructive feedback, this monograph would surely not exist. I also wish to thank Professor Mark Stein (WWU Münster) and Professor Demetrius L. Eudell (Wesleyan University, Connecticut, USA), who both served on my dissertation committee, for their thoughtful comments and suggestions.

My work on this book would not have been possible without the academic and financial support I received from many individuals and institutions: I am especially grateful to the Cusanuswerk for granting me a PhD scholarship that allowed me to complete this project in a relatively short time. Many thanks go also to the Graduate School "Practices of Literature" (GS PoL) in Münster, for providing a platform for interdisciplinary exchange and cooperation; to the Collegium for African American Research (CAAR), for giving me the opportunity to present my work-in-progress to international experts at workshops and conferences in Nantes, Atlanta and Liverpool; and to the German Academic Exchange Service (DAAD), for providing a travel grant that enabled me to attend the 2013 CAAR conference at Agnes Scott College. I also want to express my gratitude to the members of the American Studies Colloquium in Münster for their critical feedback on several chapters of the manuscript.

Last, but certainly not least, I owe more than I can express in words to my family and friends. Special thanks to my sister Christina Michels and her family, who provided me with a home in Zurich whenever I needed a break from reading and writing. I gratefully dedicate this book to my parents Anne and Hans-Peter Nehl, whose love, confidence, encouragement and unwavering emotional and intellectual support made this book possible.

Münster, April 2016, Markus Nehl

Introduction:
Slavery—An "Unmentionable" Past?

In his critically acclaimed debut novel *Open City* (2011), mainly set in New York City a few years after the terrorist attacks of 2001, Teju Cole unfolds the story of Julius, a Nigerian American psychiatric fellow at Columbia Presbyterian who spends his leisure time wandering aimlessly through the streets of Manhattan. Deconstructing prevailing notions of white American moral superiority and righteousness that especially flourished in the aftermath of 9/11, Cole employs the figure of the black intellectual urban *flâneur* to explore New York's history and legacy of slavery, colonialism and racism, focusing particularly on the mass murder of Native Americans in the seventeenth century and the systematic oppression and exploitation of blacks during and after the period of the transatlantic slave trade. Drawing attention to the devastating impact of historical racial injustices and violence on the present, Cole's novel offers an intricate view of the city as a palimpsest, a place haunted by the hidden traces of past atrocities and collective traumatic experiences.

In a key scene near the novel's end, Cole describes how Julius accidentally discovers the African Burial Ground National Monument near City Hall. Via this episode, he foregrounds the centrality of slavery to New York's economic, cultural and social development and, equally important, highlights the ways in which this history has been erased from white American public memory: The African Burial Ground, where thousands of enslaved and free people of African descent, many of them children, were laid to rest in the course of the seventeenth and eighteenth centuries, is a significant archeological site in today's lower Manhattan. As the historian Leslie M. Harris explains, the cemetery was no longer used after 1790 and, then, "covered over by roads and buildings throughout the nineteenth and twentieth centuries."[1] It was largely forgotten until 1991, when, during construction of a new 34-story office building at

---

1 | Leslie M. Harris, *In the Shadow of Slavery: African Americans in New York City, 1626-1863* (Chicago: U of Chicago P, 2003) 1.

Broadway and Duane Street, workers uncovered several graves and the remains of human bodies. Archeological excavations at the site offered valuable insights into black life and burial customs in colonial New York, drawing attention to the ways in which blacks creatively combined African and European cultural traditions. Most crucially, the (re-)discovery of the African Burial Ground showed that, between 1626 and 1827, New York's economy relied heavily on large numbers of black slaves, who were exposed to utterly dehumanizing treatment and forced to carry out various tasks, such as field work, blacksmithing, carpentry and cooking.[2]

Cole's *Open City* contributes to reconstructing the forgotten story of New York City's early black community, particularly highlighting the cruelty and violence of slavery in the North: "At the Negro Burial Ground, as it was then known, and others like it on the eastern seaboard, excavated bodies bore traces of suffering: blunt trauma, grievous bodily harm. Many of the skeletons had broken bones, evidence of the suffering they'd endured in life."[3] Cole's novel powerfully challenges myths, stereotypical assumptions and self-legitimizing interpretations of the nation's past, in general, and New York's history, in particular: To this day, many whites deny or downplay the importance of slavery to the development of the country, justify the so-called "peculiar institution" as a benevolent system or ignore the history of black enslavement altogether. Others view slavery as an exclusively southern phenomenon, trying to absolve the North from any responsibility or guilt.[4] "The fact that slavery was practiced all over the early United States," Brent Staples points out in a 2005 editorial comment in the *New York Times*, "often comes as a shock to people in places like

---

[2] | Ibid.; see also E.R. Shipp, "Black Cemetery Yields Wealth of History," *New York Times* 9 Aug. 1992, 7 July 2015 http://www.nytimes.com/1992/08/09/nyregion/black-cemetery-yields-wealth-of-history.html; David W. Dunlap, "Dig Unearths Early Black Burial Ground," *New York Times* 9 Oct. 1991, 7 July 2015 http://www.nytimes.com/1991/10/09/nyregion/dig-unearths-early-black-burial-ground.html. For more information about the history of slavery in New York City, see Harris 1-71. For a discussion of the controversy surrounding the excavation of the site and the African Burial Ground project, see Cheryl J. La Roche and Michael L. Blakey, "Seizing Intellectual Power: The Dialogue at the New York African Burial Ground," *Historical Archaeology* 31.3 (1997): 84-106.

[3] | Teju Cole, *Open City* (London: Faber & Faber, 2011) 221.

[4] | James Oliver Horton, "Presenting Slavery: The Perils of Telling America's Racial Story," *The Public Historian* 21.4 (1999): 21; Duncan Faherty, "'It's Happened Here': Slavery on the Hudson," *American Quarterly* 58.2 (2006): 456; Brent Staples, "A Convenient Amnesia About Slavery," *New York Times* 15 Dec. 2005, 7 July 2015 http://www.nytimes.com/2005/12/15/opinion/a-convenient-amnesia-about-slavery.html.

New York, where the myth of the free North has been surprisingly durable."[5] In *Open City*, Cole not only addresses what Staples describes as New York's "cultural amnesia"[6] about its past but also emphasizes the significance of slavery as a fundamental structural element of American history, society and culture.

While "American slavery is one of the last great unmentionables in public discourse,"[7] as the historian Lonnie Bunch has recently put it, over the last decades, numerous black novelists, essayists, non-fiction writers, poets, artists, and film-makers from all over the world have begun to counter this erasure of slavery from collective (white) memory and to explore the history and nature of black enslavement inside and outside the United States in a variety of genres: Among these cultural products are critically praised, commercially successful and prizewinning novels like Toni Morrison's *Beloved* (1987) and *A Mercy* (2008), books of poetry like M. NourbeSe Philip's *Zong!* (2008), graphic novels like Kyle Baker's *Nat Turner* (2008), artistic works like Kara Walker's silhouette images, plays like August Wilson's *Gem of the Ocean* (2003), television miniseries like Lawrence Hill's and Clement Virgo's *The Book of Negroes* (2015) and movies like Steve McQueen's *12 Years a Slave* (2013). According to Bunch, a film like *12 Years a Slave*, which received three Academy Awards and has attracted millions of viewers, "might help America overcome its inability to understand the centrality of slavery and its continuing impact on our society."[8]

In recent academic discourse, scholars such as Saidiya Hartman, Frank B. Wilderson III, Jared Sexton and Michelle Alexander have offered complex theoretical, philosophical, historical and political explorations of the link between the history of slavery and contemporary forms of systematic racial oppression and discrimination in the United States and elsewhere. These black intellectuals, who have been described as Afro-pessimists, "do not form anything as ostentatious as a school of thought,"[9] as Wilderson emphasizes in his 2010 study *Red, White & Black: Cinema and the Structure of U.S. Antagonisms*. And yet, influenced by the works of Frantz Fanon and Orlando Patterson, they share important assumptions about the meaning of blackness and the devastating logic of anti-blackness in our contemporary societies: Powerfully countering

---

5 | Staples, "A Convenient Amnesia About Slavery."
6 | Ibid.
7 | Lonnie Bunch, "The Director of the African-American History and Culture Museum on What Makes '12 Years a Slave' a Powerful Film," *The Smithsonian.com* 5 Nov. 2013, 26 July 2015 http://www.smithsonianmag.com/ist/?next=/smithsonian-institution/the-director-of-the-african-american-history-and-culture-museum-on-what-makes-12-years-a-slave-a-powerful-film-180947568/.
8 | Ibid.
9 | Frank B. Wilderson III, *Red, White & Black: Cinema and the Structure of U.S. Antagonisms* (Durham: Duke UP, 2010) 58.

the (white) notion of a post-racial America, they shed light on the precariousness of black life in the past and present and examine the debilitating effects of systemic white supremacy.[10]

In her path-breaking 2007 protest narrative *Lose Your Mother: A Journey along the Atlantic Slave Route*, which will be closely analyzed in chapter 3 of this study, Saidiya Hartman uses the phrase "the afterlife of slavery"[11] to reflect on the lasting impact of the transatlantic slave trade and slavery on twenty-first-century black life, to deconstruct the naïve idea of history as progress and to focus on loss, dispossession and grief as defining features of the African diaspora:[12]

If slavery persists as an issue in the political life of black America, it is not because of an antiquarian obsession with bygone days or the burden of a too-long memory, but because black lives are still imperiled and devalued by a racial calculus and a political arithmetic that were entrenched centuries ago. This is the afterlife of slavery—skewed life chances, limited access to health and education, premature death, incarceration, and impoverishment.[13]

In a way similar to Hartman, legal scholar Michelle Alexander radically challenges the prevailing (white) "narrative that emphasizes the death of slavery and Jim Crow and celebrates the nation's 'triumph over race' with the election of Barack Obama."[14] In *The New Jim Crow: Mass Incarceration in the Age of Colorblindness* (2010), Alexander focuses on the systematic discrimination of blacks within the U.S. criminal justice system. In particular, she draws attention to the high incarceration rate of black (male) Americans and, closely connected,

---

10 | See, for instance, Saidiya Hartman, *Scenes of Subjection: Terror, Slavery, and Self-Making in Nineteenth-Century America* (Oxford: Oxford UP, 1997); Saidiya Hartman, *Lose Your Mother: A Journey along the Atlantic Slave Route* (New York: Farrar, Straus and Giroux, 2007); Wilderson, *Red, White & Black*; Saidiya V. Hartman and Frank B. Wilderson III, "The Position of the Unthought," *Qui Parle* 13.2 (2003): 183-201; Jared Sexton, "'The Curtain of the Sky': An Introduction," *Critical Sociology* 36.1 (2010): 11-24; Jared Sexton, "The Social Life of Social Death: On Afro-Pessimism and Black Optimism," *InTensions* 5 (2011): 1-47; Michelle Alexander, *The New Jim Crow: Mass Incarceration in the Age of Colorblindness*, rev. ed. (2010; New York: The New Press, 2012). For a critical discussion of Afro-pessimism, see Sebastian Weier, "Forum: Consider Afro-Pessimism," *Amerikastudien/American Studies* 59.3 (2014): 419-33.
11 | Hartman, *Lose Your Mother* 6.
12 | See also Saidiya Hartman, "The Time of Slavery," *South Atlantic Quarterly* 4 (2002): 758.
13 | Hartman, *Lose Your Mother* 6.
14 | Alexander 11.

the hypervisibility and stereotypical perception of black men as criminals in public and legal discourses. "Like Jim Crow," Alexander contends, "mass incarceration marginalizes large segments of the African American community, segregates them physically (in prisons, jails, and ghettos), and then authorizes discrimination against them in voting, employment, housing, education, public benefits, and jury service."[15]

Over the last years, numerous incidents of anti-black violence have brought to the public's attention the persistent legacy of black enslavement and abjection in the United States: In August 2014, for instance, Michael Brown, an eighteen-year-old unarmed black man was shot and killed by a white police officer in Ferguson, Missouri. This not only led to street protests and violent responses by heavily militarized police forces but also provoked public discussions about structural anti-black racism and white police brutality. The police officer was not indicted for Brown's death, which resulted in further violent demonstrations.[16] According to the philosopher Charles Mills, recent events like the shooting of Michael Brown show that "in the second decade of the 21st century, nearly 150 years after the end of the Civil War and with a black president in office—black citizens are still differentially vulnerable to police violence, thereby illustrating their (our) second-class citizenship."[17] Aiming to

---

15 | Ibid. 17.
16 | In recent years, there have been numerous other incidents of racial violence: In February 2012, for instance, seventeen-year-old Trayvon Martin was shot and killed by a white neighborhood watch coordinator, who was later acquitted of second-degree murder by a jury in Florida. In November 2014, Tamir Rice, a twelve-year-old African American teenager was shot and killed by a white police officer in Cleveland, Ohio. In June 2015, nine black Americans were murdered by a white supremacist in a church in South Carolina, Charleston. See Monica Davey and Julie Bosmannov, "Protests Flare After Ferguson Police Officer Is Not Indicted," *New York Times* 24 Nov. 2014, 26 July 2015 http://www.nytimes.com/2014/11/25/us/ferguson-darren-wilson-shooting-michael-brown-grand-jury.html; Wesley Lowery, "Trayvon Martin Was Shot and Killed Three Years Ago Today," *Washington Post* 26 Feb. 2015, 26 July 2015 http://www.washingtonpost.com/news/post-nation/wp/2015/02/26/trayvon-martin-was-shot-and-killed-three-years-ago-today/; Emma G. Fitzsimmons, "Video Shows Cleveland Officer Shot Boy in 2 Seconds," *New York Times* 26 Nov. 2015, 26 July 2015 http://www.nytimes.com/2014/11/27/us/video-shows-cleveland-officer-shot-tamir-rice-2-seconds-after-pulling-up-next-to-him.html; David Remnick, "Charleston and the Age of Obama," *New Yorker* 19 June 2015, 26 July 2015 http://www.newyorker.com/news/daily-comment/charleston-and-the-age-of-obama.
17 | George Yancy, "Lost in Rawlsland: Interview with Charles Mills," *New York Times* 16 Nov. 2014, 26 July 2015 http://opinionator.blogs.nytimes.com/2014/11/16/lost-in-rawlsland/.

draw attention to the long history of black oppression and the systematic devaluation of black life in the twenty-first century, in 2012, three black female activists created the movement #BlackLivesMatter, which, as the Jamaican poet and playwright Claudia Rankine contends, "can be read as an attempt to keep mourning an open dynamic in our culture because black lives exist in a state of precariousness."[18] "If the ghost of slavery still haunts our present," Saidiya Hartman writes in *Lose Your Mother*, "it is because we are still looking for an exit from the prison."[19]

CONTEMPORARY LITERARY NEGOTIATIONS OF SLAVERY AND THE AFRICAN DIASPORA

Situated in the fields and intersections of African American, black feminist, diaspora and postcolonial studies, this work focuses on a vibrant and heterogeneous group of black authors who approach the subject of slavery from twenty-first-century perspectives. Among them are African Americans, Africans, African Canadians and African Caribbeans; former journalists, emerging scholars and distinguished professors; promising young writers and international literary celebrities. Drawing particular attention to the specific experiences of enslaved women, one of their common goals is to explore aspects of black diasporic history that have been forgotten, deliberately suppressed, neglected or marginalized in mainstream popular discussions, in earlier literary texts, in historical studies as well as in theoretical approaches. Significantly, these twenty-first-century black writers are not only concerned with U.S.-American history but also with the past of the slave trade and slavery in places such as Ghana, South Africa, Canada and Jamaica. Taken together, their texts highlight the transnational dimension of the history of slavery and the African diaspora, while at the same time paying scrupulous attention to the specificity of local historical developments and contexts.

In the following part of this chapter, after introducing the texts that I have selected for this study, I argue for a vibrant conceptualization of the African diaspora that provides a useful framework for a critical analysis of twenty-first-century literary negotiations of slavery. Moreover, this chapter gives a short overview of the emergence of neo-slave narratives in the United States in the aftermath of the Civil Rights, Black Arts and Black Power movements,

---

18 | Claudia Rankine, "The Condition of Black Life Is One of Mourning," *New York Times Magazine* 22 June 2015, 26 July 2015 http://www.nytimes.com/2015/06/22/magazine/the-condition-of-black-life-is-one-of-mourning.html.
19 | Hartman, *Lose Your Mother* 133.

focuses on recent developments within this genre and argues that the selected texts belong to a second generation of neo-slave narratives.

Set in late seventeenth-century North America, *A Mercy* (2008) is Toni Morrison's first novel after her 1987 literary masterpiece *Beloved* that explicitly returns to the theme of slavery and the Middle Passage. Focusing on the fate of Florens, a sixteen-year-old enslaved woman, *A Mercy* examines the paradigm shift from human bondage to racial slavery that occurred in the early colonial period and particularly explores the disastrous psychological effects of anti-black racism on the oppressed. Without ignoring the possibility of black resistance, Morrison's multi-perspective novel strongly emphasizes the destructive nature of chattel slavery by exploring the complexity and pain of being a slave mother, addressing the subject of intra-black violence and depicting the ultimate breakdown of a heterogeneous group of uprooted women. In *A Mercy*, Morrison draws attention to loss and grief as defining features of black life in early colonial America, employing various postmodern narrative strategies to highlight Florens's experiences of fragmentation and hopelessness.

In her innovative travelogue *Lose Your Mother* (2007), Saidiya Hartman combines fictional elements, essayistic explorations of the history of the slave trade and autobiographical passages about African American roots tourism in present-day Ghana to reflect on the disturbing legacy of slavery. Hartman, a distinguished expert on slavery, African American literature and history and a professor at Columbia University, presents a vibrant interpretation of the African diaspora and black relations: *Lose Your Mother* deconstructs the static idea of a return to an "authentic" African village and the myth of Africa as a welcoming home for black diasporic returnees, directing the reader's attention to the complicity of Africans in the slave trade and giving voice to Hartman's feelings of loss and disenchantment in Ghana. What emerges from *Lose Your Mother* is an intricate view of the black world as a complex social formation that is not only characterized by essential differences and hierarchies but also united by the common objective of fighting against anti-black racism. At the core of *Lose Your Mother* is a multi-voiced chapter called "The Dead Book," in which Hartman critically engages with the archive of slavery to highlight the ultimate impossibility of recovering the voice and story of an eighteenth-century female captive who was murdered during the Middle Passage.

Having grown up in apartheid South Africa, Yvette Christiansë is currently professor of English and Africana Studies at Barnard College specializing in postcolonial and African American literature and theory. Set in the early nineteenth century, her critically acclaimed novel *Unconfessed* (2006) unfolds the story of Sila, a female slave kidnapped from Mozambique as a child and transported to South Africa's Cape Colony. Suffering from white brutality and sexual abuse, Sila takes the life of her son Baro, desperately hoping to protect him from further pain. Christiansë's novel is based on white-authored historical documents found in the archive of slavery that reduce Sila to a piece of property and a criminal. In *Unconfessed*, Christiansë uses various sophisticated narrative strategies to write against this racist and one-sided depiction. In terms of form and content, Christiansë's novel enters into a powerful intertextual relationship with Morrison's *Beloved*: Exploring the theme of infanticide, both novels focus on the interiority of the female captive's experience and highlight the destructive psychological impact of slavery. Moreover, in a way similar to Morrison's masterpiece, *Unconfessed* self-reflexively draws attention to the limits and ethical dangers of revisiting the past of slavery.

Published in 2007, Lawrence Hill's *The Book of Negroes* is a prizewinning and best-selling novel about the life of an eighteenth-century African-born woman who is kidnapped from her native village as a child, transported across the Atlantic and sold into American slavery. Hill, an African Canadian writer and former journalist, engages in a dynamic dialogue with current discourses on the African diaspora, addressing questions of home, belonging and loss and reflecting on the impossibility of diasporic return. Focusing on the story of fugitive slaves who joined the British during the American Revolutionary War and relocated to Nova Scotia in 1783, *The Book of Negroes* particularly explores Canada's history of slavery, racial violence and segregation, deconstructing mythical conceptions of the country as a "paradise" for blacks during the time of the slave trade and slavery. Using unconvincing melodramatic plot devices, offering narrative closure and naively celebrating the healing power of literature, Hill, I argue, presents an ultimately triumphant account of an enslaved woman's life and, thus, trivializes the horrors of slavery.

Marlon James is a Caribbean-born writer and currently a professor of English and Creative Writing at Macalester College in Minnesota. His novel *The Book of Night Women* (2009), winner of the 2010 Dayton Literary Peace Prize for Fiction, highlights the destructive power of Jamaican slavery and revolves around the themes of oppression and black female resistance. Set in the late eighteenth century, James's novel focuses on the life of Lilith, the daughter of a slave woman and a white overseer, who grows up on a large sugar plantation. *The Book of Night Women* examines the intricate power relationships between slave owners, overseers, slaves and maroons, directing the reader's attention to the female slave's plight in a racist and sexist world. Moreover, tracing Lilith's transformation into a murderer, James's novel explores the role and the legitimacy of violence in the struggle for freedom. What renders *The Book of Night Women* problematic is James's decision to represent acts of anti-black violence, torture and rape in an unsparing, even pornographic, way that remains unreflected in the text. Unlike Morrison, Hartman and Christiansë, he fails to acknowledge and include the epistemological insights of black feminist scholars, such as Hortense J. Spillers, concerning the ethics of narration.

Characterized by a high level of heterogeneity, the texts I have selected for this study are set in different geographical regions and historical periods, i.e., in late seventeenth-century colonial North America (Morrison); in late eighteenth-century Jamaica (James); in eighteenth-century/early nineteenth-century West Africa, South Carolina, New York, Nova Scotia and Great Britain (Hill); in the nineteenth-century Cape Colony (Christiansë) and in twentieth-century Ghana (Hartman). In their attempt to unearth forgotten or neglected histories of slavery, they focus on spaces with specific social power structures; spaces in which meanings of race, class, gender and sexuality as well as concepts of home, belonging and exclusion are negotiated in concrete historical, social, political and cultural contexts. In analyzing these twenty-first-century literary texts, my work offers a transnational approach to the topic of writing slavery that accentuates the productive tension between local specifics and global structures:[20] It highlights the diversity and complexity of the African diaspora, while simultaneously drawing attention to dimensions that connect black diasporic subjects and communities around the world, such as traumatic experiences and memories of dislocation, violence and loss as well as dynamic forms of home-making, black agency and resistance against oppression and exploitation.

In order to acknowledge and reflect on this intricate relationship between the local and the transnational, *Transnational Black Dialogues: Re-Imagining Slavery in the Twenty-First Century* draws on a dynamic conceptual framework within the field of African diaspora studies that emphasizes the idea of "'difference within unity.'"[21] Following scholars such as Stuart Hall, Avtar Brah, Brent Hayes Edwards and Tina M. Campt,[22] this study contends that the African diaspora is a complex social and cultural, transnational network of groups marked by fundamental similarities, essential differences and internal and external hierarchies. Focusing on transnational literary and theoretical negotiations of slavery, my work is based on the conviction that it is important to contextualize

---

20 | For a similar approach in the context of black Canadian literature, see Winfried Siemerling, *The Black Atlantic Reconsidered: Black Canadian Writing, Cultural History, and the Presence of the Past* (Montreal: McGill-Queen's UP, 2015).
21 | Brent Hayes Edwards, "The Uses of Diaspora," *Social Text* 19.1 (2001): 59.
22 | Stuart Hall, "Race, Articulation, and Societies Structured in Dominance," *Black British Cultural Studies: A Reader*, eds. Houston A. Baker, Jr., Manthia Diawara and Ruth H. Lindeborg (1980; Chicago: U of Chicago P, 1996) 16-60; Stuart Hall, "Cultural Identity and Diaspora," *Identity: Community, Culture, Difference*, ed. Jonathan Rutherford (London: Lawrence and Wishart, 1990) 222-37; Avtar Brah, *Cartographies of Diaspora: Contesting Identities* (London: Routledge, 1996); Edwards 45-73; Tina M. Campt, *Other Germans: Black Germans and the Politics of Race, Gender, and Memory in the Third Reich* (Ann Arbor: U of Michigan P, 2004); Tina M. Campt, *Image Matters: Archive, Photography, and the African Diaspora in Europe* (Durham: Duke UP, 2012).

the specific history of a particular black group (such as African Canadians or African Caribbeans) and to take into account the interplay between local characteristics and the larger framework of the African diaspora.

Within the field of African diaspora studies, there is a strong focus on the history and experiences of blacks in the Atlantic world, particularly in the United States,[23] as well as a "dominance of African-American and Black British paradigms for understanding Black identity and Black cultural formations"[24] across the globe. This development, Campt contends, raises questions about the hegemony of black America in academic and public discourses on the African diaspora.[25] Furthermore, it draws attention to the (self-proclaimed) avant-garde role of African American intellectuals, scholars and writers, who have been at the forefront of articulating the complexity and richness of black life in a wide range of literary, philosophical, political and theoretical texts. Moving beyond victimization approaches, African Americans have created powerful concepts and paradigms for theorizing black diasporic identity and analyzing forms of black agency and resistance. Equally significant, they have inspired and empowered other black intellectuals, researchers and authors around the world to examine various aspects of black history both inside and outside the United States.

While twenty-first-century black writers like Christiansë, James and Hill turn their attention to exploring the past of slavery in countries like South Africa, Jamaica and Canada, they enter into a dynamic intertextual dialogue with African American literary texts about slavery—which reflects the dominance as well as the avant-garde role of black America within African diaspora discourse. Crucially, Christiansë and James, although originally from South Africa and Jamaica, respectively, are now members of the U.S. academic community. As experts in disciplines such as African American, postcolonial and gender studies, they actively participate in and contribute to the negotiation of critical theory and history, which, in turn, has an enormous influence on their literary projects: Profoundly shaped by the work of African American literary and cultural theorists and writers, Christiansë not only published a theoret-

---

23 | Paul Tiyambe Zeleza, "Rewriting the African Diaspora: Beyond the Black Atlantic," *African Affairs* 104.414 (2005): 35-68.
24 | Campt, *Other Germans* 23.
25 | For critical discussions of the dominance of African America within the field of African diaspora studies, see Tina M. Campt and Deborah A. Thomas,"Gendering Diaspora: Transnational Feminism, Diaspora and Its Hegemonies,"*Feminist Review* 90 (2008): 1-8; Campt, *Other Germans* 1-23, 168-210; Tina M.Campt, "Imagining Ourselves: What Does It Mean to Be Part of the African Diaspora?" Interview by Jean-Philippe Dedieu, *Think Africa Press* 21 Nov. 2013, 29 Jan. 2014 http://thinkafricapress.com/society/imagining-ourselves-interview-tina-campt-diaspora-photograph.

ically sophisticated monograph on the work of Toni Morrison.[26] In terms of content, aesthetics and ethics, she also participates in an intertextual dialogue with *Beloved* in her novel *Unconfessed*.[27]

WRITING AND THEORIZING SLAVERY IN THE TWENTY-FIRST CENTURY

While they shed light on different local contexts, historical events and developments, power structures and black cultural traditions, contemporary writers like Morrison, Hartman, Christiansë, Hill and James face the same aesthetic and ethical challenge of how to re-imagine slavery from twenty-first-century perspectives. Reflecting on what Hartman calls "the ethics of historical representation,"[28] this study is particularly attentive not only to the dangers inherent in writing about acts of anti-black violence, exploitation, torture and sexual abuse but also to the risks of revisiting and (re-)appropriating the archive of slavery both inside and outside the United States. Drawing on the work of black feminists such as Spillers and Deborah E. McDowell, my work contends that there are fundamental similarities and differences between Morrison's, Hartman's, Christiansë's, James's and Hill's aesthetic choices, ethical approaches and theoretical conceptions of (writing) slavery.

What makes texts like Morrison's *A Mercy*, Hartman's *Lose Your Mother* and Christiansë's *Unconfessed* so complex and powerful in both ethical and aesthetic terms, I argue, is that they creatively combine, and self-reflexively draw attention to, different narrative goals: They not only seek to reconstruct largely forgotten or suppressed memories of slavery, to counter white misrepresentations of black life, to engage with the disturbing silences and omissions in the archive, to expose the horrific violence of slavery and to address the specific vulnerability of enslaved women to (sexual) abuse. Even more significantly, writers like Morrison, Hartman and Christiansë also critically reflect on the (ultimate) impossibility of recovering the (female) slave's voice and filling the gaps in the historical records. Highly influenced by the epistemological interventions of black feminists like Spillers, they employ innovative narrative techniques, such as non-linearity, fragmentation, multi-perspectivity and self-reflexivity, to acknowledge and highlight the intricacies and risks inherent in representing scenes of exploitation and suffering and, especially, in writing about violence

---

26 | Yvette Christiansë, *Toni Morrison: An Ethical Poetics* (New York: Fordham UP, 2013).
27 | See chapter 4, "'Hertseer:' Re-Imagining Cape Slavery in Yvette Christiansë's *Unconfessed* (2006)," in this study.
28 | Saidiya Hartman, "Venus in Two Acts," *Small Axe* 12.2 (2008): 5.

against the black female body. Ultimately, texts like *A Mercy, Lose Your Mother* and *Unconfessed* culminate in the insightful claim that there are specific aspects and experiences of slavery that cannot, and should not, be put into words.

This study argues that contemporary black feminist literary negotiations of slavery like *A Mercy, Lose Your Mother* and *Unconfessed* cannot be read without taking into account their dynamic intertextual relationships to Toni Morrison's 1987 *Beloved* and, more specifically, to a particular and disturbing tendency in the reception of this masterpiece: In contemporary (African) American literature, *Beloved* stands out as one of the most influential, critically acclaimed and commercially successful literary meditations on slavery, the Middle Passage and the enduring effects of this history. The novel was translated into numerous languages and adapted into a 1998 movie starring Danny Glover and Oprah Winfrey. More importantly, it earned Morrison the Nobel Prize of Literature in 1993, which transformed her into "a global cultural figure,"[29] as Farah Jasmine Griffin has put it. Given the text's enormous international success and profound influence on academic and popular discourses, the publication of Morrison's *magnum opus* as well as its critical reception, Sabine Broeck contends, "must be marked as a watershed moment in that it put slavery, as well as the black woman's plight resulting from it, on the public agenda to a hitherto un-witnessed extent."[30]

In her insightful essay "Trauma, Agency, Kitsch and the Excesses of the Real: *Beloved* within the Field of Critical Response" (2006), Broeck offers a critical discussion of a prevailing trend in the secondary literature about *Beloved*, a novel which has been widely praised for giving voice to the formerly excluded, silenced and marginalized: Among cultural critics, (literary) scholars and other readers, Broeck argues, there is a strong tendency to offer a "kitsch"[31] interpretation of *Beloved* and to regard the novel solely as a powerful narrative of overcoming, liberation, redemption and recovery; as a triumphant tale suggesting that it is possible to work through the past, bear witness to the atrocities

---

29 | Farah Jasmine Griffin, "A 'Middle Aged Gray Haired Colored Lady' Appears on the Cover of *Newsweek*: Toni Morrison," *A New Literary History of America*, eds. Greil Marcus and Werner Sollors (Cambridge, MA: Harvard UP, 2009) 997.
30 | Sabine Broeck, "Enslavement as Regime of Western Modernity: Re-reading Gender Studies Epistemology Through Black Feminist Critique," 2008, *Sabine Broeck: Plotting Against Modernity; Critical Interventions in Race and Gender*, eds. Karin Esders, Insa Härtel and Carsten Junker (Sulzbach: Helmer, 2014) 35.
31 | Sabine Broeck, "Trauma, Agency, Kitsch and the Excesses of the Real: *Beloved* within the Field of Critical Response," 2006, *Sabine Broeck: Plotting Against Modernity; Critical Interventions in Race and Gender*, eds. Karin Esders, Insa Härtel and Carsten Junker (Sulzbach: Helmer, 2014) 247.

suffered by enslaved individuals and heal the trauma of slavery though the act of narration.

In order to support that claim, many critics have primarily focused on the novel's plot and its rather "optimistic" ending (Paul D's return to Sethe, Beloved's departure, Denver's integration into the (local) black community and her chance to go to college), without paying attention to the text's ambiguities, its complex aesthetic structure and ethical implications. According to Broeck, what is often ignored is the fact that Morrison strategically employs a variety of sophisticated narrative techniques and strategies (including fragmentation, non-realist elements, textual blanks and ruptures), reflecting on the ultimate impossibility to articulate the experiences of the dispossessed, to present a coherent story of a black woman's life in bondage and to heal the trauma of "New World" racial slavery. Marked by ambiguities, *Beloved* seeks to confront the reader with the brutal nature and persistent legacy of slavery, while commenting on the impossibility to write about this (collective) traumatic experience.[32] *Beloved*, Yvette Christiansë argues in her study *Toni Morrison: An Ethical Poetics* (2013), "does not merely fill in or supplant the previously vacant spaces of historical knowledge. It retains asymmetries and opacities, which produce a haunted text and a haunted reader."[33]

In this study, I read black feminist texts like *A Mercy*, *Lose Your Mother* and *Unconfessed* as radical intertextual responses to interpretations of *Beloved* that are based on notions of overcoming, healing and redemption: Concerned with questions of representability and ethics, Morrison, Hartman and Christiansë warn against an easy appropriation of black history and draw attention to the impossibility of working through the past in order to heal the wounds of slavery. Instead of naively and uncritically celebrating the reconciliatory power of twenty-first-century fiction, they shed light on the devastating nature of slavery to reflect on "what lived on from this history,"[34] to use Hartman's words. Thus, they engage in a dynamic dialogue with Afro-pessimist discourse. Foregrounding black experiences of loss, dispossession and grief without losing sight of forms of black agency and resistance, their texts offer a conceptualization of slavery as an utterly dehumanizing process of "thingification"[35] (Aimé Césaire), exploring the ways in which enslaved black subjects were transformed into mere commodities and objects of (sexual) exploitation.

---

32 | Ibid. 239-57; see also Broeck, "Enslavement as Regime of Western Modernity" 35; Sabine Broeck, *White Amnesia – Black Memory? American Women's Writing and History* (Frankfurt a.M.: Peter Lang, 1999) 36-40.
33 | Christiansë, *Toni Morrison* 34.
34 | Hartman, *Lose Your Mother* 130.
35 | Aimé Césaire, *Discourse on Colonialism*, trans. Joan Pinkham (1955; New York: Monthly Review Press, 2000) 42.

Analyzing crucial aesthetic, ethical and conceptual differences and similarities between texts like *A Mercy, Lose Your Mother* and *Unconfessed*, on the one hand, and *The Book of Negroes* and *The Book of Night Women*, on the other, one of the main concerns of this study is to draw attention to the risks and dangers of re-imagining slavery in the twenty-first century: What Hill shares with female writers like Morrison, Hartman and Christiansë is the desire to bring to light largely forgotten stories of slavery and to examine the specific experience of enslaved women. However, while *A Mercy, Lose Your Mother* and *Unconfessed* strongly focus on loss as a definer of black life and refuse to offer a consoling view of slavery in order to accentuate the impossibility of healing and overcoming, *The Book of Negroes* is constructed as an empowering narrative about a slave woman's triumph over slavery, suggesting that it is possible to work through and close the wounds of the past. In stark contrast to writers like Morrison, Hartman and Christiansë, Hill offers no critical reflections on the limits and ethical implications of writing about anti-black violence and slavery as "thingification" but instead highlights the liberating power of the act of narration. Using a vivid style, he presents an affirmative approach to writing and theorizing slavery, focusing especially on dynamic forms of black self-invention, home-making and renewal. Analyzing the novel's melodramatic plot structure, this study argues that *The Book of Negroes* runs the risk of playing down and trivializing the true implications and the horrors of American chattel slavery; it fails to acknowledge and express the intricate meaning of slavery as "thingification."

In *The Book of Night Women*, James, too, pays particular attention to the female slave's experience of sexual violence and oppression in a racist and male-dominated society, unfolding the story of a young black woman in late eighteenth-century Jamaica. Yet, in stark contrast to Morrison, Hartman and Christiansë, he shows the brutality of slavery in a detailed, unsparing and ultimately pornographic way, without engaging in a self-reflexive examination of the ethical dangers inherent in this narrative choice. Unlike Hill's *The Book of Negroes*, which offers an unconvincing teleological conception of history and a reductive reconciliatory interpretation of eighteenth-century black life, *The Book of Night Women* foregrounds the utterly destructive nature of slavery, underlining the impossibility for the slaves to escape the vicious circle of violence and racial oppression. By presenting the captive's experience of "thingification" in a pornographically explicit manner, however, James fails to take into account the complex (epistemological) insights of black feminist theory concerning "the ethics of historical representation,"[36] to use Hartman's phrase. Drawing on Spillers's, McDowell's, Hartman's and Angela Davis's theoretical contribu-

---

36 | Hartman, "Venus in Two Acts" 5.

tions,[37] this study contends that James subjects the enslaved to a second act of victimization and abuse, reducing his (female) characters to objects of voyeuristic desire.

I argue that both Hill and James strategically employ black female protagonists to explore the history of slavery: Not only do they seek to write themselves into the commercially successful tradition of female-authored neo-slave narratives that concentrate on the lives of enslaved women. In a self-legitimizing move, they also intend to justify their decision to depict slave women's experiences of (sexual) violence. However, both *The Book of Negroes* and *The Book of Night Women* never critically elaborate on the ethics of narration and the theoretical intricacies involved in "the practice of speaking for others"[38] (Linda Alcoff). Whereas Hill fails to articulate the true meaning of slave womanhood and motherhood by incorporating melodramatic, "fairy-tale" elements into his text, James refuses to engage in a self-reflexive examination of the dangers of representing scenes of subjection and torture in a pornographic way.

NEO-SLAVE NARRATIVES: CURRENT STATE OF RESEARCH

Exploring the history of slavery in a variety of geographical areas and historical periods, contemporary black writers like Morrison, Hartman, Christiansë, Hill and James do not write in a vacuum but enter into an energetic and fruitful dialogue with both classic slave narratives and twentieth-century neo-slave narratives. This study argues that texts like *A Mercy, Lose Your Mother, Unconfessed, The Book of Negroes* and *The Book of Night Women* are representative of a second generation of neo-slave narratives. The following short overview focuses on the emergence of neo-slave narratives in the United States in the late 1960s, explores recent developments in this genre, reflects on the complex relationship between slave and neo-slave narratives and, most importantly, argues that it is essential to distinguish between a first and a second generation of neo-slave narratives.

Since the late 1960s, numerous African American writers have written literary texts about the transatlantic slave trade and slavery. Among these works

---

37 | See Hartman, *Scenes of Subjection*; Hartman, "Venus in Two Acts" 1-14; Hortense J. Spillers, "Mama's Baby, Papa's Maybe: An American Grammar Book," *Diacritics* 17.2 (1987): 64-81; Deborah E. McDowell, ed., *Narrative of the Life of Frederick Douglass, an American Slave*, by Frederick Douglass (1845; Oxford: Oxford UP, 1999) vii-xxvii; Angela Davis, ed., *Narrative of the Life of Frederick Douglass, an American Slave*, by Frederick Douglass (1845; San Francisco: City Lights, 2010) 21-37.
38 | Linda Alcoff, "The Problem of Speaking for Others," *Cultural Critique* 20 (1991-1992): 9.

are critically praised as well as commercially successful novels like Margaret Walker's *Jubilee* (1966), Ishmael Reed's *Flight To Canada* (1976), Sherley Anne Williams's *Dessa Rose* (1986), Toni Morrison's *Beloved* (1987) and Charles Johnson's *Middle Passage* (1990). In light of the scarcity of black literary representations of slavery in the first half of the twentieth century, this orientation towards the past marked a new development in the context of African American fiction: As scholars like Ashraf H. A. Rushdy, Elizabeth Ann Beaulieu, Maria I. Diedrich and Madhu Dubey point out, it was a dynamic response to transformations in intellectual discourses and in the political, social and institutional realms of the United States; a response to transformations initiated by the Civil Rights, Black Arts and Black Power movements.[39]

One of the important changes that took place during this period was a radical reconceptualization of the historiography of slavery. In his introduction to the 1990 edition of *Black Odyssey: The African-American Ordeal in Slavery*, the historian Nathan I. Huggins presents an intriguing overview of the way U.S. historians have treated slavery over the course of time: Like the Founding Fathers of the U.S., who refused to regard racial slavery as a structural element of American history and instead constructed a racially exclusive concept of the nation, up until the transformational 1960s, U.S. historians generally created a white master narrative of American history. According to Huggins, they produced a story of constant progress that considered "racial slavery and oppression as curious abnormalities—aberrations—historical accidents to be corrected in the progressive upward reach of the nation's destiny."[40] In this dominant conceptualization of the past, there was no room for African Americans, no interest in the stories of and texts written by enslaved black men and women. In general, Huggins argues, historians "seemed to assume that a slave's testimony was self-interested special pleading and, therefore, uncreditable."[41]

The 1960s, however, marked a turning point when several historians, especially those associated with the New Left, started to adopt a bottom-up approach

---

39 | See Ashraf H. A. Rushdy, *Neo-Slave Narratives: Studies in the Social Logic of a Literary Form* (New York: Oxford UP, 1999) 1-22; Ashraf H. A. Rushdy, "The Neo-Slave Narrative," *The Cambridge Companion to the African American Novel*, ed. Maryemma Graham (Cambridge: Cambridge UP, 2004) 87; Elizabeth Ann Beaulieu, *Black Women Writers and the American Neo-Slave Narrative: Femininity Unfettered* (Westport: Greenwood Press, 1999) xiii-27; Maria I. Diedrich, "Afro-amerikanische Literatur," *Amerikanische Literaturgeschichte*, ed. Hubert Zapf, 3rd ed. (Stuttgart: Metzler, 2010) 439-40; Madhu Dubey, "Neo-Slave Narratives," *A Companion to African American Literature*, ed. Gene Andrew Jarrett (Malden, MA: Wiley-Blackwell, 2010) 332-33.
40 | Nathan Irvin Huggins, *Black Odyssey: The African-American Ordeal in Slavery* (1977; New York: Vintage, 1990) xii.
41 | Ibid. xxiv.

to history. Employing new methodologies, they began to look at the past focusing on the perspectives of African Americans and other formerly marginalized groups, such as Native Americans, Asian Americans or women. In their studies of racial slavery, they no longer ignored the testimony of slaves but began to draw on, even to concentrate exclusively on, oral histories and slave narratives.[42] As Huggins explains, scholars like John Blassingame started to examine the vital role of the black family and community, to emphasize the importance of slave religion, to shed light on the dynamic culture of the enslaved population and to reconstruct the history of organized slave rebellions and different forms of daily resistance. As a result of this important scholarly activity, (black) historians "were no longer content to understand slavery simply as an institution in which blacks labored under white dominion, mere victims subjugated to the rule and will of whites."[43] Rather, they were determined to demonstrate that enslaved black women and men were active agents in the formation of a distinctive African American culture.[44]

This new academic approach to slavery had an empowering influence on contemporary African American writers but was not the only driving force behind the emergence of neo-slave narratives. As Ashraf Rushdy argues, it is also essential to focus on important institutional developments that occurred at that time: In the late 1960s, when the Black Power movement flourished, the first Black Studies programs were established at historically white universities and colleges in the U.S., which, among other things, caused an increasing demand for black-authored texts that could be read and taught in class. With its emphasis on black self-determination, the Black Power movement, in turn, encouraged African American writers to approach the history of slavery from a black perspective.

At around the same time, the publication of *The Confessions of Nat Turner* (1967) by white Southern author William Styron evoked strong indignation among black intellectuals and Black Power advocates: They criticized the novel for its racist depiction of rebellion leader Nat Turner, its uncritical adoption of the hegemonic discourse on slavery and, as Rushdy puts it, "its presumption of assuming the voice of a slave, its uninformed appropriation of African American culture."[45] Determined to give a more accurate account of the past, African American authors like Sherley Anne Williams started to create counter-stories to Styron's controversial novel. Together, Rushdy contends, these social, polit-

---

42 | Ibid. xvi-xx. See also Rushdy, *Neo-Slave Narratives* 4; Dubey 333.
43 | Huggins xxxii.
44 | Ibid. xvi-xxxi.
45 | Rushdy, *Neo-Slave Narratives* 4.

ical, historiographical and institutional developments laid the ground for the rise of the genre of neo-slave narratives.[46]

The term "neoslave narrative" first appears in Bernard W. Bell's 1987 work *The Afro-American Novel and Its Tradition*: In a chapter on black modernism and postmodernism, Bell offers a reading of Margaret Walker's *Jubilee* (1966), which he describes as the "first major neoslave narrative: residually oral, modern narratives of escape from bondage."[47] In more recent years, Bell's neologism, which acknowledges the influence of slave narratives on postmodern black reconstructions of slavery, has been taken up by scholars like Ashraf H.A. Rushdy and Elizabeth Ann Beaulieu.

Rushdy's *Neo-Slave Narratives: Studies in the Social Logic of a Literary Form* (1999), the first extensive work on neo-slave narratives, has become a key text within the field. In comparison with Bell, Rushdy presents a more exclusive definition that characterizes neo-slave narratives as "contemporary novels that assume the form, adopt the conventions, and take on the first-person voice of the antebellum slave narrative."[48] Rushdy offers an excellent overview of the historical contexts out of which the genre of neo-slave narrative emerged. In his analysis of *Flight to Canada* (1976) by Ishmael Reed, *Dessa Rose* (1986) by Sherley Anne Williams, *Oxherding Tale* (1982) and *Middle Passage* (1990) by Charles Johnson, he draws on an extended meaning of intertextuality, which refers to the relationships that exist between literary texts as well as to "the ways texts mediate the social conditions of their formal production."[49] Rushdy shows that the three selected authors of neo-slave narratives from the 1970s, 1980s and early 1990s actively participate in discourses of the 1960s: They comment on the heated controversy surrounding Styron's text, contribute to historiographical discussions about slavery and, equally significant, critically reflect on the legacies of the Civil Rights and Black Power movements. By employing the form of the classic slave narrative, a genre in which black American subjectivity was first articulated, they demonstrate the rise of a new black political consciousness.[50] Primarily "concerned with tracing how a specific literary form emerged and evolved in response to developments in the public sphere,"[51] Rushdy's study, I argue, fails to explore the influence of black feminist criticism on neo-slave narrative authors and to provide a systematic reflection on the ethical implications and dangers of re-imagining chattel slavery from a twentieth-cen-

---

46 | Ibid. 1-22, 90; see also Rushdy, "The Neo-Slave Narrative" 87-98.
47 | Bernard W. Bell, *The Afro-American Novel and Its Tradition* (Amherst: U of Massachusetts P, 1987) 289.
48 | Rushdy, *Neo-Slave Narratives* 3.
49 | Ibid. 14.
50 | Ibid. 1-22.
51 | Ibid. 5.

tury perspective. Furthermore, Rushdy does not acknowledge and examine the transnational dimension of the genre of neo-slave narratives, ignoring the fact that "Caribbean and Black British writers have also turned back toward slavery,"[52] as Arlene R. Keizer contends.

Beaulieu is one of the first scholars to approach the genre of neo-slave narratives from the vantage point of black feminism: In her seminal study *Black Women Writers and the American Neo-Slave Narrative: Femininity Unfettered* (1999), Beaulieu argues that twentieth-century female writers like Sherley Anne Williams, Toni Morrison and J. California Cooper "choose to author neo-slave narratives to reinscribe history from the point of view of the black woman, most specifically the nineteenth-century enslaved mother."[53] As Beaulieu points out, highly influenced by the revisionist scholarship of black feminists such as Angela Davis and Deborah Gray White, these black women writers are determined

to rectify the historic invisibility of the enslaved woman by exploding the oversimplified stereotype of black women as genderless work animals capable only of matching a man's work production in the field and of breeding, and by producing viable alternative models of enslaved women, models that continue to inspire black women today.[54]

According to Beaulieu, writers like Morrison, Williams and Cooper depict female slaves as strong and complex characters, "as mothers capable of loving and caring for their children in spite of the obstacles placed in their way by slavery and slave masters."[55] By exploring the intricate meaning of motherhood under slavery, they engage in a powerful rewriting of male-authored slave narratives that primarily focus on themes like black manhood and literacy.[56] While her study offers a complex meditation on intertextual relations between slave and neo-slave narratives, Beaulieu fails to examine differences and similarities between contemporary black female and male writers in terms of aesthetic choices and theoretical conceptions of (writing) slavery.[57] Moreover, like Rushdy, she does not systematically reflect on questions concerning the ethics of narration, i.e., the dangers inherent in representing acts of exploitation and violence against the black (female) body. Crucially, she also ignores the transnational nature of the genre of neo-slave narratives.

---

52 | Arlene R. Keizer, *Black Subjects: Identity Formation in the Contemporary Narrative of Slavery* (Ithaca: Cornell UP, 2004) 4.
53 | Beaulieu xv.
54 | Ibid. 25.
55 | Ibid. 14.
56 | Ibid. 13-14.
57 | For a similar critique of Beaulieu's study, see also Keizer 4.

In a way similar to Beaulieu, Angelyn Mitchell offers a compelling analysis of twentieth-century representations of slavery by black female writers. In her study *The Freedom to Remember: Narrative, Slavery, and Gender in Contemporary Black Women's Fiction* (2002), she concentrates on literary works such as Octavia Butler's *Kindred* (1979), Sherley Anne Williams's *Dessa Rose* (1986), Toni Morrison's *Beloved* (1987), J. California Cooper's *Family* (1992) and Lorene Carey's *The Price of a Child* (1995). According to Mitchell, these selected postmodern novels do not primarily deal with the condition of enslavement but rather explore "the nature of freedom—of affranchisement—for those who were formerly enslaved."[58] Therefore, Mitchell does not use the term neo-slave narratives to characterize these female-authored texts but instead introduces the category of "liberatory narratives."

Mitchell shows that the "liberatory narratives" are deeply embedded in a black women's literary tradition. In particular, they stand in a dialogic relationship with Harriet Jacob's classic slave narrative *Incidents in the Life of a Slave Girl* (1861) and, from a twentieth-century perspective, shed light on issues like black motherhood and community. Inspired by contemporary black feminist discourse, they write about formerly ignored aspects of slavery and delve into the inner life of female slaves. According to Mitchell, by challenging the white master narrative of slavery that reduces black women to disempowered objects, the "liberatory narrative" has a healing effect on contemporary (black) audiences: It is intended "to liberate its readers from the shackles of the past by asking them to look at the whole of slavery, especially as it involved Black women."[59] The novels under consideration, Mitchell argues, "are liberatory not only in content and form, but in their projected and ideal reception as well."[60]

Mitchell's study fails to take into account that, as Keizer puts it, many (female-authored) neo-slave narratives do "not qualify as liberatory, either for their characters or their readers."[61] In *Transnational Black Dialogues*, I argue that writers like Morrison, Hartman and Christiansë not only self-reflexively elaborate on the impossibility of working through the past in order to heal the trauma of slavery but also highlight the enduring effects of slavery on later black generations. Refusing to give a consoling view of black slave life, they reflect on what Hartman calls "the future created by"[62] slavery. Focusing on loss, grief and dispossession as defining features of the African diaspora, their texts cannot be described as "liberatory narratives."

---

58 | Angelyn Mitchell, *The Freedom to Remember: Narrative, Slavery, and Gender in Contemporary Black Women's Fiction* (New Brunswick: Rutgers UP, 2002) 4.
59 | Ibid. 146.
60 | Ibid. 21.
61 | Keizer 4.
62 | Hartman, *Lose Your Mother* 133.

In recent years, scholars like Keizer have started to explore the transnational dimension of the genre of neo-slave narratives, moving beyond an exclusive focus on literary negotiations of U.S.-American slavery. In her monograph *Black Subjects: Identity Formation in the Contemporary Narrative of Slavery* (2004), Keizer shows that both Caribbean and African American writers participate in discourses on African diasporic identity and challenge established Western concepts of subjectivity, such as psychoanalysis and performance theory. What unites authors like Derek Walcott and Morrison, despite their exploration of different geographical regions, is their attempt to deconstruct static and essentialized understandings of black identity, "while maintaining a sense of the integrity of creolized black cultures in the Americas and showing how black subjectivities are produced and contested within these cultures."[63] The authors do not return to the period of slavery primarily to call attention to the history of black subjugation and contemporary forms of racial oppression but rather, Keizer contends, "to explore the process of self-creation under extremely oppressive conditions."[64] In particular, they theorize about the complex nature of black diasporic resistance. In a way similar to Rushdy, Keizer reads these twentieth-century neo-slave narratives as responses to the social, cultural and political movements of the 1960s.[65] While Keizer acknowledges that novels about slavery "have emerged from every site in the diaspora where people of African descent are present in significant numbers,"[66] she focuses exclusively on African American and Caribbean authors. Moreover, primarily concerned with examining the authors' concepts of subjectivity, she does not critically reflect on questions of representability and ethics.

Transnational Black Dialogues offers an innovative transnational approach to recent developments in the genre of neo-slave narratives: Rushdy, Beaulieu and Mitchell are exclusively concerned with late twentieth-century African American writers whose neo-slave narratives primarily reconstruct the history of slavery in the United States in the nineteenth century and critically reflect on discourses associated with the Civil Rights, Black Arts and Black Power Movements; in other words, their studies are striking examples of the dominance of African America within African diaspora discourse. By contrast, I also include twenty-first-century black writers with different cultural backgrounds (e.g. African Canadian, South African, African American and African Caribbean) who examine the link between the history of slavery and twenty-first-century black life; who enter into an intertextual discussion with African diaspora theory, slave narratives, earlier neo-slave narratives and African American literature

---

63 | Keizer 11.
64 | Ibid.
65 | Ibid. 1-20.
66 | Ibid. 4.

more generally; who shed light on a variety of places and periods, such as late eighteenth-century Jamaica and early nineteenth-century South Africa.[67]

Unlike Keizer, whose primary goal is to highlight the relationship between black Caribbean/American authors' concepts of subjectivity and Western theories of identity, I offer a systematic investigation of continuities and discontinuities between twentieth-century and recent neo-slave narratives. In contrast to Keizer's *Black Subjects*, my work draws on diaspora theory to analyze the complex tension between local black histories and the global framework of the African diaspora, while paying particular attention to the ethical and aesthetic implications of writing chattel slavery from today's point of view.

SECOND-GENERATION NEO-SLAVE NARRATIVES

Significantly, in current academic discourse, the term neo-slave narrative is not uncontested: A major point of criticism is that the prevailing definitions of this genre are too restrictive to cover the heterogeneity and diversity of contemporary representations of slavery. In *Black Subjects*, for instance, Keizer argues that Bell's definition in *The Afro-American Novel and Its Tradition* "limits the scope of these works because of its focus on the movement from enslavement to freedom, the trajectory of the traditional slave narrative."[68] Keizer also criticizes Rushdy for concentrating "even more narrowly on the influence of the antebellum slave narrative, analyzing only those contemporary novels that clearly and explicitly reference nineteenth-century, first-person, literate slave testimony."[69] Many literary texts that deal with slavery, Keizer contends, are not first-person accounts and therefore depart from the tradition of slave narratives. Thus, in order to consider a larger group of texts, she introduces "the category of contemporary narratives of slavery."[70] In a similar way, in *Laughing Fit to Kill: Black Humor in the Fictions of Slavery* (2008), Glenda R. Carpio employs the broad term "fictions of slavery" to refer to a heterogeneous mixture of genres,

---

67 | While I acknowledge that Francophone authors, such as Maryse Condé and Patrick Chamoiseau, and many other non-Anglophone writers have turned their attention to exploring the history of slavery and the slave trade, I focus exclusively on texts written in English to limit the scope of my study. For a discussion of Francophone Caribbean authors of slavery, see Judith Misrahi-Barak, ed., *Revisiting Slave Narratives/ Les avatars contemporains des récits d'esclaves* (Montpellier: Université Montpellier III, 2005).
68 | Keizer 3.
69 | Ibid.
70 | Ibid. 4.

including plays, short stories, novels and visual art, from the Civil Rights era to the present.[71]

While I agree that Bell's and Rushdy's definitions are narrow, the term neo-slave narrative captures the complex intertextual relationship between slave narratives and contemporary literary representations of slavery. No one has better described this dynamic interaction than Toni Morrison: In her seminal 1987 essay "The Site of Memory," she offers an insightful reflection on key characteristics of the slave narrative and her role as a contemporary black female writer. As Morrison explains, slave narrative authors like Olaudah Equiano, Frederick Douglass and Harriet Ann Jacobs primarily addressed—or rather: had to address—a white audience: "In shaping the experience to make it palatable to those who were in a position to alleviate it, they were silent about many things, and they 'forgot' many other things," Morrison argues. "There was a careful selection of the instances that they would record and a careful rendering of those that they chose to describe."[72] In Morrison's view, her task as a postmodern novelist is to shed light on previously suppressed topics such as the female captive's experience of sexual violence, to explore the interior life of the enslaved and to find ways "how to rip that veil drawn over 'proceedings too terrible to relate.'"[73]

In their attempt to appropriate the past of slavery, in their struggle for black self-representation, black writers like Morrison refused to submit to the expectations of a white audience; they envisioned a reader from their own cultural matrix instead of a white audience:[74] "I write what I have recently begun to call village literature, fiction that is really for the village, for the tribe,"[75] Morrison says in a 1981 interview with Thomas LeClair. In other words, in texts like *Beloved*, she has a reader in mind who is familiar with African American oral traditions, myths, tales and folklore; a reader who is ready and culturally competent to take part "in the act of creating the story."[76] As Diedrich explains, Morrison's concept of "village literature" must be interpreted as a "construction

---

71 | Glenda R. Carpio, *Laughing Fit to Kill: Black Humor in the Fictions of Slavery* (New York: Oxford UP, 2008).
72 | Toni Morrison, "The Site of Memory," *Inventing the Truth: The Art and Craft of Memoir*, eds. Russell Baker and William Zinsser, 2nd ed. (Boston: Houghton Mifflin, 1995) 91.
73 | Ibid.
74 | Diedrich, "Afro-amerikanische Literatur" 439-43.
75 | Thomas LeClair, "The Language Must Not Sweat: A Conversation with Toni Morrison," *Conversations with Toni Morrison*, ed. Danille Taylor-Guthrie (Jackson: UP of Mississippi, 1994) 120.
76 | Maria I. Diedrich, "'Things Fall Apart?' The Black Critical Controversy Over Toni Morrison's *Beloved*," *Amerikastudien/American Studies* 34.2. (1989): 176.

of her ideal target group; it is a model which bears little resemblance to her actual audience,"[77] yet is both self-empowering and liberating.

In this study, I argue that twenty-first-century black writers continue to write about formerly ignored or marginalized aspects of slavery and, in doing so, enter into a dialogue with both the antebellum slave narrative and twentieth-century neo-slave narratives. Crucially, writers like Morrison, Hartman and Christiansë not only try to fill in the gaps of the historical record but also self-reflexively comment on the dangers and limits inherent in their attempt to reconstruct the history of slavery from today's perspective. In *Transnational Black Dialogues*, I use the term neo-slave narrative in a broad sense to refer to different genres, such as novels and travelogues, and texts written from different perspectives, not only first-person accounts.

As far as the category of second-generation neo-slave narratives is concerned, the notion of succeeding generations is not without its pitfalls. As Mark Stein points out in a study on black British fiction, the idea of different generations suggests that it is possible to draw clear lines of demarcation between one group of authors/texts and another.[78] Moreover, Stein maintains, it implies "an organic connection between the literature of different writers who may or may not stand in a *relationship of entailment*."[79] While it is true that the linearity the term conveys is problematic,[80] I use the concept of the generation to draw attention to fundamental continuities and important discontinuities between neo-slave narrative authors of the 1960s, 1970s, 1980s and early 1990s and twenty-first-century writers with regard to form, content, theoretical conceptions of slavery, social and political contexts and publishing opportunities. Crucially, this study is based on the conviction that the lines between the first and the second generation are not strict. Toni Morrison, for instance, is a pioneer as well as the most famous and commercially successful representative of the first generation. With *A Mercy*, however, she has written a text that contributes to a significant broadening of the genre of neo-slave narratives, most notably by focusing on the paradigm shift from human bondage to racial slavery in early North America and by entering into a powerful intertextual dialogue with *Beloved* and the critical reception of her *magnum opus*. I argue that *A Mercy* is a second-generation neo-slave narrative.

In terms of publishing opportunities, second-generation neo-slave narrative writers like Hartman, Christiansë, Hill and James benefit from the struggles, accomplishments and the huge commercial success of the first generation: In

---

77 | Ibid. 175.
78 | Mark Stein, *Black British Literature: Novels of Transformation* (Columbus: Ohio State UP, 2004) 5-7.
79 | Ibid. 6; italics in the original.
80 | Ibid. 7.

the 1960s, 1970s and 1980s, black authors like Sherley Anne Williams faced considerable difficulties in finding a publisher for their short stories and novels, suffering from racial discrimination and harassment in a white-dominated publishing world: "From her attempted entry into the fiction marketplace, Williams learned that the field of cultural production contained the same inequities as the social terrain of the United States,"[81] Rushdy contends. While some white editors categorically refused to publish the work of black Americans altogether, others forced black writers to revise their manuscripts significantly to appeal to a white audience.[82] In the 1980s, Williams eventually found a publisher for her novel *Dessa Rose* (1986). Significantly, she was urged by her white editor at HarperCollins to include an author's note at the beginning of her neo-slave narrative, informing her readers that *Dessa Rose* is a work of fiction. As Rushdy puts it, Williams's novel "was being treated like an antebellum slave narrative, her authority questioned the same way fugitive slaves' had been."[83]

However difficult it was for twentieth-century black writers to enter the white literary marketplace, many of their novels became international best-sellers: Most impressively, Alex Haley's neo-slave narrative *Roots: The Saga of an American Family* (1976) was translated into more than twenty languages, received the Pulitzer Prize, sold almost nine million copies and was adapted into an eight-part, ABC television miniseries that attracted more than 130 million viewers from all over the world.[84] Today, decades after the first publication of *Roots*, there is a large and growing market for black literary texts about slavery: Given the commercial success story of African American writers like Haley and Nobel Prize winner Morrison, publishers within and outside the United States are highly interested in printing and promoting the work of neo-slave narrative authors. In recent years, texts such as Hartman's *Lose Your Mother*, Hill's *The Book of Negroes* and James's *The Book of Night Women* have been published by major houses, i.e., by Farrar, Straus and Giroux, Norton and Riverhead Books, respectively.

Over the last decades, there has also been a change in terms of the intended readership of neo-slave narratives; a shift away from an exclusive orientation towards a "village" audience: Honored by notable literary awards, neo-slave narratives have been and continue to be read by a large group of both black and

---

81 | Rushdy, *Neo-Slave Narratives* 141.
82 | Paul C. Rosenblatt, "Reading Novels as a Social Science Researcher," *The Impact of Racism on African American Families: Literature as Social Science* (Surrey: Ashgate, 2014) 22-23.
83 | Rushdy, *Neo-Slave Narratives* 141.
84 | Eric Bennett, "Alexander Palmer (Alex) Haley, 1921-1992," *Africana: The Encyclopedia of the African and African American Experience*, vol. 3, eds. Kwame Anthony Appiah and Henry Louis Gates, Jr., 2nd ed. (Oxford: Oxford UP, 2005) 131.

white readers from across the world. Hill's *The Book of Negroes*, for instance, has been translated into many different languages, such as French, German and Dutch, and has sold hundreds of thousands of copies. Like Haley's *Roots*, the novel was turned into an incredibly popular miniseries: Directed by Clement Virgo, it premiered on CBC Television in early 2015 and was watched by more than 1.6 million viewers in Canada.[85] Today, neo-slave narratives authors like Hill see black and white readers as their intended audience; their texts are rather written for the "global village." Against this background, this study is particularly attentive to the risks inherent in specific narrative strategies employed by contemporary writers to appeal to a large readership, such as the explicit rendering of acts of violence, torture and sexual abuse, as in James's *The Book of Night Women*.

Most twentieth-century neo-slave narrative authors were not only professors at American universities and colleges but also supporters of the social, cultural and political movements of the 1960s: As Rushdy emphasizes, Ishmael Reed, Sherley Anne Williams and Charles Johnson, for example, "began writing in the sixties when each first became enamored of and then disenchanted with the politics of Black Power."[86] In their neo-slave narratives, they focus on "particular Black Power issues—especially the politics of property, identity, and violence—as a way of commenting on the failures of the New Left and articulating their hopes for whatever comes next."[87] For many second-generation neo-slave narrative authors, the Civil Rights, Black Arts and Black Power movements mark a turning point in the history of blacks in the United States and elsewhere. Yet, in their literary texts, I argue, they do not necessarily (and explicitly) reflect on the discourse of the 1960s but rather examine the connection between the period of slavery and forms of systemic racism in the twenty-first century. While they are profoundly influenced by the avant-garde work of African American writers, they contribute to an enormous broadening of the genre of neo-slave narratives by exploring the transnational dimension of the history of slavery, by creatively combining different narrative forms and strate-

---

85 | Ted Bishop, "Introduction," *Dear Sir, I Intend to Burn Your Book: An Anatomy of a Book Burning*, by Lawrence Hill (Edmonton: U of Alberta P, 2013) xiv; Jane Taber, "How *The Book of Negroes*, a Profound Yet Unknown Canadian Story, Became a Miniseries," *Globe and Mail* 2 Jan. 2015, 21 Jan. 2015 http://www.theglobeandmail.com/arts/television/an-unknown-canadian-story-brings-book-of-negros-to-tv/article22275312/; Lawrence Hill, "Adaptation: Rewriting *The Book of Negroes* For the Small Screen," *The Walrus* Jan./ Feb. 2015, 21 Jan. 2015 http://thewalrus.ca/adaptation/; Katie Bailey, "The Book of Negroes Debuts to 1.7M Viewers," *Playback* 8 Jan. 2015, 23 July 2015 http://playbackonline.ca/2015/01/08/book-of-negroes-debuts-to-1-7m-viewers/.
86 | Rushdy, *Neo-Slave Narratives* 5.
87 | Ibid.

gies and by entering into a powerful dialogue with contemporary discourses on the African diaspora and on the ethics of narration.

Structure

Chapter 1, "The Concept of the African Diaspora and the Notion of Difference," lays the theoretical foundations for my analysis of second-generation neo-slave narratives. I focus especially on recent critical interventions in the field of (black) diaspora studies that seek to explore the complexity and diversity of black diasporic experiences by adopting a transnational perspective. Drawing on and engaging with the works of scholars like Stuart Hall, Brent Hayes Edwards, Avtar Brah and Tina M. Campt, I argue for a conceptualization of the African diaspora that is grounded on the idea of difference: Such an interpretation acknowledges and highlights the specificity of local black contexts and histories, while at the same time reflecting on the larger framework and the dialogic nature of the African diaspora. In particular, it draws attention to power differences and hierarchical structures within and between black diasporic groups. I contend that this vibrant view of diaspora is both an intricate framework and a powerful analytical tool for the examination of second-generation neo-slave narratives.

The following chapters (2-6) on Morrison's, Hartman's, Christiansë's, Hill's and James's neo-slave narratives are not arranged chronologically according to their date of publication. Rather, I begin my analysis with a discussion of Morrison's *A Mercy* to illustrate the complex intertextual relationship between first- and second-generation neo-slave narratives. This part is followed by chapters on *Lose Your Mother* and *Unconfessed* because these texts participate in a fruitful dialogue with *A Mercy* about the ethical challenges, implications and dangers of writing and theorizing slavery. Before closing with an epilogue, I focus on *The Book of Negroes* and *The Book of Night Women*, examining and highlighting fundamental differences between the female- and male-authored texts in my study.

Chapter 2, "From Human Bondage to Racial Slavery: Toni Morrison's *A Mercy* (2008)," reads Morrison's ninth novel *A Mercy* as an intertextual intervention against reductive reconciliatory interpretations of *Beloved* in both scholarly and public discussions: Focusing on Morrison's intricate depiction of the plight and vulnerability of enslaved women in late seventeenth-century North America, I demonstrate that *A Mercy* sheds light on the permanent and debilitating psychological effects of sexual exploitation, oppression and humiliation in order to accentuate the impossibility of working through, and closing the wounds of, slavery. Drawing attention to the novel's emphasis on loss and exploration of intra-black conflicts, the chapter illustrates that *A Mercy* engages in an intertextual dialogue with both Afro-pessimist discourse and black diaspora (feminist) theory. Moreover, I show that Morrison employs complex narrative techniques (for instance, non-linearity and self-reflexivity) to capture her black female protagonist's experiences of uprootedness and dissolution and to reflect on the limits of black self-invention. Chapter 2 also examines Morrison's representation of the paradigm shift from human bondage to racial slavery that took place in the early colonial period, arguing that *A Mercy* foregrounds the socio-psychological conditions under which anti-black racism developed and flourished in North America.

In Chapter 3, "Rethinking the African Diaspora: Saidiya Hartman's *Lose Your Mother* (2007)," I explore how Hartman's innovative travelogue contributes to a critical re-negotiation of the concept of the African diaspora and Paul Gilroy's paradigm of the black Atlantic: *Lose Your Mother*, I contend, challenges static interpretations of black diasporic identity grounded on authenticity, continuity and tradition, engaging in an Afro-pessimistic rewriting of Alex Haley's famous neo-slave narrative *Roots* (1976) and focusing on loss, dispossession, grief and mourning as central features of black life. Equally significant, Hartman's text deconstructs dominant narratives of black relations based on similarity and unanimity, drawing attention to differences, gaps, social inequalities and hierarchies between (and among) African Americans and Africans.

Furthermore, drawing on Spillers's and Morrison's works, chapter 3 analyzes Hartman's ambitious project to explore the experiences of an eighteenth-century slave woman during the Middle Passage: I demonstrate that Hartman offers a highly self-reflexive and multi-perspective account to engage with the silences in the archive, to comment on the ethical dangers inherent in her attempt to address the female captive's (sexual) abuse and to underscore the (ultimate) impossibility of recovering the slave's voice and healing the wounds of slavery.

Chapter 4, "'Hertseer:' Re-Imagining Cape Slavery in Yvette Christiansë's *Unconfessed* (2006)," focuses on Christiansë's critical encounter with and fictional (re-)appropriation of the colonial archive, examining the complex ways in which *Unconfessed* deconstructs the received and racist representation of Sila van de Kaap, an early nineteenth-century Cape slave, as a piece of property and murderer. Drawing attention to intertextual links between *Beloved* and *Unconfessed*, I show that Christiansë's text not only highlights the cruelty of Cape slavery and the female slaves' devastating experiences of (sexual) violence but also self-reflexively elaborates on the ultimate impossibility of reconstructing Sila's life. In a way similar to Hartman and Morrison, Christiansë refuses to engage in a therapeutic literary project as she resists the temptation to fill in the gaps and silences of the archive and to transform the slave woman's story of loss into a narrative of overcoming.

Chapter 5, "Transnational Diasporic Journeys in Lawrence Hill's *The Book of Negroes* (2007)," illustrates that Hill's best-selling neo-slave narrative presents a distinct transnational perspective on slavery and black life in the eighteenth-century world: Exploring the meaning of home for black women and men kidnapped from their ancestral lands and sold into American slavery, *The Book of Negroes*, I contend, focuses on the impossibility of going back to any "authentic" place of origin in Africa; at the same time, it sheds light on complex forms of black self-invention and home-making and struggles for freedom and racial equality in North America, West Africa and Europe. Thus, Hill's novel actively participates in contemporary discussions about the African diaspora, deconstructing static and essentialist understandings of black culture and re-writing important historical events, such as the experiences of African Americans during and after the American Revolutionary War, from a black perspective. In particular, I show that *The Book of Negroes* challenges mythical conceptions of Canada as a "paradise" for blacks during the period of the transatlantic slave trade and slavery by depicting the black protagonist's experiences of racial violence and utter disillusionment in Nova Scotia.

Moreover, chapter 5 critically examines the novel's aesthetic devices and its theoretical conception of slavery: Drawing attention especially to the novel's melodramatic plot devices and "fairy-tale" ending, I argue that Hill, unlike Morrison, Hartman and Christiansë, fails to acknowledge and explore the full meaning of racial slavery as a dehumanizing system of "thingification." Unlike *A Mercy*, *Lose Your Mother* and *Unconfessed*, *The Book of Negroes* ultimately highlights the triumph over slavery, conveying the disturbing message that it is possible to overcome the traumatic experiences of slavery.

Chapter 6, "A Vicious Circle of Violence: Revisiting Jamaican Slavery in Marlon James's *The Book of Night Women* (2009)," analyzes James's prizewinning novel about slavery in late eighteenth-century Jamaica. Drawing on the works of Hartman, Spillers, McDowell and Davis and highlighting crucial differences between *A Mercy*, *Unconfessed* and *Lose Your Mother*, on the one hand, and *The Book of Night Women*, on the other, I delineate how James exposes the enslaved to a second act of victimization and violence by representing the horrors of slavery and, in particular, the slave women's sexual abuse and oppression in a pornographic way, without reflecting on the ethical dangers of depicting scenes of torture and subjection.

Examining James's intertextual engagement with Afro-pessimist discourse, I show that one of the novel's primary goals is to draw attention to the utterly dehumanizing nature of Caribbean slavery, focusing on the captives' experience of being caught in a vicious circle of repression, counter-violence and retaliation: While *The Book of Night Women* foregrounds the (female) slaves' determination and willingness to offer (violent) resistance, it ultimately stresses the impossibility to escape racial oppression. Examining James's depiction of his female protagonist's transformation into a murderer, I illustrate that *The Book of Night Women* enters into a dynamic dialogue with Richard Wright's *Native Son* (1940): Both novels not only reflect on the (potentially) liberating power of violent action for subjugated individuals but also emphasize the ultimate destructive nature of violence.

1 The Concept of the African Diaspora and the Notion of Difference

Introduction

In academic discourse in general and cultural studies in particular, the Greek term diaspora has emerged as a key analytical concept to shed light on different processes of (violent) dispersal and resettlement of groups, often caused by a collective traumatic event that continues to haunt later generations. Closely linked to the complex history and fate of the Jewish people, diaspora was first used in the so-called Septuagint, a translated version of the Hebrew scriptures. In this Greek text, which was created in the third and second centuries B.C.E., the word did not refer to a specific historical event of displacement, such as the Babylonian captivity. Rather, it was introduced in a more general sense to describe the situation of Jews living in a foreign place outside the region of Palestine. While there were many successful Jewish individuals in the diaspora, this experience was perceived as negative and tragic.[1] In its original usage in the Septuagint, Martin Baumann contends, diaspora was interpreted "as a preparation, an intermediate situation until the final divine gathering in Jerusalem."[2] In other words, in this early conception of diaspora, there was a distinct theological and spiritual dimension and a strong focus on an eventual return to Palestine.[3]

Throughout history, black artists, writers and intellectuals have explored the similarities and differences between Jewish and black experiences. They have focused on a wide range of diasporic themes, such as the scattering of black communities in the context of the transatlantic slave trade or the role of

---

1 | See Martin Baumann, "Diaspora: Genealogies of Semantics and Transcultural Comparison," *Numen* 47.3 (2000): 313-18.
2 | Ibid. 317.
3 | Ibid.

the African mother continent.[4] However, as sociologist Robin Cohen emphasizes, over the centuries, "the classical use of the term, usually capitalized as Diaspora and used only in the singular, was mainly confined to the study of the Jewish experience."[5] It was only in the second half of the twentieth century, in the context of decolonization movements in Africa and the Civil Rights movement in the United States, that historians and intellectuals started to employ the term African diaspora to address "the status and prospects of persons of African descent around the world as well as at home."[6] Since then, in the academic world and in popular discourse, diaspora has become a widely used concept to reflect on questions of black identity, home and belonging and to analyze power structures, processes of exclusion and forms of black resistance. In particular, in many studies and discussions, it is employed as a framework to shed light on aspects that connect black individuals and groups across national and cultural borders.[7] As the historian Tina M. Campt notes, given its popularity, diaspora is often seen as "*the* requisite approach or theoretical model through which one should (or perhaps must) understand all formations of Black community, regardless of historical, geographical, or cultural context."[8] Of course, this development is problematic: As a mere buzzword without paying attention to the specificity of a given black group, the notion of the African diaspora has no analytical value.

Without doubt, the frequent use of the phrase with regard to black social formations is closely connected with a more general and rapid proliferation of the term diaspora in the humanities and social sciences. Especially since the 1980s, it is no longer primarily used for an analysis of Jewish, Armenian, Irish, Greek and black communities.[9] In a 1996 essay, Khachig Tölölyan, a prominent expert in the field and editor of *Diaspora: A Journal of Transnational Studies*, observes that, over the last years, the centuries-old concept of diaspora—once mainly associated with grief, misery, hopelessness and displacement—has been

---

4 | George Shepperson, "African Diaspora: Concept and Context," *Global Dimensions of the African Diaspora*, ed. Joseph E. Harris, 2nd ed. (Washington, D.C.: Howard UP, 1993) 46; Edwards 45; Tiffany Ruby Patterson and Robin D. G. Kelley, "Unfinished Migrations: Reflections on the African Diaspora and the Making of the Modern World," *African Studies Review* 43.1 (2000): 14.
5 | Robin Cohen, *Global Diasporas: An Introduction*, 2nd ed. (New York: Routledge, 2008) 1.
6 | Shepperson 41.
7 | Campt, *Other Germans* 171-72; Edwards 45.
8 | Campt, *Other Germans* 174; italics in the original.
9 | Baumann 322; Rogers Brubaker, "The 'Diaspora' Diaspora," *Ethnic and Racial Studies* 28.1 (2005): 1-2; Khachig Tölölyan, "The Contemporary Discourse of Diaspora Studies," *Comparative Studies of South Asia, Africa and the Middle East* 27.3 (2007): 648.

refashioned and transformed to celebrate migration and mobility[10] and to refer to a wide variety of dispersed formations, such as "exile groups, overseas communities, ethnic and racial minorities."[11] The risk is, Tölölyan argues, that diaspora is turned into "a promiscuously capacious category that is taken to include all the adjacent phenomena to which it is linked."[12] In a similar vein, in a paper called "The 'Diaspora' Diaspora" (2005), Rogers Brubaker reflects on the problematic overuse of the word, which "loses its discriminating power—its ability to pick out phenomena, to make distinctions."[13] The fact that diaspora becomes a universalized concept, "paradoxically, means the disappearance of diaspora."[14]

While it is true that the concept is not without its flaws, especially if it is employed in an all-embracing sense and ahistorical manner, my study is based on the conviction that the notion of the African diaspora provides a useful framework for a critical analysis and illuminating comparison of second-generation neo-slave narratives. In the following, I will focus on recent diaspora theories, especially on postmodern concepts from the field of cultural studies that attempt to analyze the complexity of diasporic experience by adopting a transnational perspective. In particular, I will show that the theories under discussion give very different answers to the key question as to what can be regarded as points of connection between members and groups of a diaspora.[15] Following theorists like Stuart Hall, Avtar Brah, Brent Hayes Edwards and Tina M. Campt, this chapter offers a vibrant interpretation of the African diaspora that is based on "difference." Such a conceptualization attends to the specificity of a given black community without losing sight of the larger framework of the African diaspora.

DISPERSAL, LOSS AND THE STATIC IDEA OF RETURN

In recent scholarly discourse on diasporic formations, there have been several attempts to identify characteristics that serve as unifying links between members of a diaspora group. One prominent example of such an approach is William Safran's paper "Diasporas in Modern Societies: Myths of Homeland and Return" (1991), which provides us with a precise definition of the concept of diaspora based on the history of the Jewish people. Safran, a political scientist, argues that diasporic groups are "expatriate minority communities whose

---

10 | Khachig Tölölyan, "Rethinking Diaspora(s): Stateless Power in the Transnational Moment," *Diaspora: A Journal of Transnational Studies* 5.1 (1996): 3, 8-9, 28.
11 | Ibid. 3.
12 | Ibid. 8.
13 | Brubaker 3.
14 | Ibid.
15 | For similiar concerns, see Campt, *Other Germans* 171-72.

members share"[16] a number of essential features: They (or their forbears) have been shaped by an event of dispersal from their homeland to unfamiliar locations, where they suffer from a sense of loss and displacement. In the diaspora, they keep alive memories of their ancestral—and often idealized—home and are dedicated "to the maintenance or restoration"[17] of their mother country. In Safran's view, members of a diaspora are united by the idea or desire to go back to their place of origin.[18] Since this model of diaspora highlights "the permanence of community through time and space,"[19] to quote Christine Chivallon, it can be described as static. Referring to the Jewish diaspora, it primarily focuses on "the afflictions, isolation and insecurity of living in a foreign place."[20] Diasporic subjects are primarily seen as victims of displacement rather than as active agents shaping their own lives.[21]

In his seminal essay "Diasporas" (1994), a survey of contemporary theories, James Clifford offers an important and often-cited response to Safran's approach and criticizes his decision to define the diaspora concept "by recourse to an 'ideal type.'"[22] According to Clifford, Safran's interpretation is too restrictive because it is "oriented by continuous cultural connections to a source and by a teleology of 'return.'"[23] A closer look at the history of the Jewish people, Clifford contends, reveals a much more complex story than the one indicated in Safran's list. Moreover, his interpretation does not apply to the heterogeneous experiences of African, Caribbean or South Asian diasporic formations. In many cases, "the transnational connections linking diasporas need not be

---

16 | William Safran, "Diasporas in Modern Societies: Myths of Homeland and Return," *Diaspora: A Journal of Transnational Studies* 1 (1991): 83.
17 | Ibid. 84.
18 | Ibid. 83-84. See also James Clifford, "Diasporas," *Cultural Anthropology* 9.3 (1994): 304-05; Cohen 6.
19 | Christine Chivallon, "Beyond Gilroy's Black Atlantic: The Experience of the African Diaspora," trans. Karen E. Fields, *Diaspora: A Journal of Transnational Studies* 11.3 (2002): 360.
20 | Cohen 22.
21 | In 2010/2011, I was actively involved in writing the research proposal for the Marie Skłodowska-Curie Initial Training Program "Diasporic Constructions of Home and Belonging" (CoHaB), offering a short overview of the paradigm shift from a static view of diaspora (associated with scholars like William Safran) to a dynamic interpretation (proposed by scholars like Stuart Hall, Paul Gilroy, James Clifford and Avtar Brah). See Florian Kläger and Klaus Stierstorfer, "Introduction," *Diasporic Constructions of Home and Belonging*, eds. Kläger and Stierstorfer (Berlin: De Gruyter, 2015) 1-7.
22 | Clifford 306.
23 | Ibid.

articulated primarily through a real or symbolic homeland."[24] Clifford urges us "to recognize the strong entailment of Jewish history on the language of diaspora without making that history a definitive model."[25]

DIASPORA AS ARTICULATION AND DIFFERENCE

It is the work of the cultural studies theorist Stuart Hall that has paved the way for a paradigm shift within (African) diaspora studies[26] by focusing our attention to difference, the theory of articulation and the concept of hybridity. His essay "Race, Articulation, and Societies Structured in Dominance" (1980) is not directly concerned with questions of diaspora but an important theoretical starting point for a conception of diaspora as articulation.[27] The text, a complex engagement with theories by Karl Marx, Ernesto Laclau and Louis Althusser, seeks to address a number of problems in current scholarship on "racially structured social formations."[28] In particular, Hall criticizes one-sided scholarly approaches that deal solely with economic aspects and ignore the complexity as well as the "historical specificity"[29] of a given social structure. What is important for our purpose here is that Hall traces "the emergence of a new theoretical paradigm"[30] for the study of social formations: it takes its inspiration from Marx's understanding of the American plantation system as "an articulation between different modes of production."[31]

Determined to move beyond (economic) reductionism, Hall urges us to think of a social formation "as a complex articulated structure."[32] In this theoretical context, the term "articulation" refers to a possible but not necessary linkage between dissimilar elements (of a specific society). It evokes, Hall explains in an interview with Lawrence Grossberg, a connection that can be made, unmade and remade.[33] As an illustration, Hall uses the image of a truck

---

24 | Ibid.
25 | Ibid. For an overview of Clifford's critique, see also Ruth Mayer, *Diaspora: Eine kritische Begriffsbestimmung* (Bielefeld: transcript, 2005) 10-12.
26 | See also footnote 21 in this chapter.
27 | See, for instance, Edwards 59-60; Campt, *Image Matters* 37.
28 | Hall, "Race, Articulation, and Societies Structured in Dominance" 16.
29 | Ibid. 50.
30 | Ibid.
31 | Ibid. 33.
32 | Ibid.
33 | Lawrence Grossberg, "On Postmodernism and Articulation: An Interview with Stuart Hall," *Stuart Hall: Critical Dialogues in Cultural Studies*, eds. David Morley and Kuan-Hsing Chen (London: Routledge, 1996) 141.

"where the front (cab) and back (trailer) can, but need not necessarily, be"[34] articulated with each other. According to Hall, the concept of articulation helps us to see "how specific ideological elements come, under certain conditions, to cohere together within a discourse."[35] What is crucial for our discussion is Hall's claim that such an articulated structure is inevitably a unity "in which things are related, as much through their differences as through their similarities."[36] It is this idea of the complexity of social groups that Hall takes up in his theoretical work on diasporic formations.[37]

In his seminal text "Cultural Identity and Diaspora" (1990), Hall refers to two conceptualizations of cultural identity that, paradoxically, stand in opposition to each other but are also interrelated. The first one, which has influenced black representatives of the Négritude and Pan-African movements, is based on the notions of continuity, similarity and authenticity. In this static interpretation, members of a specific cultural group are linked by collective experiences and codes; they share an essential (authentic) identity that does not change over time and that can be unearthed or articulated through artistic practices.[38] The second understanding of cultural identity introduces the ideas of discontinuity and difference. It is grounded on the insight that cultural identities are not stable and resistant to changes but rather "subject to the continuous 'play' of history, culture and power."[39] As a result, this dynamic view acknowledges that there are important similarities between individuals of the same culture as well as "critical points of deep and significant *difference*."[40]

According to Hall, it is precisely the tension between continuity and discontinuity, similarity and difference that characterizes diasporic life. He illustrates this point by exploring the dynamics of Caribbean diasporic identity, which he understands as a creative fusion of African, European, Asian and American influences, as a dynamic process of "being" and "becoming."[41] The transatlantic slave trade united a heterogeneous group of Africans with different ethnic, linguistic and religious backgrounds: they created a unique culture in the so-called "New World" based on established traditions and new forms as well as on shared experiences and/or memories of slavery, forced migration, anti-black violence and colonialism. In Hall's view, the Caribbean experience of diaspora is not defined by the existence of, and the wish to return to, a common home-

---

34 | Ibid.
35 | Ibid.
36 | Hall, "Race, Articulation, and Societies Structured in Dominance" 38.
37 | Edwards 60.
38 | Hall, "Cultural Identity and Diaspora" 223.
39 | Ibid. 225.
40 | Ibid.; italics in the original.
41 | Ibid.

land associated with authenticity. It is rather characterized by a shared history of forced deportation and racial oppression as well as "by the recognition of a necessary heterogeneity and diversity; by a conception of 'identity' which lives with and through, not despite, difference; by *hybridity*."[42]

CONTINUITY AND INNOVATION: GILROY'S TRANSNATIONAL PARADIGM OF THE BLACK ATLANTIC

In its emphasis on hybridity and on the fluidity of identities, Hall's essay shares important concerns with Paul Gilroy's *The Black Atlantic: Modernity and Double Consciousness* (1993).[43] Gilroy argues against the view "that cultures always flow into patterns congruent with the borders of essentially homogeneous nation states."[44] Such a nation-centered perspective does not capture the complex experiences of black diasporic individuals and groups. Adopting a transnational approach, his study uses the image of the Atlantic Ocean in a metaphorical way to refer to a hybrid system of interactions between black people from different cultural and national backgrounds. The ocean image, in turn, is closely linked with that of the ship "in motion across the spaces between Europe, America, Africa, and the Caribbean."[45] A powerful symbol of black agency, the image of the ship illustrates the exchange of thoughts, concepts and cultural products as well as the various journeys of black intellectuals like W.E.B. Du Bois and Richard Wright. However, in its evocation of the slave vessel and the transatlantic slave trade, it is also a reminder of the traumatic experience of the Middle Passage, focusing our attention to the complex entanglement of racial slavery and Western modernity.[46]

In Gilroy's work, the transnational network of the black Atlantic is conceptualized as a vibrant "counterculture of modernity."[47] There is the powerful argument that, throughout history, black intellectuals and writers have not only been engaged in Western intellectual discourse. They have also contributed to a rethinking of well-established views articulated by European philosophers like Hegel. Determined to challenge any simplistic distinction between center and periphery, Gilroy contends that members of the black Atlantic "stand simulta-

---

42 | Ibid. 235; italics in the original.
43 | See Chivallon 359-60; Mayer 84.
44 | Paul Gilroy, *The Black Atlantic: Modernity and Double Consciousness* (Cambridge: Harvard UP, 1993) 5.
45 | Ibid. 4.
46 | See ibid. 4, 17.
47 | Ibid. 5.

neously both inside and outside the western culture."⁴⁸ In order to illustrate this claim, Gilroy offers a reading of the writings of black intellectuals like Frederick Douglass. He argues that Douglass's depiction of his fight with the slave-breaker Edward Covey can be interpreted as a revisionary account of Hegel's famous master-slave dialectic. In contrast to Hegel's text, Douglass's narrative deals with a slave who is no longer willing to accept the authority of his master. At the risk of death, he decides to revolt against the white man and, after a violent fight, emerges as a self-confident subject.⁴⁹ For Gilroy, this passage has a larger philosophical meaning in that the slave's orientation towards "death rather than bondage articulates a principle of negativity that is opposed to the formal logic and rational calculation characteristic of modern western thinking."⁵⁰ By exploring the past from the perspective of the enslaved, Gilroy seeks to deconstruct the vision of "history as progress"⁵¹ and to highlight the conjunction of civilization and inhumanity on which Western modernity is based.⁵²

What unites the members of the counterculture of the black Atlantic is not only a shared history and collective memory of suffering, oppression and anti-black violence, which is epitomized by "the catastrophic rupture of the middle passage,"⁵³ but also a long tradition of resistance and struggle for black liberation and citizenship across national borders. It is a unique history that has resulted in a rich and diverse artistic and literary heritage. As a hybrid cultural product, black music plays an essential part in Gilroy's concept. Created at the intersection of different black cultures, it serves to demonstrate that black "identity can be understood neither as a fixed essence nor as a vague and utterly contingent construction."⁵⁴ In other words, it can be regarded as a model that allows us to move beyond a static opposition between an essentialist view of black identity based on tradition and a pluralist perspective, which rests on the conviction that "the pursuit of any unifying dynamic or underlying structure of feeling in contemporary black cultures is utterly misplaced."⁵⁵ According to Gilroy, the history of the black Atlantic is marked by both continuity and innovation. In emphasizing the complex relationship between "roots" and "routes" (to use Gilroy's play on words), *The Black Atlantic* offers a critical perspective on the ideology of Afrocentrism and its belief in the purity of black culture.

---

48 | Ibid. 48-49.
49 | See ibid. 60-71.
50 | Ibid. 68.
51 | Ibid. 55.
52 | Ibid. 55, 63.
53 | Ibid. 197.
54 | Ibid. 102.
55 | Ibid. 80.

Reflecting a larger trend in contemporary academic discourse to challenge concepts like authenticity, nationality and tradition, *The Black Atlantic* has been widely celebrated as a seminal text within the field of (African) diaspora studies.[56] Focusing our attention to different forms of black agency, it provides a powerful alternative "to the older tales of unrelenting diasporic victimization,"[57] to quote Paul Tiyambe Zeleza. In terms of terminology, many experts in the field agree that the phrase black Atlantic appropriately captures the idea of a dynamic contact zone between black people without emphasizing a close and stable connection to a specific national or cultural origin.[58]

(POWER) DIFFERENCES AND GAPS: RETHINKING THE CONCEPT OF THE BLACK ATLANTIC

While it is still considered a highly influential study of black diasporic life, increasing numbers of scholars are arguing for a rethinking of *The Black Atlantic*. A major point of critique is that, despite its transnational perspective, Gilroy's text focuses primarily on African American history and culture, taking the experiences of a selected number of African American male artists or intellectuals as the norm and the trauma of the Middle Passage as a unifying concept within the black world.[59] Using the framework of the Atlantic, it is not concerned with interactions and links between groups and members of the African diaspora outside Western contexts and the Anglophone sphere.[60] While Europe serves as an inspiring and transformative place for African Americans, there are hardly any references to the role of Africa within the counterculture of the black Atlantic or to exchanges between Africans and other black individuals.[61] Furthermore, as black feminist scholars like Michelle M. Wright contend, Gilroy does not reflect on the specific experience of black women in the diaspora, failing to take into account that "the category of race can never be fully divorced from the related categories of gender and sexuality."[62]

Turning to questions of hegemony within the formation of the African diaspora, anthropologist Jacqueline Nassy Brown is one of the first to warn against an uncritical celebration of Gilroy's paradigm. As she argues in "Black

---

56 | Mayer 83; see also Chivallon 359.
57 | Zeleza 35.
58 | Mayer 81.
59 | Michelle M. Wright, *Becoming Black: Creating Identity in the African Diaspora* (Durham: Duke UP, 2004) 2-6; Zeleza 37; Mayer 110.
60 | Zeleza 37; Edwards 63.
61 | Mayer 110-11; Zeleza 37.
62 | Wright, *Becoming Black* 6.

Liverpool, Black America, and the Gendering of Diasporic Space" (1998), the hybrid cultural formation of the black Atlantic is constructed as an ideal community without hierarchical structures or exclusion. Centered on the idea of "universal participation across national divides,"[63] it fails to pay attention to power differences and inequalities between and within black diasporic groups. In particular, Gilroy's work does not reflect on "the way American hegemony has determined the lopsided nature of transatlantic exchanges, forging as a result relations of antagonism among blacks transnationally."[64] In Brown's view, *The Black Atlantic* emphasizes the positive aspects of intercultural interactions without considering and problematizing the dominance of African American culture and the (potential) marginalization of other black diasporic groups.

In his thoughtful essay "The Uses of Diaspora" (2001), Brent Hayes Edwards criticizes the tendency within current (U.S.-American) academic discourse to equate diaspora with the transnational paradigm of the black Atlantic, although this conflation of concepts is not suggested by Gilroy.[65] Edwards urges us to reflect on the multifaceted dimension of the concept of the African diaspora by considering the origin of the use of the term in black academic circles in the middle of the twentieth century. Paying special attention to the work of the historian George Shepperson (who is generally considered one of the first intellectuals to employ the phrase in black scholarship), Edwards shows that the orientation towards diaspora as an analytical concept is an important intervention and epistemological contribution to the discourse of black internationalism in the 1960s. In particular, it has to be regarded as a critical reflection on Pan-Africanism and its focus "on vanguardist collaboration toward a unified articulation of the interests of 'African peoples' at the level of international policy."[66] According to Edwards, the word African diaspora is introduced to take account of ideological differences and linguistic divisions existing between and within different groups of African descent in different parts of the world. It is taken up "to break with a depoliticizing emphasis on 'unity' and unidirectional return"[67] to Africa and "forces us to consider discourses of cultural and political linkage only through and across difference."[68] Diaspora is a perfect choice because it "has none of the 'overtones' that make a term like *Pan-Africanism* already contested terrain."[69]

---

63 | Jacqueline Nassy Brown, "Black Liverpool, Black America, and the Gendering of Diasporic Space," *Cultural Anthropology* 13.3 (1998): 296.
64 | Ibid. 297.
65 | Edwards 45.
66 | Ibid. 46.
67 | Ibid. 55.
68 | Ibid. 64.
69 | Ibid. 54; italics in the original.

Taking inspiration from an essay by Léopold Senghor, Edwards uses the term *décalage* to reflect on the complex structure of the African diaspora and the concept of difference. "[O]ne of the many French words that resists translation into English,"[70] *décalage* refers to an incongruity, a fissure in time or a gap in space. In Edwards's concept, it serves as a model to focus our attention to points of disagreement and untranslatability that are inevitably part of any interaction between black diasporic groups:[71] "*[D]écalage* is the kernel of precisely that which cannot be transferred or exchanged, the received biases that refuse to pass over when one crosses the water."[72] In a paradoxical way, for Edwards, it is precisely the fact that there are such striking differences or insurmountable gaps between black communities which "allows the African diaspora to 'step' and 'move' in various articulations."[73] In order to illustrate this intricate view of diaspora, which recalls Hall's theory of articulation, Edwards draws on the image of a joint of the body. It is a place of connection, where different parts of the body are joined together, but also a place of separation. Ultimately, "it is *only* difference—the separation between bones or members—that allows movement."[74]

"THE DYNAMICS OF DIFFERENCE:" CAMPT'S MODEL OF THE AFRICAN DIASPORA

Combining fieldwork in Germany with theoretical analysis, the historian Tina M. Campt has written a groundbreaking study that moves beyond an exclusive focus on similarities between black diasporic formations and illuminates the idea of difference. Adopting an interdisciplinary and transnational perspective, her work *Other Germans: Black Germans and the Politics of Race, Gender, and Memory in the Third Reich* (2004) is situated in the fields and intersections of Holocaust studies, German studies, African diaspora studies and memory studies. Focusing on conceptions of national identity and the complex interplay between race and gender, it addresses the history and diverse experiences of Germans of African descent during the Nazi era. In her close reading of the oral accounts of two Afro-Germans who were born in the 1920s, Campt sheds light on the emergence and articulation of black subjectivity in the "Third Reich." Emphasizing the significance of local contexts and everyday practices, she directs our attention not only to processes of exclusion and discrimination against Afro-Germans; she also identifies forms of inclusion and black resistance. By

---

70 | Ibid. 65.
71 | See also Hartman, *Lose Your Mother* 239, 244.
72 | Edwards 65; italics in the original.
73 | Ibid. 66.
74 | Ibid.; italics in the original.

placing the memories of black individuals at the center of analysis, Campt provides more than a new perspective on the Holocaust and the Nazi regime: she draws on her interview partners' narratives to engage in a critical rethinking of dominant understandings of the African diaspora.[75]

Influenced by the work of Brown and Edwards, Campt observes that "scholarship theorizing Black community and cultural formations often relies on a discourse of diasporic relation in which similarity and commonality are privileged."[76] Most notably, in many discussions of diaspora, there is a tendency to explore the history of black diasporic groups through the eyes of black British or African American culture. According to Campt, this is a manifestation of power differences and hierarchies between black communities around the world that are the result of "different histories of racialization, colonization, and imperialism."[77] The recurrent reference to African America, in particular, "may be read as a discourse that refers not so much to a relation of equity than of hegemony."[78] Moreover, this development directs our attention to the avant-garde role of African American authors, scholars and intellectuals: Over decades, they have been at the forefront of exploring the development and nature of the African diaspora and the complexity of black life. Primarily focused on the American context, their ideas and explanations have become dominant concepts used to describe and interpret the experiences of other black individuals and groups, without considering local specificities.

Examining the complex relation between Afro-German history and that of other black diasporic societies, Campt highlights the heterogeneity of black experiences. Warning against generalizations, she urges us to approach diaspora "with an awareness and articulation of its limits in regard to those Black communities whose histories do not necessarily or comfortably conform to dominant models,"[79] especially to Gilroy's influential paradigm. Unlike members of the black Atlantic, Afro-Germans are not necessarily linked by a common history of transatlantic movement, collective displacement and enslavement. In many cases, they do not share the same ideas of home and belonging and concepts of community. Moreover, their experiences of resistance differ from those of other people of African descent.[80] And yet, in academic contexts and popular discourse, black Germans are frequently "assumed to identify with histories of

---

75 | Campt, *Other Germans* 1-23.
76 | Ibid. 169.
77 | Ibid. 178.
78 | Ibid.
79 | Ibid. 174.
80 | Ibid. 180-81.

struggle (most often those of Africans, Caribbeans, or African-Americans) in which Afro-Germans are not seen as active participants."[81]

In *Other Germans*, Campt offers a more constructive view of black diasporic relations. In her analysis of her interviews with Afro-Germans, she turns our attention to "moments of difference, discrepancy, and translation"[82] that are at the heart of transnational interactions between different black diasporic communities. Focusing on the negotiation of black identity, she calls for an understanding of the African diaspora as a dynamic "set of relations constructed actively by communities for specific purposes."[83] Campt emphasizes that there are significant differences between black groups (based on different histories of racial oppression and resistance, experiences of belonging and processes of subject formation) which cannot be ignored and should not be translated. To sum up, what emerges from Campt's explorations on the history of Afro-Germans is the insight that the African diaspora has to be conceptualized "as a formation that is not solely or even primarily about relations of unity and similarity, but more often and quite profoundly about the dynamics of *difference*."[84] In Campt's view, it is essential to contextualize the history of a particular black diasporic group and to consider the tension between the local specificity of a given community and the larger framework of the African diaspora.

---

81 | Ibid. 180.
82 | Ibid. 23.
83 | Ibid. 173. This view echoes Jacqueline Nassy Brown's understanding of diaspora "as a *counter/part* relation built on cultural and historical equivalences." As Brown explains: "To posit *equivalences* is to put meaningful differences (such as distinct colonial histories) on the same analytical plane at the start, in order to then expose the ways they come to bear in social practice. The backslash in *counter/part* and the stress that may be put on either side of it index shifting relations of antagonism and affinity; these latter terms depend equally on *difference* while highlighting two possibilities for what people can do with it." Jacqueline Nassy Brown, *Dropping Anchor, Setting Sail: Geographies of Race in Black Liverpool* (Princeton: Princeton UP, 2005) 99-100; italics in the original.
84 | Campt, *Other Germans* 169; italics in the original.

Negotiations of Power at the Local Level: Brah's Concept of "Diaspora Space"

The concept of diaspora, Campt's work suggests, not only refers to forms of migration and displacement but also, and essentially, to processes of arrival, dwelling and home-making in specific local contexts.[85] While it is essential to focus on the complex relationship between different groups of the African diaspora, it is also of utmost importance to shed light on internal power differences and tensions at the local level.[86] Avtar Brah's concept of "diaspora space" offers a framework for an analysis of such fissures and negotiations of power. In her influential study *Cartographies of Diaspora: Contesting Identities* (1996), Brah urges scholars of diaspora studies to consider the precise circumstances of dispersion from a center, to think about the following questions when analyzing diasporic journeys, "What socio-economic, political, and cultural conditions mark the trajectories of these journeys? What regimes of power inscribe the formation of a specific diaspora?"[87] Furthermore, like Campt, she asks us to pay attention to the conditions of arrival and the power structures that exist or emerge within a given diasporic community and between different diasporic and indigenous groups.[88] Brah argues for "a multi-axial understanding of power"[89] based on a number of categories like gender, race, class, sexuality and religion.

Such a conceptualization calls into question a static distinction between "minority" and "majority;" Brah's theory points to the "ways in which a group constituted as a 'minority' along one dimension of differentiation may be constructed as a 'majority' along another."[90] In a similar way, depending on the category under consideration, an individual may at the same time belong to a "majority" group and a "minority" community. Putting a strong emphasis on diasporic agency, Brah highlights the interactions that occur between different diasporic groups without the intervention of the supposed dominant group. Through such exchanges, diasporic groups "continually challenge the minoritising and peripheralising impulses of the cultures of dominance."[91]

In addition to deconstructing the distinction between "minority" and "majority," Brah is particularly interested in exploring the meaning of home for diasporic subjects. As she contends, "home" is not only "a mythic place of desire

---

85 | Ibid. 7; see also Campt, *Image Matters* 25, 54.
86 | Campt and Thomas, "Gendering Diaspora: Transnational Feminism, Diaspora and Its Hegemonies" 3.
87 | Brah 182.
88 | Ibid. 182-86.
89 | Ibid. 189.
90 | Ibid.
91 | Ibid. 210.

in the diasporic imagination."[92] It is also the physical and psychological experience of a particular place at a particular moment, a place in the diaspora where identities are negotiated and transformed. In other words, for Brah, the diaspora experience is not only about memories of the past or a sense of displacement and dislocation; it is also closely linked to the idea of location.[93] Expanding on this idea, in a 2013 interview, Campt emphasizes the dialogic character of the African diaspora, arguing that "diaspora is what happens when you're in one place and still have to connect to and utilize the resources of other black communities to make sense of your own."[94] In Campt's view, it is essential to explore the connections and differences between different black diasporic groups in different locations.

In *Cartographies of Diaspora*, Brah shows that a diasporic place can be charged with different connotations, depending on generational and individual differences. Potentially, it is a place where possibilities emerge. In many cases, however, borders play a prominent role in the diaspora. Drawing on Gloria Anzaldua's work, Brah uses the term "border" in a literal sense (a line that divides geographical areas) and in a metaphorical way to address social, cultural, racial and sexual lines of division.[95] "Diaspora space" as proposed by Brah, then, is the place where the concepts of "diaspora, border, and dis/location" intersect, where "boundaries of inclusion and exclusion, of belonging and otherness, of 'us' and 'them', are contested."[96]

To conclude, in Brah's theory, "diaspora space" is a hybrid formation that consists of diasporic[97] and non-diasporic groups (such as indigenous communities) engaged in interactions that challenge static interpretations of diasporic identity and that subvert the hegemony of the supposed dominant culture. However, given the hierarchies and power structures that exist between and within these different groups, it is not a "postmodern playground of 'anything goes', where all kinds of identities are equally valuable and available as if in a 'multicultural supermarket',[98] to quote John McLeod, but a space where diasporic members are confronted with discourses of exclusion and oppression.

---

92 | Ibid. 192.
93 | Ibid. 192-93.
94 | Campt, "Imagining Ourselves."
95 | Brah 198.
96 | Ibid. 208, 209.
97 | Noteworthy, Brah's theory of "diaspora space" is not restricted to the study of a specific diasporic group, such as African Americans in the United States.
98 | John McLeod, *Beginning Postcolonialism*, 2nd ed. (Manchester: Manchester UP, 2000) 260.

THE CONCEPT OF THE AFRICAN DIASPORA AS A CONCEPTUAL FRAMEWORK AND ANALYTICAL TOOL

Transnational Black Dialogues is based on the conviction that the concept of the African diaspora offers an intricate framework in which to situate second-generation neo-slave narratives. Drawing on the work of scholars such as Stuart Hall, Avtar Brah, Brent Hayes Edwards and Tina M. Campt, it argues for a dynamic understanding of diaspora that stresses the idea of "'difference within unity.'"[99] With Campt, this study contends that the African diaspora is a complex transnational network of groups characterized by internal and external hierarchies; a social, cultural and political "formation that is not solely or even primarily about relations of unity and similarity, but more often and quite profoundly about the dynamics of *difference*."[100]

Morrison's *A Mercy*, Hartman's *Lose Your Mother*, Christiansë's *Unconfessed*, Hill's *The Book of Negroes* and James's *The Book of Night Women* are set in different geographical locations and historical periods, e.g. in late seventeenth-century mainland North America, in late eighteenth-century Jamaica and in early nineteenth-century South Africa. Taken together, as a heterogeneous body of texts, these second-generation neo-slave narratives foreground the diversity of the African diaspora and explore the transnational dimension of the history of slavery. At the same time, focusing on different spaces with specific social power structures, they pay close attention to the particularities of local contexts and histories. In *Transnational Black Dialogues*, I show that these twenty-first-century literary texts engage in a dynamic dialogue with contemporary African diaspora theory, participating in and contributing to current debates on the relationship between the local and the global, on the meaning of home, on the complex interplay between "roots" and "routes," on (power) differences and hierarchies within and between black diasporic groups as well as on the enduring legacy of slavery.

Following Campt, this study argues that it is essential to contextualize the specific history of a given black community (e.g. African Canadians, African Caribbeans and South Africans) as well as to examine the complex relation between local contexts and the larger framework of the African diaspora. Characterized by similarities, differences and hierarchies between and within black communities around the world, the African diaspora is, to use Campt's words, "a vibrant site of analysis, investment, and aspiration."[101] In my study, this vibrant understanding of diaspora is both a conceptual framework and an analytical tool for my analysis of Morrison's *A Mercy*, Hartman's *Lose Your Mother*, Christiansë's *Unconfessed*, Hill's *The Book of Negroes* and James's *The Book of Night Women*.

---

99 | Edwards 59.
100 | Campt, *Other Germans* 169; italics in the original.
101 | Ibid. 23.

2 From Human Bondage to Racial Slavery: Toni Morrison's *A Mercy* (2008)

INTRODUCTION

No author is more closely associated with the genre of neo-slave narratives than the African American writer, scholar, intellectual and Nobel Laureate Toni Morrison. Her 1987 *Beloved* is one of the most famous, critically praised and commercially successful novels about the transatlantic slave trade, the dehumanizing nature of chattel slavery and the devastating impact of this history on later generations of African Americans. Written from a black feminist perspective, it offers a thoughtful meditation on the complexity and pain of black womanhood and motherhood under slavery. Since its initial publication in the late 1980s, *Beloved* has provoked public and academic debates about the nature and legacy of black enslavement, countering the erasure of slavery from collective (white) American memory. Moreover, it has inspired numerous black novelists, poets and non-fiction authors to write about the past of slavery both in the United States and in other parts of the world.[1]

Published in 2008, *A Mercy* is Morrison's first novel after *Beloved* that deals explicitly with the experience of the Middle Passage and the history of slavery in the "New World." Whereas *Beloved* explores the haunting and persistent presence of racial slavery by focusing on the life of an (ex-)slave in the period before and after the Civil War, *A Mercy* is set in late seventeenth-century North America (1682-1690)—a time in which different types of human bondage, such as slavery and white indentureship, co-existed. Thus, Morrison's 2008 novel expands the genre of neo-slave narratives that, in their original form, primarily deal with the African American experience of slavery in the nineteenth century. At the heart of *A Mercy* is an exploration of the paradigm shift from human bondage

---

1 | For a discussion of the significance of Morrison's *Beloved* in American literature and culture, see also my introduction to *Transnational Black Dialogues*; see also Broeck, "Trauma, Agency, Kitsch and the Excesses of the Real" 239-57; Broeck, "Enslavement as Regime of Western Modernity" 34-36.

to racial slavery that took place in the early North American colonies. Crucially, Morrison's novel particularly examines the socio-psychological conditions under which anti-black racism developed and flourished in the "New World."

In her 2006 essay "Trauma, Agency, Kitsch and the Excesses of the Real," Sabine Broeck calls attention to a prevalent and disturbing trend in the critical reception of Morrison's first neo-slave narrative *Beloved*:[2] Over the last decades, many scholars and cultural critics have presented what Broeck describes as a "kitsch"[3] interpretation of Morrison's best-seller. Primarily concentrating on the novel's plot and, more specifically, its seemingly "optimistic" ending (i.e., Beloved's disappearance, Paul D's reunion with Sethe and Denver's successful struggle for self-determination), they have analyzed *Beloved* solely as a narrative of liberation and redemption; as a text that ultimately articulates the possibility of working through and healing the trauma of slavery.

According to Broeck, these critics have failed to take into account *Beloved*'s inner ambiguities and complex ethical agenda: Employing innovative narrative strategies (e.g. fragmentation and textual blanks), Morrison not only brings to light forgotten or suppressed memories of slavery and the Middle Passage but also critically reflects on the ultimate impossibility of bearing witness to this traumatic experience and of closing the wounds of this past.[4] In fact, as Yvette Christiansë contends, one of Morrison's most significant achievements is that she "complicates and resists our desire to read her fiction as a simple kind of memory work defined by the positive recovery of that which has been left out of the historical record."[5] And yet, despite Morrison's effort to challenge the idea of the reconciliatory power of neo-slave narratives, most readers and critics continue to "treat the fiction as being precisely that: a consoling filling in of blank spaces, a giving voice to the long-muted subjects of history."[6]

Like her *magnum opus Beloved*, Morrison's ninth novel *A Mercy* is a multi-perspective, highly fragmented, self-reflexive, non-linear and poetic text full of unresolved tensions and inner ambiguities. This complex narrative form, I argue, reflects the black slave characters' experiences of uprootedness, sexual abuse and fragmentation in late seventeenth-century North America. Without denying the possibility of black agency and resistance, *A Mercy* highlights the crushing power of chattel slavery and the traumatizing and debilitating effects of racial discrimination and oppression, particularly drawing attention to the hardships of slave motherhood and the suffering caused by the separation of slave families.

---

2 | See also the introduction to this study.
3 | Broeck, "Trauma, Agency, Kitsch and the Excesses of the Real" 247.
4 | Ibid. 239-57; see also Broeck, *White Amnesia – Black Memory?* 36-40.
5 | Christiansë, *Toni Morrison* 46.
6 | Ibid. 35.

I read Morrison's *A Mercy* as a powerful black feminist reflection on—and intertextual intervention against—reductive reconciliatory interpretations of *Beloved* in academic and public discourses.[7] In a way similar to Saidiya Hartman's *Lose Your Mother*, Yvette Christiansë's *Unconfessed* and Marlon James's *The Book of Night Women*, *A Mercy* provides a conceptualization of slavery as a dehumanizing and destructive system of exploitation and "thingification." Instead of foregrounding the healing power of black solidarity, love, interracial cooperation, literacy and creative work in the life of the slave protagonist Florens, Morrison addresses the complex theme of intra-black violence, sheds light on the ultimate breakdown of a multiracial group of uprooted women and directs the reader's attention to the limits of black self-invention in the early colonial period. Focusing on loss and grief as defining elements of black (slave) life, *A Mercy* participates in a constructive discussion with Afro-pessimism about the meaning of (anti-)blackness.[8] Significantly, like Hartman's *Lose Your Mother* and Christiansë's *Unconfessed*, Morrison's novel self-reflexively engages with questions of representability and ethics as it comments on and highlights the impossibility of giving a coherent account of Florens's life and of working through and closing the wounds of slavery.

In terms of structure, this chapter opens with a critical discussion of Morrison's representation of a seventeenth-century transatlantic journey from England to America by a group of (forced) lower-class white female migrants. Examining the concept of human bondage in all its variety, *A Mercy* draws attention to the plight of lower-class women and, more specifically, the misogynistic nature of the "mail-order bride system" in the patriarchal Atlantic world of the seventeenth century. And yet, Morrison, I argue, foregrounds race as a central dimension of modern transatlantic history and never allows the reader to lose sight of the differences in the experiences of African captives during the Middle Passage and (forced) European migrants.

After giving a short historical overview of slavery and black life in seventeenth-century mainland North America, I will focus on Morrison's exploration of the meaning of "thingification" and the novel's rendering of Florens's experiences of anti-black racism. I will show that *A Mercy* especially foregrounds the debilitating psychological effects of racial discrimination and oppression on the black enslaved protagonist. Moreover, this chapter analyzes the novel's depiction of Florens's complex (violent) relationship with a free black man, before examining the relevance Morrison attributes to the breakdown of the female

---

7 | For a similar interpretation of Morrison's *A Mercy*, see also Maria I. Diedrich, "'The Burden of Our Theories' Genealogies:' Lessons in Decolonization of Gender," *Sabine Broeck: Plotting Against Modernity; Critical Interventions in Race and Gender*, eds. Karin Esders, Insa Härtel and Carsten Junker (Sulzbach: Helmer, 2014) 269.
8 | See also Wilderson 58.

community on the Vaark farm in Milton, in upstate New York.[9] In the last part, I will demonstrate that Morrison strategically employs specific narrative and aesthetic strategies, including self-reflexivity and non-linearity, to capture Florens's traumatic experiences of loss, dissolution and fragmentation.

ON BOARD THE *ANGELUS*: REBEKKA'S TRANSATLANTIC JOURNEY TO AMERICA

"How long will it take will she get lost will he be there will he come will some vagrant rape her?"[10] In the middle of *A Mercy*, Morrison introduces the reader to the thoughts of sixteen-year-old Rebekka, a lower-class white woman born in seventeenth-century London. Rebekka is sold by her parents to get married to Jacob Vaark, an Anglo-Dutch trader, who has recently inherited a tract of land in one of the American colonies but needs a wife in order to receive the property. As a "mail-order bride" expected to raise a family with a stranger in a foreign land, Rebekka faces an uncertain future. Morrison strategically uses a stream-of-consciousness technique to highlight the precariousness of Rebekka's situation and to give deep insight into the white woman's anxious state of mind. While *A Mercy* explores the misogynistic nature of the seventeenth-century "mail-order bride system," the novel also suggests that America holds the promise of a better future for Rebekka: Her departure from Europe means leaving behind a town full of crime and poverty (that is, London during the Restoration) and getting rid of family members who treat her with indifference and contempt.

The stream-of-consciousness passage quoted above marks the beginning of a chapter written from Rebekka's perspective, several years after her arrival in the "New World." Focusing on race as a defining characteristic of American life, Morrison explores Rebekka's transformation from a lower-class woman to a mistress over slaves and servants, from the daughter of a poor waterman to the wife of an ambitious farmer. And yet, challenging mythical conceptions of the "New World" as a paradise for (poor) white Europeans, *A Mercy* does not offer a triumphant account of Rebekka's American experience but instead draws

---

9 | In *Toni Morrison: An Ethical Poetics*, Christiansë tries to identify the location of the Vaark farm: "Vaark's journey passes 'Fort Orange: Cape Henry: Nieuw Amsterdam; Wiltwyck,' and he passes through Algonquin, Susquehanna, Chesapeake, and Lenape territories. [...] Since Fort Orange is present-day Albany, Vaark's directions suggest that he has come from upstate New York." Christiansë, *Toni Morrison* 263.
10 | Toni Morrison, *A Mercy: A Novel* (New York: Random House Large Print, 2008) 117. All further references to this novel (M) will be cited in the text and will refer to this edition.

attention to the omnipresence of death and illness in the lives of white immigrants: Rebekka not only has to cope with the loss of Jacob and her children but also suffers from smallpox, one of the most dreaded diseases in colonial America.[11] Confined to bed, in a state of fever, she starts to look back on her past.

Rebekka's story is one of migration that involves a six-week transatlantic passage on board the *Angelus*, in the steerage of the vessel, "a dark space below next to the animal stalls" (M 133). Highlighting the degrading and dehumanizing treatment of lower-class European women in the seventeenth century, Morrison shows that Rebekka is still traumatized by the memory of the water, the constricted space, the darkness and unhygienic conditions on her voyage to America: "Light and weather streamed from a hatch; a tub for waste sat beside a keg of cider; a basket and a rope where food could be let down and the basket retrieved" (M 133). As a lower-class passenger, there are only a few moments when Rebekka is allowed to leave the darkness and spend an hour on deck. Throughout the journey, she is forced to defecate in front of strangers.

Of course, Rebekka is not an African captive and the *Angelus* is not a slave ship transporting human cargo from Africa to the Americas. Still, given the terrible conditions in the steerage, a space that resembles a prison, Morrison evokes the imagery of the Middle Passage in this scene. At the same time, however, *A Mercy* never allows the reader to forget the essential differences in the experiences of poor white female migrants and enslaved people of African descent: Unlike black slaves torn from family and kin, exposed to extreme forms of violence and transformed into movable commodities, Rebekka has not been brutally kidnapped and put in chains. As a free white woman, she has a number of choices: She is the one who makes the decision to run away, to hide somewhere in London or to board the ship to America.

Unlike enslaved individuals violently taken to an unknown location,[12] Rebekka knows, however vaguely, the destination of her journey. Her future is not that of a slave denied subjecthood and reduced to an object but that of a slave mistress. Therefore, although Morrison conjures up certain images of the Middle Passage in this chapter, it would be highly reductive and misleading to describe Rebekka's sea voyage across the Atlantic as a "white Middle Passage:"[13] This is a term used by the African American social historian Lerone Bennett,

---

11 | For an overview of the history of smallpox in the early colonial period, see Gerald N. Grob, *The Deadly Truth: A History of Disease in America* (Cambridge, MA: Harvard UP, 2002) 72-74.
12 | See Maria I. Diedrich and Werner Sollors, "Introduction," *The Black Columbiad: Defining Moments in African American Literature and Culture*, eds. Diedrich and Sollors (Cambridge, MA: Harvard UP, 1994) 4-5.
13 | Lerone Bennett, Jr., *The Shaping of Black America: The Struggles and Triumphs of African-Americans, 1619 to the 1990s* (New York: Penguin Books, 1975) 45.

Jr. in his 1975 study *The Shaping of Black America: The Struggles and Triumphs of African-Americans*, when he refers to the transatlantic passage by white indentured servants. For Rebekka, the journey is an extremely traumatizing experience but it differs fundamentally from the situation of African captives who, as Maria I. Diedrich and Werner Sollors put it, "were herded together on slave vessels by beings whom they could only perceive as evil spirits, skinless and savage creatures, as early slave narratives relate."[14]

In *A Mercy*, Rebekka's experience on board the *Angelus* is as much about degradation based on class as it is about white female solidarity. Below deck, she stays with a group of "exiled, thrown-away" (M 135) female migrants, who face a future of unpaid labor in America: thieves like Dorothea and ten-year-old Patty or prostitutes like Judith and Lydia, "ordered to choose between prison or exile" (M 133). However different their stories are, the women share a sense of displacement but show no signs of resignation, creating a space of resistance against patriarchal forms of oppression: "Women of and for men, in those few moments they were neither" (M 139). Without downplaying the hardships on board the *Angelus*, this scene accentuates the power of female cooperation in the face of misogyny and oppression.

Morrison's representation of a transatlantic journey from Europe to America by a group of (forced) female migrants directs our attention to one of the novel's central concerns: Marked by a polyphony of voices, a variety of narrative perspectives, *A Mercy* explores the concept of human bondage in all its diversity, particularly drawing attention to the plight of lower-class women in the patriarchal Atlantic world of the seventeenth century. While Morrison never loses sight of the possibility of female resistance, her novel depicts a culture in which lower-class white women are exploited, sold and bought as property. By focusing on this inhuman trade in women, *A Mercy* contributes to an enormous broadening of the genre of neo-slave narratives usually primarily dedicated to the reconstruction of black history. It addresses the horrors of the Middle Passage, the crushing power of chattel slavery and the plight of poor European migrants in the late seventeenth century, without conflating the experiences of African slaves, on the one hand, and lower-class white women and indentured servants, on the other. This is a crucial difference to Bennett's approach in *The Shaping of Black America*: His usage of the term "white Middle Passage"[15] implies that white indentured servants were exposed to the same forms of violence, humiliation and "thingification" as African captives during the Middle Passage.

Significantly, *A Mercy* is not only concerned with the history of European migration to America in the seventeenth century. It also explores the complex web of power relations between enslaved and free individuals of African de-

---

14 | Diedrich and Sollors 4.
15 | Bennett, Jr. 45.

scent, Native Americans and whites in mainland North America. Before examining a key scene of the novel that offers a striking example of anti-black racism, I will give a short historical overview of the period the novel is set in: It is a time of significant transformations associated with the rise of the plantation system and what the historian Ira Berlin describes as the change "from a society with slaves to a slave society."[16]

HISTORICAL CONTEXT: RACE IN SEVENTEENTH-CENTURY NORTH AMERICA

Over the last decades, Berlin's work has played a crucial role in reshaping our understanding of chattel slavery and (early) black life in the "New World." One of Berlin's central arguments is that slavery differed from region to region in mainland North America and took on different forms over the years, decades and centuries. In his influential study *Generations of Captivity: A History of African-American Slaves* (2003), he pays scrupulous attention to the particularities of places like New Netherland and Virginia and distinguishes between different generations of slaves, such as the charter generations and the plantation generations.[17] Within the historiography of American slavery, in general, and early black life, in particular, Berlin's "segmented approach pushed aside older studies that tended to homogenize African American experiences over time and to focus largely on the antebellum South,"[18] to use Graham R. Hodges's words.

As Berlin has shown, so-called "Atlantic creoles were among the first Africans transported to the mainland"[19] in the sixteenth century. These women and men of mixed European-African ancestry were fluent in several African and European languages and well-informed about the commercial system of the Atlantic world. Some of them were shipped to the "New World" as slaves, whereas others arrived in the Americas as interpreters or members of ships' crews.[20] Together, these Atlantic creoles "became black America's charter generations."[21]

---

16 | Ira Berlin, *Generations of Captivity: A History of African-American Slaves* (2003; Cambridge, MA: Harvard UP, 2004) 55.
17 | Ibid. 2-31.
18 | Graham Russell Hodges, "Historiography of Early Black Life," *Encyclopedia of African American History, 1619-1895: From the Colonial Period to the Age of Frederick Douglass*, ed. Paul Finkelman, vol. 2 (Oxford: Oxford UP, 2006) 169.
19 | Berlin, *Generations of Captivity* 30.
20 | Ibid. 2-31. See also Ira Berlin, *The Making of African America: The Four Great Migrations* (New York: Penguin, 2010) 67-68.
21 | Berlin, *Generations of Captivity* 30.

According to Berlin, Atlantic creoles successfully used their skills and knowledge to build a new home in mainland North America. In seventeenth-century New Netherland, where some of them were enslaved by the Dutch, Atlantic creoles created their own families, took part in religious activities of the colony and managed to live semi-independent lives. They worked together with European servants and, occasionally, they owned slaves, demonstrating that, as Berlin puts it, "race—like lineage and religion—was just one of many markers in the social order."[22] In many cases, in the Dutch colony of New Netherland but also in English colonies like Virginia and Maryland, enslaved Atlantic creoles achieved their freedom.[23] In contrast to slave societies, these early American colonies can be described as societies with slaves, in which different systems of labor (slavery, indenture and free wage labor) co-existed and slavery was "marginal to the central productive processes."[24]

A large number of white European migrants to the New World arrived as indentured servants. Unable to pay their transatlantic passage, they had to rely on the financial support of others. In order to repay their debts, they were forced to work for a master for a fixed number of years.[25] Like slaves, they were subjects of abuse, such as overwork, violent beatings and sexual assault.[26] In contrast to African captives, they had a number of rights: "They could sue and testify in court, though they could not vote. They could not engage in trade, but they could own property,"[27] Paul Spickard explains in *Almost All Aliens: Immigration, Race, and Colonialism in American History and Identity* (2007). Of utmost importance, their status as servants was not passed on to their daughters and sons, though additional years could be added to their terms.[28] Brought together as people in bondage, enslaved women and men of African descent and white indentured servants built relationships and cooperated in acts of (violent) resistance.[29]

The most famous interracial insurgency in the seventeenth century was Bacon's Rebellion (1676), an uprising led by the white planter Nathaniel Bacon against the leaders of the colony of Virginia: "Bacon developed plans in 1675

---

22 | Ibid. 33.
23 | Ibid. 31-39. See also Berlin, *The Making of African America* 68.
24 | Berlin, *Generations of Captivity* 9.
25 | Winthrop D. Jordan, *The White Man's Burden: Historical Origins of Racism in the United States* (Oxford: Oxford UP, 1974) 28.
26 | Paul Spickard, *Almost All Aliens: Immigration, Race, and Colonialism in American History and Identity* (New York: Routledge, 2007) 61.
27 | Ibid.
28 | Ibid.
29 | Edmund S. Morgan, *American Slavery, American Freedom: The Ordeal of Colonial Virginia* (New York: Norton, 1975) 327.

to seize Native American lands in order to acquire more property for himself and others and nullify the threat of Indian raids," Michelle Alexander explains. "When the planter elite in Virginia refused to provide militia support for his scheme, Bacon retaliated, leading an attack on the elite, their homes, and their property."[30] In the course of the uprising, Bacon's troops set fire to Jamestown and killed hundreds of Native Americans. Significantly, large numbers of white servants and black slaves participated in the rebellion, hoping to obtain the freedom promised by Bacon and his followers. However, the uprising was suppressed shortly after Bacon's death in October 1676.[31]

In the late seventeenth century, the plantation system began to emerge in the Chesapeake region, creating an enormous demand for laborers. In the aftermath of Bacon's Rebellion, white planters were afraid of further acts of collaboration between poor whites and blacks. They started to replace white servants with black slaves, which were kidnapped from Africa and directly taken to the Chesapeake region in large numbers.[32] As a result, a colony like Virginia changed from a society with slaves to a slave society, in which black slaves were the main source of labor. Treated as chattel, the newly arrived Africans and their descendants were exposed to extreme violence and brutality. In contrast to members of the charter generations, they had few chances to establish families, to live independently and to escape slavery.[33] Of utmost importance, in the second half of the seventeenth century, racist laws were introduced to "recognize permanent, inherited slave status for African immigrant workers."[34]

In *A Mercy*, Morrison explores this period of dramatic changes for blacks by focusing on the fate of Florens, a sixteen-year-old slave woman. The following sub-chapter analyzes Morrison's representation of Florens's encounter with a group of white women and men in a small village presumably inhabited by Puritans. Examining the complex meaning of "thingification," it is a key scene in the novel which directs our attention to the socio-psychological conditions under which anti-black racism developed and flourished in seventeenth-century North America.

---

30 | Alexander 24.
31 | Kathleen M. Brown, "Bacon's Rebellion," *The Oxford Encyclopedia of American Social History*, ed. Lynn Dumenil, vol. 1 (Oxford: Oxford UP, 2012) 99-100.
32 | Berlin, *Generations of Captivity* 53-55; Berlin, *The Making of African America* 68-69; Spickard 4, 69-67; Morgan 328.
33 | Berlin, *Generations of Captivity* 6-9, 53-67; Berlin, *The Making of African America* 68.
34 | Spickard 71.

"A THING APART:" FLORENS'S ENCOUNTER WITH THE PURITANS

Born as a slave in Maryland, Florens grows up on a tobacco farm owned by the Portuguese slaveholder D'Ortega, who is compelled to offer some of his slaves to his creditor Jacob Vaark. Subjected to exploitation and sexual abuse by her master and mistress, Florens's mother desperately begs Jacob to choose her daughter, wishing to protect her from rape and violence on D'Ortega's plantation. Florens, who is taken to Jacob's farm in upstate New York, does not know—and will never learn—the motives behind her mother's action. As a result, for the rest of the novel, she is overwhelmed by a profound sense of loss, rejection and loneliness.

When her new mistress Rebekka suffers from smallpox, the young black woman embarks on a dangerous journey to find her lover, a free black man simply called the Blacksmith, who knows how to cure Rebekka's illness. At nightfall, Florens comes into a small Puritan village, a place where religious extremism and xenophobia go hand in hand: The scene is set in 1690, more than a decade after Bacon's Rebellion, when anti-black laws had already been passed. It is also the period of witchcraft accusations in New England, just a few years before the notorious incidents in places like Salem in colonial Massachusetts, "a time of tensions epitomized by contests between religious practices and calls for unity against ungodliness."[35] The Puritan villagers in *A Mercy* are described as being full of fear, hate, distrust and prejudices: They believe in the existence of Satan and accuse Jane, a white girl suffering from a squint, of being a demon, primarily because of Jane's physical handicap. When the Puritans discover Florens, however, they no longer focus on Jane but turn on the black woman. Based on their social status as free white individuals, the villagers judge from a position of supposed moral and racial superiority and identify Florens as a dangerous being. In the Puritans' view, it is Florens's skin color, her blackness, which makes her the devil's servant. Although a letter written by Rebekka provides information on Florens and her journey, they reduce the black woman to an embodiment of evil.

What follows is a scene that Aimé Césaire would describe as a process of "thingification," a passage that reminds us of the inhuman and degrading treatment of slaves at slave auctions: Afraid to touch her, the Puritans order Florens to take off all her clothes and start to examine her feet, teeth and private parts. Between Florens and the white men and women, there is, to use Césaire's words, "[n]o human contact, but relations of domination and submission."[36] Based on racial prejudice and ignorance, the Puritans regard Florens as an ob-

---
35 | Christiansë, *Toni Morrison* 59.
36 | Césaire 42.

ject, a thing, examining her "across distances without recognition" (M 186). Focusing on the devaluation and objectification of blackness in a white-dominated community, the scene in the Puritan village evokes the slave market, i.e., the fate of future generations of African Americans treated as chattel in a racist nation. It anticipates a society in which the concepts of slavery and race are closely intertwined and blackness is equated with inferiority.

Crucially, *A Mercy* not only directs the reader's attention to the process of exclusion and dehumanization itself but, in a passage that echoes Frantz Fanon's reflections on anti-blackness in his influential work *Black Skin, White Masks* (1952), it sheds light on the devastating psychological effects of this act of othering on Florens.[37] Morrison's slave protagonist, Christiansë argues, "is as exploded at the surface of the skin as is Fanon, who finds himself the object of a look that does not seek reciprocity but only fixity and subjugation."[38] While Florens manages to escape from the Puritans with Jane's help, she will never forget the racialized gaze of her white interrogators, the eyes of the villagers which "stare and decide if [her] navel is in the right place if [her] knees bend backward like the forelegs of a dog" (M 189). Reduced to a thing, she begins to believe in her supposed inferiority, to feel like "a thing apart" (M 189):

Inside I am shrinking. I climb the streambed under watching trees and know I am not the same. I am losing something with every step I take. I can feel the drain. Something precious is leaving me. I am a thing apart. With the letter I belong and am lawful. Without it I am a weak calf abandon by the herd, a turtle without shell, a minion with no telltale signs but a darkness I am born with, outside, yes, but inside as well and the inside dark is small, feathered and toothy. Is that what my mother knows? Why she chooses me to live without? Not the outside dark we share, a minha mãe and me, but the inside one we don't. Is this dying mine alone? Is the clawing feathery thing the only life in me? (M 189-90)

Like Hartman's *Lose Your Mother*, Christiansë's *Unconfessed* and James's *The Book of Night Women*, *A Mercy* engages in a discussion with Afro-pessimist discourse about the destructive nature of anti-blackness, focusing on grief, loss and mourning as definers of black life: In the passage quoted above, Morrison strategically uses specific metaphors from the semantic field of animals to express Florens's feelings of despair and insecurity, drawing attention to the slave woman's transformation into a weaker and more vulnerable person. *A Mercy* explores how Florens's experience of "thingification" in the Puritan

---

37 | Frantz Fanon, *Black Skin, White Masks*, trans. Richard Philcox (1952; New York: Grove Press, 2008). For a similar interpretation of Morrison's representation of Florens's traumatizing experience in the Puritan village, see Christiansë, *Toni Morrison* 58.
38 | Christiansë, *Toni Morrison* 58.

village destroys the black woman's self-esteem—and how the incident brings back excruciatingly painful memories of Florens's separation from her mother.

Focusing on the traumatizing effects of the destruction of slave families on slave children, Morrison has her black protagonist suffer from self-hatred and self-alienation: Florens interprets her mother's behavior on D'Ortega's plantation as an act of abandonment, blames herself for being rejected, thinks that her mother has given her away because she behaves like a beast, a monster with feathers and claws. This scene shows that Florens has internalized the Puritans' racist image, a conception of the black subject as a non-human being. It is this internalization of black inferiority that Fanon identifies as one of the most destructive effects of colonialism on the colonized.[39]

INTRA-BLACK VIOLENCE: FLORENS'S NIGHTMARISH REUNION WITH THE BLACKSMITH

Morrison offers an interpretation of diaspora that "is embedded within a multi-axial understanding of power,"[40] to use Avtar Brah's words: Highlighting the intersections between race, class, gender and sexuality, *A Mercy* not only explores the complexity of black-white relations in early North America but also addresses intra-black tensions, conflicts and violence through Florens. The novel demonstrates that the African diaspora is a social formation marked by internal hierarchical structures—or what Tina Campt and Deborah Thomas describe as "asymmetrical relations of power."[41]

Instead of foregrounding the healing power of love between a black woman and a black man, Morrison constructs Florens's reunion with the Blacksmith as a nightmare scenario: Destabilized by the Puritans' treatment and filled with jealousy, Florens attacks Malaik, an orphan adopted by her lover. Without listening to her story, the Blacksmith pushes Florens away, hits her and accuses her of being "a slave by choice" (M 233). His feelings of resentment and hostility towards Florens are a direct response to the woman's violent outburst; he is also repelled by Florens's strong and unquestioning attachment to him.

However, given the Blacksmith's status, there is another explanation for his reaction: As a free man who is allowed to "marry, own things, travel, sell his own labor" (M 73), the Blacksmith belongs to a higher social sphere, although he is not a white person. A talented healer and professional craftsman

---

39 | See Fanon, *Black Skin, White Masks* 2.
40 | Brah 189.
41 | Campt and Thomas, "Gendering Diaspora: Transnational Feminism, Diaspora and Its Hegemonies" 3.

from New Amsterdam, he can be described as an "Atlantic creole."[42] As Berlin explains, "whatever tragedy befell them, Atlantic creoles did not arrive in the New World as deracinated chattels stripped of their past and without resources to meet the future."[43] In most cases, they were familiar with various cultural contexts, spoke several African and European languages, took part in important commercial activities and worked as craftsmen, traders or hunters together with Europeans. In other words, their experiences differed fundamentally from those of later generations of Africans reduced to chattel in North America.[44]

A Mercy shows that the Blacksmith's status is threatened by the social and political changes that take place in the early colonial period: the conflation of race and slavery. In order to demonstrate his liberty and strengthen his position of power, the Blacksmith, Valerie Babb argues, "must maintain a clear demarcation between his free blackness and Florens's enslaved blackness."[45] In this sense, the Blacksmith's rejection of, and hostility towards, Florens is more than a way to assert his authority and manhood; it is a means to keep his distance from slavery.[46] Depicting the intricate relationship between a female captive and a free black man, A Mercy reflects on the complexity of black life and the specific vulnerability of enslaved women in seventeenth-century North America: Instead of offering a triumphant account of a love affair, Morrison directs the reader's attention to violent conflicts, negotiations of power and hierarchies based on race and gender within the black diasporic community.

Examining the complex theme of intra-black violence, Morrison's *A Mercy* contributes to a radical re-writing of American history from a black feminist perspective and enters into a powerful intertextual dialogue with slave narratives: As Maria I. Diedrich has shown, black antebellum writers like Frederick Douglass had to address "a predominantly white audience who were to be won as allies against slavery and racism."[47] Seeking to draw attention to the slaves' moral superiority over their white oppressors, they focused on "black protagonists whom no form of violence and injustice could dehumanize; suffering, instead of brutalizing their victims, ennobled them."[48] One of Morrison's central concerns in texts like *Beloved* and *A Mercy* is to challenge this strict dichotomy between black victimhood and white guilt culture: Her novels stress the brutalizing impact of

---

42 | Berlin, *Generations of Captivity* 23-39. See also my short overview of the historical period Morrison's *A Mercy* is set in.
43 | Berlin, *Generations of Captivity* 32.
44 | See ibid. 23-39.
45 | Valerie Babb, "E Pluribus Unum? The American Origins Narrative in Toni Morrison's *A Mercy*," *MELUS* 36.2 (2011): 154.
46 | See ibid.
47 | Diedrich, "'Things Fall Apart?'" 181.
48 | Ibid.

chattel slavery on both blacks and whites, deconstructing static interpretations of black communities as homogenous groups of passive victims. Giving voice to the specific plight of slave women, Morrison shows that black female captives not only suffered from the same forms of white violence as their fellow male slaves; they were also subjected to (sexual) abuse by black men.[49]

In the late 1980s, shortly after the publication of *Beloved*, Morrison was sharply criticized by black male intellectuals and writers like Ishmael Reed and Stanley Crouch for focusing explicitly on forms of disloyalty, violence and corruption within the black community and, particularly, for representing black male protagonists as both victims of white racism and oppressors of black women. These black male critics, Diedrich explains, were dismayed by the author's radical feminist project and envious of the critical and popular success of Morrison's novels.[50] Significantly, while Morrison's literary work has "aroused the ire of many male competitors,"[51] it has inspired and encouraged numerous black female writers, including second-generation neo-slave narrative authors like Yvette Christiansë, to adopt a radical black feminist perspective, to shed light on the specific experiences of black women, to address the theme of intra-black violence under slavery. As I will argue in chapter 4 of this study, in *Unconfessed*, Christiansë examines the ways in which enslaved men like Jeptha try to restore some sense of self-worth and self-control by humiliating and oppressing female slaves like Sila, the novel's protagonist.

In *A Mercy*, Morrison ends the scene in the Blacksmith's cabin by exploring the detrimental effects of humiliation on Florens: she attacks, and probably kills, her lover. In her description of the struggle with the Blacksmith, Morrison's first-person narrator reuses the image of a beast with feathers and claws to characterize her behavior: "Feathers lifting, I unfold. The claws scratch and scratch until the hammer is in my hand" (M 233). This quotation is another indication that Florens has developed a self-image that is consistent with the Puritans' racist conception. Focusing on the transformation of despair and fear into violence, *A Mercy* illustrates that Florens sees no other option but to attack the Blacksmith in order to express her feelings of utter hopelessness.

Exploring the complex nature of white-black and black-black relations in the early colonies, Morrison makes sure that the reader recognizes the differences between Florens's reactions in the Puritan village and in the Blacksmith's cabin. Born as a slave, exposed to the cruelty of white men and women, Florens has internalized notions of white supremacy and privilege. This is the main reason

---

49 | Ibid. 175-86; see also Maria I. Diedrich, *Ausbruch aus der Knechtschaft: Das Amerikanische Slave Narrative zwischen Unabhängigkeitserklärung und Bürgerkrieg* (Stuttgart: Franz Steiner, 1986) 78-83.
50 | Diedrich, "'Things Fall Apart?'" 175-86.
51 | Ibid. 177.

why she does not attack the Puritans when they treat her like a thing and reduce her to "flesh,"[52] to use Hortense J. Spillers's term. At the same time, Morrison represents the Puritans' examination as an utterly traumatizing experience that continues to haunt the slave woman for the rest of her life. Florens's violent act against the Blacksmith is primarily a result of the dehumanization she has experienced in the Puritan village. While she is powerless to destroy the white-controlled power structure, she strikes back when the Blacksmith humiliates and hurts her. Instead of celebrating Florens's reunion with her lover, the scene in the Blacksmith's cabin highlights the destructive and enduring impact of anti-black violence on relationships within the black community.

BORDERS AND BORDER CROSSINGS ON THE VAARK FARM

As an enslaved woman, Florens's fate depends on the decisions of her white mistress. The black protagonist's destiny is entwined with that of the little community on the Vaark farm, a heterogeneous group of displaced women. Brought together in a specific place at a particular moment in time, these individuals are part of a "diaspora space,"[53] to use Brah's term, in which meanings of home and relations of power are negotiated. Based on "a multi-axial understanding of power,"[54] Brah's theory helps to explore the complex hierarchical structures in late seventeenth-century North America as depicted in *A Mercy*. In the following, I will show that Morrison constructs Rebekka's farm in Milton as a highly ambivalent space. While her novel focuses on individual transformations and border crossings, it also draws attention to acts of othering and discrimination against Native Americans and African Americans on the Vaark farm.

In *A Mercy*, Morrison depicts all of her female characters as uprooted individuals who suffer from their separation from home and family. Having witnessed the destruction of her native village, Lina, a Native American servant, is plagued by survivor guilt. She is traumatized by images of dead infants, of peo-

---

52 | In her influential essay "Mama's Baby, Papa's Maybe: An American Grammar Book," Spillers differentiates between "body" and "flesh:" "But I would make a distinction between 'body' and 'flesh' and impose that distinction as the central one between captive and liberated subject-positions. In that sense, before the 'body' there is the 'flesh,' that zero degree of social conceptualization that does not escape concealment under the brush of discourse, or the reflexes of iconography. [...] If we think of the 'flesh' as a primary narrative, then we mean its seared, divided, ripped-apartness, riveted to the ship's hole, fallen, or 'escaped' overboard." Spillers, "Mama's Baby, Papa's Maybe: An American Grammar Book" 67.
53 | Brah 178-210.
54 | Ibid. 189.

ple dying next to her, of family members suffering from pain. In the course of the novel, however, she finds her own way of coping with loss and rootlessness. In a state of loneliness and anger, she makes the important decision "to fortify herself" (M 78). Not only does she begin to talk to animals and plants, which reveals her deep love for nature. She also starts to embrace her traumatic past as a source of power and inspiration and to combine her Native American cultural heritage with European influences: "Relying on memory and her own resources, she cobbled together neglected rites, merged Europe medicine with native, scripture with lore, and recalled or invented the hidden meaning of things" (M 78). In this passage, Morrison presents a dynamic and anti-essentialist view of cultural identity based on the interplay between tradition and innovation, continuity and discontinuity. For Lina, at least at this point in the novel, Rebekka's farm represents a place of potential possibilities, a place in which hybridity is practiced and celebrated as a means to survive. Nevertheless, Lina still feels "*a homing desire*,"[55] to use Brah's phrase, and suffers from not being able to live with her family in a Native American village.[56]

Her loneliness is alleviated by the arrival of Rebekka, who, as a European "mail-order bride" transformed into an American mistress, becomes a member of the dominant group. Despite initial mutual dislike and despite differences in status, Lina and Rebekka realize that they need each other to meet the challenges they face: "Together, by trial and error they learned; what kept the foxes away; how and when to handle and spread manure; the difference between lethal and edible and the sweet taste of timothy grass [...]" (M 86-7). In other words, each day, as a Native American servant and a free white mistress, they participate in interactions that challenge hierarchical structures based on ethnicity and class; following Brah, they deconstruct the static distinction between "minority" and "majority."[57]

However, Morrison does not offer an uncritical celebration of interracial female solidarity. Whereas Lina readily accepts Florens as a new member of their community and cares for her like a mother, Morrison has Sorrow suffer a different fate. Sorrow is introduced as a survivor of a shipwreck, a "mongrelized" (M 198) girl with red hair and black teeth struggling with a past of abuse. According to Anissa Wardi, she can be regarded as an embodiment of the Middle Passage. A homeless child used to a life on water, she "marks the 'sorrow' of the Africans'

---

55 | Ibid. 193; italics in the original.
56 | Mar Gallego-Durán, "'Nobody Teaches you to Be a Woman': Female Identity, Community and Motherhood in Toni Morrison's A Mercy," *Toni Morrison's A Mercy: Critical Approaches*, eds. Shirley A. Stave and Justine Tally (Newcastle upon Tyne: Cambridge Scholars Publishing, 2011) 108.
57 | Brah 189.

displacement and forced habitation of the slave ships."[58] Morrison represents Rebekka's farm as a place where borders are erected that exclude and dehumanize Sorrow. Given her status as a "mongrelized" (M 198) woman, the white and Native American community members treat Sorrow with distrust or contempt since she does not fit into the racial order of their society. The white characters see her as a threat to the supposed "racial purity" and "superiority" of their race; Lina thinks that Sorrow suffers from a curse. "In the community's eyes, Sorrow is less than human and will always be other in this society of foreign codes,"[59] as Evelyn Jaffe Schreiber argues. Nevertheless, *A Mercy* shows how Sorrow goes through a process of change after giving birth to a daughter, finding a way to resist the hostility she endures.[60]

Given Lina's negative attitude toward Sorrow, there are first hints that the household on the Vaark farm is rather a patchwork of orphans than a family. Therefore, it does not really come as a surprise that the community breaks down after Jacob's death: It leaves the women without a provider and causes Rebekka's emotional disorder. Focusing on Rebekka's transformation from a poor migrant into a resentful and brutal mistress who destroys the network of female solidarity on the Vaark farm, *A Mercy* draws attention to the demoralizing effect of chattel slavery on white female slaveholders; a theme that also plays a crucial role in antebellum slave narratives and in neo-slave narratives like James's *The Book of Night Women*.[61] In *A Mercy*, Morrison shows how Rebekka begins to beat one of her female servants, takes down Lina's hammock and offers Florens for sale, although the black young woman has saved her life (M 254). It is her status that allows Rebekka to erect what Brah would call boundaries of exclusion. As a free white woman, she is authorized by law to reduce Florens to chattel, i.e., movable property. In this "diaspora space" in late seventeenth-century North America, race becomes a defining feature. Whereas the white indentured servant Scully is happy about some of the first wages he receives from Rebekka and looks forward to the end of his servitude, Florens faces a future in which slavery and blackness will be closely intertwined, in which blacks will be systematically treated as non-human beings. Exploring

---

58 | Anissa Wardi, "The Politics of 'Home' in *A Mercy*," *Toni Morrison's A Mercy: Critical Approaches*, eds. Shirley A. Stave and Justine Tally (Newcastle upon Tyne: Cambridge Scholars Publishing, 2011) 27.
59 | Evelyn Jaffe Schreiber, "Personal and Cultural Memory in *A Mercy*," *Toni Morrison: Memory and Meaning*, eds. Adrienne Lanier Seward and Justine Tally (Jackson: UP of Mississippi, 2014) 89.
60 | See also Michel Martin, "Toni Morrison on Human Bondage and a Post-Racial Age," *NPR* 26 Dec. 2008, 1 Sept. 2015 http://m.npr.org/story/98679703.
61 | See chapter 6, "A Vicious Circle of Violence: Revisiting Jamaican Slavery in Marlon James's *The Book of Night Women* (2009)," in this study.

the paradigm shift from human bondage to racial slavery through characters like Scully, Rebekka and Florens, *A Mercy* reveals the centrality of violence and loss in the lives of black American slaves in the late seventeenth century.

DISSOLUTION AND REINVENTION?—POSTMODERN NEGOTIATIONS OF SLAVERY

> [...] modern life begins with slavery ... From a woman's point of view, in terms of confronting the problems of where the world is now, black women had to deal with "post-modern" problems in the nineteenth century and earlier. These things had to be addressed by black people a long time ago. Certain kinds of dissolution, the loss of and the need to reconstruct certain kinds of stability.[62]

This famous quotation by Toni Morrison is taken from a 1993 interview with Paul Gilroy, a conversation focusing on *Beloved* and the complex relationship between racial slavery and Western modernity. Foregrounding the instability and fragmentation of black (female) identity under chattel slavery, Morrison's work shows that enslaved people of African descent must be considered "the first truly modern people,"[63] as Gilroy puts it. While Morrison highlights black women's experiences of discontinuity and disruption (generally associated with postmodernism),[64] she also refers to the possibility of diasporic resistance, the necessity for enslaved subjects to develop specific strategies in order to survive.[65] This is one of the central themes that Morrison explores in her neo-slave narratives.

Although they are set in different historical contexts, both *Beloved* and *A Mercy* unfold the stories of black women who are exposed to the horrors of slavery and racism but try to find a way to live with fragmentation and pain. In order to capture Florens's quest for recognition and self-control in *A Mercy*, Morrison strategically employs a variety of postmodern narrative strategies, such as metafiction, self-reflexivity and non-linearity. Whereas several chapters are third-per-

---

62 | Paul Gilroy, "Living Memory: A Meeting with Toni Morrison," *Small Acts: Thoughts on the Politics of Black Cultures* (London: Serpent's Tail, 1993) 178; second ellipsis in the original.
63 | Ibid.
64 | See, for instance, Linda Hutcheon, *A Poetics of Postmodernism: History, Theory and Fiction* (New York: Routledge, 1988) 3.
65 | Gilroy, "Living Memory: A Meeting with Toni Morrison" 178.

son narratives focalized through characters like Lina and Rebekka, every other chapter is told from Florens's first-person point of view. Written in a poetic language, Florens's account is full of ambiguities and uncertainties, flashbacks and fragmented memories. This narrative form, I argue, reflects Florens's experiences of loss and dissolution caused by the painful separation from her mother, the encounter with the Puritans and the Blacksmith's rejection.

This is already evident at the beginning of *A Mercy:* Morrison opens the novel without any introduction, leaving us in a state of disorientation, which, in turn, reflects her black protagonist's emotional condition: "Don't be afraid. My telling can't hurt you in spite of what I have done and I promise to lie quietly in the dark [...]" (M 3). For the reader, at this point in the text, it is neither possible to identify the narrator and narratee of the "confession" (M 3) nor to understand the facts and circumstances of the deed the narrator refers to. Moreover, it is not possible to decipher the meaning of images and signs, such as the "dog's profile" or the "corn-husk doll" (M 3). The beginning of Florens's account is not only highly mysterious but also self-reflexive. While the narrator reveals her intention to explain her act of violence, she refers to the limits of her ability to comprehend her environment and accentuates the impossibility to reconstruct her past accurately: "Often there are too many signs, or a bright omen clouds up too fast. I sort them and try to recall, yet I know I am missing much [...]" (M 4). In the following, Florens combines memories of her childhood on D'Ortega's plantation with recollections of her life on Rebekka's farm and descriptions of her journey to the Blacksmith. It is the reader's task to put together these fragments and to combine them with information provided by other characters.

Later in the novel, in *A Mercy*'s penultimate chapter, Florens once again explicitly refers to the act of telling her story. The scene is set on the Vaark farm in Milton, a couple of months after Florens's violent struggle with the Blacksmith. Rebekka, now turned into a slave mistress, has ordered her slaves and servants not to go into her dead husband's splendid house. In the darkness of the night, however, Florens feels save enough to act against her mistress and to enter the building. She cannot forget her encounter with the Puritans and her humiliation by the Blacksmith; she knows that her mistress plans to sell her. And yet, never losing sight of the possibility of black agency, Morrison shows how Florens emerges as an active woman and begins to carve her story (the story we have been reading) into the walls and the floor of one of the rooms: "I am holding light in one hand and carving letters with the others. My arms ache but I have need to tell you this" (M 263).

In a literal and metaphorical sense, the act of writing is extremely difficult and painful for Florens but she feels the necessity of bearing witness to slavery. Her story is a confession addressed to the Blacksmith, an attempt to explain her violent behavior by informing her lover about her experience of "thingification" in the Puritan village: "I know my withering is born in the Widow's closet" (M

262). While Florens reflects on the cruelty of her deed and the hopelessness of her situation, she also finds a new sense of self-worth, through the very act of remembering and writing: "I am become wilderness but I am also Florens. In full" (M 264). By developing a more complex self-image, she tries to move beyond the negative image the Blacksmith has created of her. Therefore, her first-person account is not only a declaration of guilt but also a means to embrace her blackness and her history.[66]

Within the African American literary tradition, in general, and in the context of slave narratives, in particular, the concepts of literacy, writing, self-determination and freedom are closely connected. In their autobiographical texts, many slave narrative authors focused on the importance of reading and writing in their struggle for freedom and recognition.[67] In *A Mercy*, Morrison explores the role of literacy in the period of slavery by telling, as Christiansë puts it, "the story of a slave who can write even before the emergence of slave narrative"[68] as a genre. In Maryland, Florens's "teacher is a Catholic priest who defies the codes against such instruction for slaves, which determine that the acquisition of literacy will be, as for so many slaves to come, shrouded in secrecy."[69]

While Morrison conceptualizes Florens's creative act in her master's house as an expression of black agency, she refuses to offer a triumphant reconstruction of Florens's life as a slave and identity as a writer. At the end of Florens's first-person account, Morrison puts a strong emphasis on loss rather than on renewal, highlighting the impossibility of closing the wounds caused by Florens's separation from her family: "I will keep one sadness. That all this time I cannot know what my mother is telling me" (M 264). While Florens's writing serves as a means to address the cruelty she has experienced, it cannot be interpreted as an act of self-liberation and overcoming. Since she cannot enter into a dialogue with her mother, Florens will never get an answer to the central question of her life: Why did her mother give her away on D'Ortega's farm? Via this scene, Morrison challenges the idea of slavery fiction as a form of therapy and healing, focusing instead on the destructive and enduring effects of chattel slavery on her black female protagonist. This is what makes *A Mercy* a powerful intertextual response to reductive reconciliatory, "kitsch" interpretations of *Beloved* in public and academic discourse.

Crucially, Florens's text in her dead master's house will never be read. It is not written for a broad audience but a single reader, i.e., the Blacksmith, who is illiterate (and probably dead): "You won't read my telling," Florens remarks.

---

66 | See also Gallego-Durán, "Nobody Teaches you to Be a Woman" 112-13.
67 | See Henry Louis Gates, Jr., "Introduction," *The Classic Slave Narratives* (New York: Signet Classics, 2002) 1.
68 | Christiansë, *Toni Morrison* 53.
69 | Ibid.

"You read the world but not the letters of talk. [...] If you never read this, no one will" (M 263). In *A Mercy*, it is the reader who is encouraged to take on the Blacksmith's role, the task of a listener and witness. Unlike the characters in the story, the reader is in a privileged position to encounter and combine different narrative perspectives. While Florens is left with a deep sense of grief because she does not know her mother's story, the reader has the chance to delve into her mother's past, to explore her thoughts and feelings in the novel's last chapter.

"An Open Wound That Cannot Heal:"
The Hardships of Black Womanhood

The mother's "letter" to Florens, a powerful meditation on the hardships of black womanhood and motherhood under slavery, is an attempt to explain her behavior on D'Ortega's farm. Born as a free person in Africa, Florens's mother is enslaved in the course of a war caused by a dispute between African tribal leaders. Taken to the coast, she is sold to white slave traders and shipped to the "New World," where she becomes a victim of rape. Whereas *Beloved* directs our attention to the ethical risks and ultimate impossibility of writing the Middle Passage,[70] *A Mercy* offers a short narrative description of the terrible journey across the Atlantic Ocean, focusing in particular on the tragic stories of slaves who, driven to utmost despair, see no other option but to commit suicide. Depicting the barbarity of the transatlantic slave trade, Morrison represents the Middle Passage as a defining event in the life of Florens's mother, a trauma which continues to haunt the enslaved woman for the rest of her life.

After having recounted the horrors on board the slave ship and the female captive's painful experiences of sexual abuse in Barbados and Maryland, Morrison has Florens's mother refer to the day when Jacob arrives on D'Ortega's plantation. Her account of the precariousness of black women's lives under slavery serves as the basis for understanding the scene on the farm in Maryland. Florens's mother knows that there is no way to protect her daughter from the violence of slavery. Giving Florens away is the only possibility to rescue her from the hands of the slave owner D'Ortega, the only chance to save her from rape on this particular plantation. Since she sees Jacob as a man of relative kindness and integrity, she desperately urges him to buy Florens. Like *Beloved* and Christiansë's *Unconfessed*, *A Mercy* explores the complexity and pain of what it means to be a slave mother in a society in which enslaved children are always in danger of being beaten, raped, sold or killed. The following passage captures Florens's mother's moral dilemma:

---

70 | See Broeck, "Enslavement as Regime of Western Modernity" 35.

One chance, I thought. There is no protection but there is difference. You stood there in those shoes and the tall man laughed and said he would take me to close the debt. I knew Senhor would not allow it. I said you. Take you, my daughter. Because I saw the tall man see you as a human child, not pieces of eight. I knelt before him. Hoping for a miracle. He said yes. It was not a miracle. Bestowed by God. It was a mercy. Offered by a human. (M 272-73)

Florens's mother reads Jacob's decision to take her daughter as an act of humanity (a form of "mercy" to which the novel's title refers) because the Anglo-Dutch trader saves Florens from being raped by D'Ortega. However, Morrison makes sure that the reader is familiar with Jacob's perspective: his materialistic attitude and self-centered behavior; his desire to increase his property; his efforts to assert his authority as a white man; his determination to exert power over women, his servants and slaves; last but not least, his decision to invest in the slave trade to construct a new, impressive house on his farm in Milton.[71] According to his own statement, Jacob is only interested in the trade in goods, not in the buying and selling of human beings (M 39). Behind his initial refusal to take slaves from D'Ortega, however, there is no moral rejection of the institution of slavery: It is only the insight that the trade in slaves causes "too much trouble" (M 36) that initially deters him from accepting D'Ortega's offer. At the same time, he is neither willing to cancel the debts of the slave owner nor intent upon filing a lawsuit against the man.

In this vexed situation, Morrison has Jacob discover Florens, a potential companion and servant for his wife Rebekka, who has lost all her children: "This one here, swimming in horrible shoes, appeared to be about the same age as Patrician, and if she got kicked in the head by a mare, the loss would not rock Rebekka so" (M 42). This quotation reveals that Jacob sees Florens only as a slave, an unfree person who, if necessary, can be easily replaced by any other worker. His decision to choose Florens is not at all an act of human solidarity; it is a pragmatic solution to his dispute with D'Ortega, the only way to close his deal with the slave owner without financial losses. While Morrison depicts the Anglo-Dutch trader as a man who shows pity for injured and ill-treated animals, she emphasizes that Jacob is unable to empathize with Florens and her mother.[72] "Animals," Christiansë contends, "remain the safe, easy recipients of his form of mercy; humans trapped in slavery are not animal enough for this."[73]

---

71 | See also Mar Gallego-Durán, "'Newness Trembles Me'? Representations of White Masculinity in Toni Morrison's *A Mercy*," *Toni Morrison: Memory and Meaning*, eds. Adrienne Lanier Seward and Justine Tally (Jackson: UP of Mississippi, 2014) 244-49.
72 | Christiansë, *Toni Morrison* 214-15.
73 | Ibid. 215.

Juxtaposing the perspectives of Jacob and Florens's mother, *A Mercy* draws attention to the hypocrisy of white slaveholders like Jacob and accentuates the impossibility for black women to escape racial violence and rape in seventeenth-century North America: "There is no protection," Florens's mother remarks. "To be female in this place is to be an open wound that cannot heal. Even if scars form, the festering is ever below" (M 267). Exploring the utterly dehumanizing nature of chattel slavery as "thingification" through a black feminist and Afro-pessimistic perspective, *A Mercy* draws attention to the enduring impact of physical and sexual abuse and the separation of slave families upon female captives. For Florens and her mother, it is impossible to overcome their traumatic experiences of humiliation and exploitation, to (re-)gain some sense of wholeness. Their only hope is to find a way to live with loss and despair, and this is also the future chattel slavery designs for them and their offspring.

Conclusion

Published more than two decades after her groundbreaking and best-selling novel *Beloved*, Morrison's *A Mercy* makes a crucial contribution to examining the complex history and nature of the African diaspora in the early colonial period. Tracing the paradigm shift from human bondage to racial slavery through characters like Florens, Rebekka and Scully, Morrison highlights the social and political construction of blackness and whiteness and, equally important, places a strong emphasis on loss, fragmentation, uprootedness and anti-black violence as defining characteristics in the lives of black slaves in late seventeenth-century North America. Written from a radical black feminist perspective, Morrison's novel accentuates the crushing power of chattel slavery as "thingification" by exploring the traumatic impact of the destruction of slave families on mother and child.

In terms of aesthetics, ethics and theorizing slavery, *A Mercy*, I argue, is a powerful intertextual response to the "kitsch reception" of *Beloved*: *A Mercy* never loses sight of the possibility of black agency under slavery, exploring how Florens emerges as a writer after being treated as a demon in the Puritan village, after being rejected and humiliated by the Blacksmith. However, and this is a crucial point, Morrison resists the temptation to offer an ultimately triumphant and consoling account of chattel slavery and Florens's life, to provide narrative closure and to construct a "happy ending." Not only does she draw attention to the destructive and enduring effects of anti-blackness on relationships within the black community (i.e., the Blacksmith's attack on Florens; Florens's violent response) and the brutalizing impact of slavery on white (female) slaveholders (i.e., the breakdown of the Vaark community after Rebekka's transformation into a resentful mistress). Morrison also foregrounds the impossibility for female captives to escape sexual abuse and violence and to sustain or restore familial bonds: "[O]ne of the monstrous things that slavery in this country caused was the breakup of families," Morrison explains in a 2008 interview with Michel Martin. In *A Mercy*, she goes on to explain, "there was an urgent request or an encouragement for me to make it possible for Florens to hear and know and understand why her mother gave her away. And I resisted it completely because the truth is, she would never know."[74]

In *A Mercy*, Christiansë argues, "Morrison is never simply recuperative and never triumphalist, thus avoiding the conservatism of such gestures."[75] Instead of celebrating Florens's act of writing as a powerful and lasting triumph over the dehumanizing influence of slavery, the novel insinuates that the black protagonist "might even burn down the house and, with it, the story that she has been writing."[76] Ultimately, *A Mercy* is not about healing but about the impossibility of successfully working through, and thus leaving behind, the trauma of slavery.[77] Engaging in a dialogue with Afro-pessimism, *A Mercy* enters into the early period of chattel slavery in mainland North America to trace the origins of the history of anti-blackness, to reflect on the meaning of blackness[78] in the past and in the present.

---

74 | Martin, "Toni Morrison on Human Bondage and a Post-Racial Age."
75 | Christiansë, *Toni Morrison* 60.
76 | Ibid.
77 | For similar reflections on Morrison's *Beloved*, see Broeck, "Trauma, Agency, Kitsch and the Excesses of the Real" 243.
78 | See also Wilderson 58.

3 Rethinking the African Diaspora: Saidiya Hartman's *Lose Your Mother* (2007)

INTRODUCTION

A cultural historian and expert on slavery at Columbia University, Saidiya Hartman is one of the most distinguished scholars in the field of African American studies. Her widely recognized monograph *Scenes of Subjection: Terror, Slavery, and Self-Making in Nineteenth-Century America* (1997) focuses on everyday acts of anti-black violence and forms of black resistance during and after the time of racial slavery in the United States, seeking "to illuminate the terror of the mundane and quotidian rather than exploit the shocking spectacle."[1] Drawing on a wide variety of archival sources, including slave testimony, newspaper articles, government documents and other white-authored texts, Hartman is particularly concerned with the risks and limits of reconstructing and articulating the slave's experience[2]—a topic that also defines her later work.

Like Hortense J. Spillers, Jared Sexton, Frank B. Wilderson and a number of other (contemporary) black scholars, Hartman has been called an Afro-pessimist. These intellectuals share theoretical, philosophical and political assumptions about the meaning of (anti-)blackness in the United States and in other parts of the world.[3] Focusing on structural forms of white supremacy and the precariousness of black life in the twenty-first century, they draw attention to the enduring and destructive effects of slavery and black abjection—what Hartman describes as "the afterlife of slavery."[4] Deconstructing the idea of a post-racial America, they agree that, as Wilderson puts it, "the election of a

---

1 | Hartman, *Scenes of Subjection* 4.
2 | Ibid. 10-14.
3 | Wilderson 1-32, 58. See also my introduction to *Transnational Black Dialogues*. For a critical discussion of Afro-pessimism, see Weier 419-33.
4 | Hartman, *Lose Your Mother* 6. All further references to Hartman's *Lose Your Mother* (LYM) will be cited in the text.

Black president aside, police brutality, mass incarceration, segregated and substandard schools and housing, astronomical rates of HIV infection, and the threat of being turned away en masse at the polls still constitute the lived experience of Black life."[5]

In her second-generation neo-slave narrative *Lose Your Mother: A Journey along the Atlantic Slave Route* (2007), Hartman explores the complex relation between the past of slavery and the present, crossing the boundaries of genres: Her text is an innovative mélange of fictional elements, essayistic reflections on the history of the slave trade and autobiographical passages about her experiences as a Fulbright scholar in Ghana in 1997. Focusing on Hartman's attempt to trace the stories of African captives, *Lose Your Mother* sheds light on a number of burning topics that resonate in contemporary public discourse and academic contexts: the lasting and disturbing legacy of racial slavery; the black diasporic subject's quest for home and belonging; the discourse of roots tourism in Ghana; links and differences between African Americans and Africans and the limits and dangers of representing slavery in the twenty-first century. "All of these concerns about time, eventfulness, the life world of the human commodity," Hartman explains in a conversation, "required a hybrid form, a personal narrative, a historical meditation, and a metadiscourse on history."[6]

Combining autobiographical writing with theoretical considerations on the relationship between Africa and the African diaspora, Hartman's travelogue describes a literal journey through Ghana as well as a metaphorical one: Beginning with a depiction of her feelings of estrangement, *Lose Your Mother* reveals how Hartman's encounters with local residents on the coast and in the Ghanaian hinterland influence her interpretation of the transatlantic slave trade and slavery, her understanding of transnational relations between black communities and her identity as an *African* American. At the end of her journey, she privileges a view of the black world as a complex formation marked by essential differences and hierarchies but also by similarities.

In terms of structure, this chapter begins with an exploration of Ghana's status as a symbol of hope and place of residence for African Americans in the late 1950s and 1960s. Moreover, I will examine the impact of Alex Haley's famous neo-slave narrative *Roots* (1976) on diasporic constructions of Africa and public discussions about the history of racial slavery in the late twentieth century. In addition, I will focus on Ghana's popularity among black American visitors and emigrants in the 1990s as well as on contemporary forms of roots

---

5 | Wilderson 10.
6 | Saidiya Hartman, Eva Hoffman and Daniel Mendelsohn, "Memoirs of Return: Saidiya Hartman, Eva Hoffman, and Daniel Mendelsohn in Conversation with Nancy K. Miller," *Rites of Return: Diaspora Poetics and the Politics of Memory*, eds. Marianne Hirsch and Nancy K. Miller (New York: Columbia UP, 2011) 111.

tourism encouraged by popular TV documentaries and modern DNA technology. After this contextualization, the chapter shows that *Lose Your Mother* calls for a paradigm shift in our understanding of relations between Africa and its diaspora. Engaging in an Afro-pessimistic rewriting of Haley's novel, Hartman's text discards the concept of a return to an ancestral village and the idea of a family reunion in Africa. Discussing the active participation of Africans in the slave trade and drawing attention to Hartman's experiences of loss and estrangement in Ghana, *Lose Your Mother* challenges the myth of "mother Africa" as a welcoming home for black diasporic returnees and deconstructs a static understanding of the African diaspora grounded on authenticity, continuity and roots.

Most crucially, Hartman's text moves beyond a view of the black world as a transnational community linked by common historical experiences of dispossession. Focusing on Hartman's emphasis on difference, I will examine the ways in which *Lose Your Mother* contributes to a powerful re-negotiation of Paul Gilroy's concept of the black Atlantic and the discourse of roots tourism in Ghana. Moreover, I will demonstrate that Hartman ends her travelogue by developing a new perspective on the African diaspora and transnational black relations. The last part of this chapter sheds light on Hartman's critical (re-)appropriation of the archive of slavery, analyzing her attempt to explore the experiences of a young African woman who was murdered during the Middle Passage.

FREEDOM DREAMERS AND ROOT SEEKERS: BLACK AMERICANS IN POST-INDEPENDENCE GHANA

Ghana's political independence from Great Britain in 1957 marked a crucial moment in the history of Africa and the African diaspora. All over the world, black individuals welcomed and celebrated the establishment of the new country, the first sub-Saharan nation to break away from colonial rule. For many people of African descent, the events in Ghana were a source of hope and opportunity, inspiring and energizing them to resist racial oppression and colonial domination in their countries of origin.[7] As the historian Kevin K. Gaines explains, in the late 1950s and 1960s, Ghana not only emerged as a symbol of black freedom, "a beacon for the black world's liberatory aspirations."[8] It also became a place of residence and refuge for black expatriates, who were drawn

---

7 | Kevin K. Gaines, *American Africans in Ghana: Black Expatriates and the Civil Rights Era* (Chapel Hill: U of North Carolina P, 2006) 1-26; Bayo Holsey, *Routes of Remembrance: Refashioning the Slave Trade in Ghana* (Chicago: U of Chicago P, 2008) 128.
8 | Gaines 26.

by the vision of a free black community and the idea of a pan-African identity articulated by Kwame Nkrumah, Ghana's first president.[9]

In his public speeches and writings, Nkrumah stressed the importance of solidarity between different black groups in political and economic affairs. In the years following independence, he actively recruited African Americans and other members of the African diaspora to live and work in Ghana and to assist in the process of nation-building. Many black Americans, in particular professionals, writers, activists and political refugees, readily accepted his invitation to relocate to West Africa. Among those who visited the country or even migrated to Ghana were well-known African American intellectuals, such as Richard Wright, Maya Angelou and W.E.B. Du Bois. In the midst of a period of social and political unrest in the U.S., at a time when the Civil Rights movement was at its height, many black Americans dreamed of a country without anti-black violence. Sympathizing with the anticolonial movements in Africa, they were inclined to take part in the global struggle against racial oppression. For these expatriates, crossing the Atlantic Ocean to settle in Ghana not only provided a way to escape from the laws of Jim Crow and to create a free black state:[10] Moving to Africa also "satisfied an idealized desire for a return to their homeland,"[11] as Bayo Holsey puts it.

In her memoir *All God's Children Need Travelling Shoes* (1986), a reflection on her time in Ghana in the early 1960s, the African American poet and writer Maya Angelou expresses such a longing for home. Although she also refers to experiences of disappointment and conflicts with local residents, she embraces the static idea of return:

The prodigal child, having strayed, been stolen or sold from the land of her fathers, having squandered her mother's gifts and having laid down in cruel gutters, had at last arisen and directed herself back to the welcoming arms of the family where she would be bathed, clothed with fine raiment and seated at the welcoming table.[12]

In this passage, Angelou presents a highly idealized and mythical image of Africa as a haven for African American returnees. While the slave's deportation across the Atlantic and life in America is depicted as a descent into hell, Angelou draws on images associated with familial love, care and support to describe the warm welcome she receives in Africa. Highlighting her status as a resilient, proud and victorious slave descendant, she strategically reconstructs

---

9 | Ibid. 6.
10 | Holsey 153-54; Gaines 1-26, 44.
11 | Holsey 154.
12 | Maya Angelou, *All God's Children Need Travelling Shoes* (1986; London: Virago, 2012) 21.

her African experience as a triumphant success story. Written for an (African) American reader, her text suggests that it is possible to put an end to the history of dispossession and grief and to reconnect with Africa.

Crucially, there are significant absences and silences in *All God's Children Need Travelling Shoes*. Unwilling to relinquish her dream of diasporic homecoming and rebirth in Africa, Angelou deliberately avoids addressing questions of historical guilt: Throughout her autobiographical text, she refuses to discuss the active participation of Africans in the transatlantic slave trade because this history stands in stark contrast to her vision of Africa as a promised land for black diasporic women and men. Desperate and determined to find a sense of belonging in Ghana, she ignores the fact that many of her ancestors were kidnapped and sold into transatlantic slavery by other Africans. Strategically constructed as a narrative of liberation and healing, Angelou's text prioritizes solidarity and unity between people of African descent, failing to reflect on past experiences of betrayal and acts of complicity between European slave traders and Africans. Angelou can maintain her narrative of African return, belonging and healing only because she firmly bases it on narrative strategies of avoidance and silencing.

As victims of racism and segregation in the U.S., many African Americans like Angelou dreamed of a new and better life in Ghana in the 1950s and 1960s. In their attempt to reinvent and refashion themselves on the African continent, they struggled to shake off the ghosts of slavery and colonialism. Turning away from narratives of despair and defeat, they sought to recover and revitalize the history of ancient Africa as an era of glory and splendor. Notably, on the political level in Ghana, a similar tendency to focus on Africa's noble past could be observed: Determined to challenge Western myths of African cultural inferiority, backwardness and savagery, Nkrumah called for stories of black self-determination, self-reliance and freedom. Under his leadership, "Ghana" was chosen as the nation's new official name, evoking the history of the old and well-known West African kingdom rather than that of the transatlantic slave trade (see LYM 40).[13]

For many expatriates in Ghana, the dream of creating a new society and starting a new life in Africa was destroyed in 1966, when Nkrumah's government was overthrown in a military and police coup. After the president's ouster, most of the black exiles left the country and decided to go back to the U.S. to participate in the struggle for civil rights and social justice there and to retain and celebrate their connections to Africa (see LYM 37).[14] "Nkrumah's Ghana,"

---

13 | See also Holsey 60.
14 | See also Gaines 244-46.

Gaines contends, "had changed the lives of these men and women and had endowed them with a unique perspective on the politics of the African diaspora."[15]

A decade later, in the late 1970s, a wide public debate about the link between Africa and its diaspora emerged in the United States. This discussion was caused by the publication of Alex Haley's *Roots: The Saga of an American Family* (1976), one of the most famous and commercially successful first-generation neo-slave narratives. In *Roots*, Haley delves into his (slave) ancestors' past, beginning with an exploration of the life of Kunta Kinte in eighteenth-century West Africa. At the heart of the novel is Haley's description of a journey to Juffure, a small town in Gambia and Kinte's supposed birthplace. By highlighting the possibility to identify his African roots and to return to his ancestral village, Haley constructs a static view of Africa and the African diaspora grounded on continuity, authenticity and tradition. Notably, focusing on seven generations of African Americans, *Roots* not only sheds light on oppression and dispossession in Africa and in the "New World" but also on experiences of survival and fights for black freedom. In particular, it deals with the history of African royals and elites, emphasizing the connection between African Americans and ancient African kingdoms.[16]

Shortly after the novel's publication, *Roots* was transformed into an incredibly popular television miniseries, attracting more than 130 million viewers from all over the world.[17] Given its popularity and commercial success, Haley's text had an enormous influence on (African American) conceptions of Africa and interpretations of the slave trade. Representing slaves as noble characters and strong survivors rather than as passive victims, it encouraged black diasporic subjects to explore the past of racial slavery and, most crucially, to embrace their African origins. In the wake of *Roots*, Americans, in general, and African Americans, in particular, developed an enormous interest in family genealogies. Like Haley, many black Americans embarked on a journey to African countries like Ghana to trace their roots and discover their ethnic and cultural heritage.[18]

Many scholars agree that *Roots* offers an empowering vision of black American history, challenging interpretations of slavery that rely exclusively on nar-

---

15 | Ibid. 245.
16 | Kamari Maxine Clarke, "Mapping Transnationality: Roots Tourism and the Institutionalization of Ethnic Heritage," *Globalization and Race: Transformations in the Cultural Production of Blackness*, eds. Kamari Maxine Clarke and Deborah A. Thomas (Durham: Duke UP, 2006) 140-41; Marianne Hirsch and Nancy K. Miller, "Introduction," *Rites of Return: Diaspora Poetics and the Politics of Memory*, eds. Hirsch and Miller (New York: Columbia UP, 2011) 1-2.
17 | Clarke 140. See also my introduction to *Transnational Black Dialogues*.
18 | Holsey 155; Clarke 141.

ratives of victimization and passivity. At the same time, the novel has been criticized for its teleological construction of history:[19] According to Holsey, *Roots* is "a triumphant tale that does not attend to continuing forms of oppression."[20] Celebrating the triumph over slavery, it differs fundamentally from texts like Toni Morrison's *Beloved* "in which the terror of slavery is always a haunting presence."[21]

In the 1990s, when Hartman spent a year in Ghana as a Fulbright Scholar, the West African nation continued to attract thousands of African Americans, in particular (class-privileged) tourists, entrepreneurs, retirees and celebrities. More than a decade after the airing of *Roots*, several factors contributed to the country's continuing popularity among black visitors and emigrants from the United States: While Ghana struggled with economic problems and high rates of poverty and unemployment, it was known for its stable democratic system and hospitality towards foreign visitors. Wishing to delve into the history of the transatlantic slave trade, many black Americans were drawn by Ghana's wide array of historic sites and monuments, such as former slave dungeons and castles. The Ghanaian government finally recognized the enormous economic potential of diaspora tourism and explicitly invited African Americans and other individuals of African descent to travel or relocate to Ghana and invest in the country. Financially supported by U.S.-American organizations, institutions and agencies like USAID, in the early 1990s, Ghana started to renovate and restore the castles in Elmina and Cape Coast, which, as a result, emerged as immensely popular and highly frequented tourist attractions. In order to increase the number of tourists, the administration even intended to create a special visa program for black diasporic individuals in 2005.[22]

In the new millennium, still, many African Americans are driven by the longing to trace their ancestral origins. This desire is fueled by contemporary TV series about root seekers and modern DNA technology: Most recently and prominently, the cultural critic and Harvard professor Henry Louis Gates, Jr. presented a twenty-first-century version of Haley's *Roots*, encouraging black Americans to explore their family histories and connections to Africa. In his PBS documentary *African American Lives* (2006), Gates sets out to identify the ancestral African roots of a number of African American celebrities like talk show icon Oprah Winfrey, singer Tina Turner and actor Morgan Freeman.

---

19 | Holsey 155; Clarke 141.
20 | Holsey 155-56.
21 | Ibid. 156.
22 | Gaines 282-83; Lydia Polgreen, "Ghana's Uneasy Embrace of Slavery's Diaspora," *New York Times* 27 Dec. 2005: A1+; Holsey 156-62; Edward M. Bruner, "Tourism in Ghana: The Representation of Slavery and the Return of the Black Diaspora," *American Anthropologist* 98.2 (1996): 290-91.

Working together with leading scientists, he not only draws on genealogical documents, archival sources and online databases but also uses DNA testing to construct narratives of recovery and healing.[23] "For the first time since the seventeenth century," Gates argues, "we are able, symbolically at least, to reverse the Middle Passage. Our ancestors brought something with them that not even the slave trade could take away: their own distinctive strands of DNA."[24] Like Haley in the 1970s, Gates offers a static interpretation of the African diaspora focusing on roots, authenticity and the possibility of return and healing.

While *African American Lives* was extremely successful in commercial terms and followed by a number of other genealogical series like *Faces of America* (2010),[25] Gates's documentaries provoked sharp criticism from scholars working in the fields of critical race theory, African American and African diaspora studies. For instance, in a 2006 essay in *The Nation*, the legal scholar and Columbia professor Patricia J. Williams urges "us to be less romantic about what all this DNA swabbing reveals."[26] Focusing on the social construction of (black) diasporic identity, she emphasizes that the longing to return to an African homeland "is in our heads, not in our mitochondria."[27] Critically reflecting on Gates's decision to use DNA testing, Williams argues that "if we biologize our history, we will forever be less than we could be."[28]

---

23 | Henry Louis Gates, Jr., *In Search of Our Roots: How 19 Extraordinary African Americans Reclaimed Their Past* (New York: Crown Publishers, 2010) 1-14; Henry Louis Gates, Jr., "Exactly How 'Black' Is Black America? 100 Amazing Facts About the Negro: Find out the Percentage of African Ancestry in Black Americans," *The Root.com* 11 Feb. 2013, 11 Apr. 2014 http://www.theroot.com/articles/history/2013/02/how_mixed_are_african_americans.html; see also Hirsch, "Introduction" 2.
24 | Gates, *In Search of Our Roots* 10.
25 | See Meg Greene, *Henry Louis Gates, Jr.: A Biography* (Santa Barbara, CA: Greenwood, 2012) 160.
26 | Patricia J. Williams, "Emotional Truth," *The Nation* 16 Feb. 2006, 23 Sept. 2014 http://www.thenation.com/article/emotional-truth.
27 | Ibid.
28 | Ibid.

KINLESS AND UPROOTED: A STRANGER IN AFRICA

In newspaper reviews and scholarly articles, Hartman's *Lose Your Mother* has been described as "an anti-*Roots*" story, an alternative narrative to Haley's popular novel.[29] Indeed, there are significant differences between both texts: Whereas, in *Roots*, Haley crosses the Atlantic to explore and strengthen his ties to Africa and to find his ancestral village, Hartman had abandoned the concept of black diasporic return long before her Fulbright year. In contrast to Haley, she does not intend to celebrate Africa's noble past and discover the history of royal families and ancient kingdoms. Rather, as a scholar of slavery and "a descendant of the enslaved" (LYM 6), she struggles to trace the paths of those Africans captured by slave raiders and predatory groups, forcibly transported to the coast of West Africa and shipped to foreign lands on the other side of the Atlantic.

Instead of embracing her African roots and searching for information about distant ancestors, she seeks to reconstruct the experiences of strangers, the story of "the commoners, the unwilling and coerced migrants who created a new culture in the hostile world of the Americas" (LYM 7). In Ghana, she visits formers slave castles and dungeons, slave markets and fortified towns, determined to confront and excavate the history of African captives and "the transatlantic system of *thingification*,"[30] to use Sabine Broeck's words. By deconstructing a static view of black diasporic identity based on roots and authenticity, Hartman engages in an Afro-pessimistic rewriting of Haley's text and a critical re-negotiation of the concept of the African diaspora; she sets herself apart from thousands of other black Americans who—encouraged by new DNA technology—hope to reconnect to an African mother country and spend money on genetic tests "to construct a family tree."[31]

While Hartman shows no interest in searching for her origins and tracing family genealogies, she attests to her emotional connection to Africa, having "dreamed of living in Ghana" (LYM 56) since her time in college in the 1980s.

---

29 | See G. Pascal Zachary, "Valiant Battle to Reconstruct Ties to Africa," *San Francisco Chronicle Book Review* 28 Jan. 2007: M1+; Marcus Wood, "Round Table: Review of Saidiya Hartman, *Lose Your Mother: A Journey along the Atlantic Slave Route*," *Journal of American Studies* 44.1 (2010): 9-11; Hartman, "Memoirs of Return" 112-13.
30 | Broeck, "Enslavement as Regime of Western Modernity" 37; italics in the original.
31 | Amy Harmon, "Blacks Pin Hope on DNA to Fill in Slavery's Gaps in Family Trees," *New York Times* 25 July 2005: A1+. In *Lose Your Mother*, Hartman discusses this "article in *The New York Times* about African Americans attempting to fill in the blank spaces of their history with DNA tests." Hartman strongly opposes the use of DNA technology to trace ancestral roots and refers to "the ambiguous and inconclusive results" of such DNA tests (LYM 90).

Like so many other black diasporic subjects, she longs for a place to call home, a country without anti-black racism and humiliation, a nation in which she does not "feel like a problem" (LYM 57). Instead of looking for a specific geographical place in West Africa, she strives for a more general sense of belonging in the world. However, as a woman of African descent, she also hopes to be welcomed as a friend by the Ghanaians. Focusing on her encounters with local residents, her travelogue is marked by ambiguity. As Hartman explains in a conversation with Nancy K. Miller, Eva Hoffman and Daniel Mendelsohn, "Like every oppositional narrative, *Lose Your Mother* is haunted by the thing it writes against—the desire for home—and, at the same time, I was acutely aware that I would always be outside home."[32]

As Hartman illustrates, Ghana does not at all feel like a welcoming place. From the beginning of her journey, right from the moment she steps off the bus in Elmina, she is treated as a stranger, "a wandering seed bereft of the possibility of taking root" (LYM 4). Instead of embracing her as a long-missing sister, the Ghanaians, in a distancing move, call her *obruni*, a term used for privileged and wealthy foreigners and visitors from other countries.[33] In Ghana, she suffers from a sense of alienation and loss similar to her experiences of exclusion in the United States. Realizing that her skin color does not necessarily make her a beloved family member, in the course of her stay in Ghana, she learns to accept her status as an outsider: "After all, I was a stranger from across the sea" (LYM 4).

In *Strangers to Ourselves* (1991 [1988]), the philosopher Julia Kristeva describes the condition of being a foreigner, alien or outsider as follows: "Not belonging to any place, any time, any love. A lost origin, the impossibility to take root, a rummaging memory, the present in abeyance."[34] This conception of the stranger as an uprooted, displaced and unloved person neither belonging

---

32 | Hartman, "Memoirs of Return" 113.

33 | In *Routes of Remembrance: Refashioning the Slave Trade in Ghana*, Holsey offers an explanation of the term *obruni* or *oburoni*: "Oburoni (or buronyi in Fante) is an Akan word that has become a bone of contention between Ghanaians and blacks in the diaspora, who, having been told that *oburoni* means 'white man,' find themselves to their dismay called by this term. In actuality *oburoni* means 'those who come from over the horizon.' This is not a racial label then but rather a demonstration of the ways in which Ghanaians often identify people by the places from which they come, in quite literal terms. Indeed, the Americanness of African Americans is quite significant from the point of view of Ghanaians. For them, African American and white tourists sometimes occupy the same mental space; they are all privileged foreigners." Holsey 220; italics in the original.

34 | Julia Kristeva, *Strangers to Ourselves*, trans. Leon S. Roudiez (1988; New York: Columbia UP, 1991) 7.

to a specific place nor—and this is a crucial point—to any specific historical moment captures Hartman's experience as a member of the African diaspora. "Being a stranger," Hartman argues, "concerns not only matters of familiarity, belonging, and exclusion but as well involves a particular relation to the past" (LYM 17).

In *Lose Your Mother*, Hartman sheds light on the complex interrelation between the past and the present, exploring "the historical links between Ghana and the African diaspora."[35] On her journey, many Ghanaians immediately and correctly identify her as a slave descendant, a woman whose ancestors were kidnapped and taken to the Americas. As a black American visitor, a stranger in Africa, she is a living reminder of the horror of the Middle Passage, "the vestige of the dead" (LYM 18). Whereas Angelou and Haley focus on black agency and heroic survival, Hartman employs death metaphors to express the horrors of slavery and the enduring effects of this history on African American identity, to reflect on "the incomplete project of freedom."[36] An enslaved person, Hartman argues, is a foreigner and outsider separated from home and loved ones. Based on this characterization, she interprets the term *obruni* as a reference to her forebears' status as non-kin: In the era of the slave trade, Africans did not give away and sell their friends and family members, she contends, but individuals they perceived, often conveniently so, as social outcasts, criminals and strangers from other parts of the country (LYM 5). For Hartman, *obruni* evokes this history of relations between different African individuals and groups. By drawing our attention to regional, ethnic, religious and class cleavages within West African societies, she counters the notion of a single African culture, a view that emerged in the period of the transatlantic slave trade and European colonialism.[37] "Africa was never one identity," Hartman contends, "but plural and contested ones" (LYM 231).

In a way similar to Morrison's *A Mercy* and Christiansë's *Unconfessed*, *Lose Your Mother* refuses to offer a consoling interpretation of slavery: What results from Hartman's engagement with the past is a deep sense of loss that cannot be redeemed or healed, and the death metaphors she insists on using express just that. As its title suggests, *Lose Your Mother* urges African American readers and other members of the African diaspora to discard mythical and romanticizing conceptions of "mother Africa" as a paradise and home for black dias-

---

35 | Holsey 220.
36 | Hartman, "Venus in Two Acts" 4.
37 | See Maria I. Diedrich, "'As if Freedom Were a City Waiting for Them in the Distance:' The American Revolution and the Black Hessian Subject," *Transnational American Studies*, ed. Udo J. Hebel (Heidelberg: Winter, 2012) 102.

poric returnees.[38] Having witnessed the failures of the twentieth-century black liberation movements, Hartman is unable to conceive of Africa as a place that promises renewal and rebirth. Unlike black expatriates in the late 1950s and 1960s, who traveled to Ghana hoping to recover their African roots and build a free back nation, she belongs to a new generation of African Americans who are skeptical about the realization of political, economic and social justice for black women and men: "My arrival in Ghana was not auspicious. Mine was an age not of dreaming but of disenchantment" (LYM 38). As Hartman points out, even in Nkrumah's Ghana in the 1960s, many black Americans like Maya Angelou could embrace "mother Africa" only by consciously ignoring a past that spelt African complicity in the slave trade and slavery. In *All God's Children Need Travelling Shoes*, Angelou thus intentionally avoids a confrontation with the history of the transatlantic slave trade and the experiences of her enslaved ancestors by initially staying away from the former slave castle in Cape Coast. What she longs for in Ghana is to be "accepted as an African,"[39] and she can achieve that only by closing her eyes to African guilt. This is a crucial difference between Angelou's memoir and *Lose Your Mother*: For Hartman, exploring the history of racial slavery has a larger significance than the desire to blend into Ghanaian society (LYM 41-42).

In her travelogue, Hartman offers a self-reflexive comment on the meaning of the past for the present and the relevance of her project to explore the stories of the enslaved: Tracing the route of African captives, visiting the slave castles in Ghana and, most crucially, writing about slavery cannot simply be equated with "an antiquarian obsession with bygone days" (LYM 6). Rather, it is a highly political endeavor that highlights the painful connection between our time and the period of the slave trade,[40] the enduring effects of slavery on contemporary black life. Like Wilderson and other Afro-pessimists, Hartman argues that the legacy of racial slavery manifests itself in a shorter life expectancy, a higher risk of poverty and fewer educational opportunities for blacks (LYM 6). By turning to the past of loss and despair in order to reflect on the present, *Lose Your Mother*

---

38 | Broeck, "Enslavement as Regime of Western Modernity" 37; Judie Newman, "Round Table: Review of Saidiya Hartman, *Lose Your Mother: A Journey along the Atlantic Slave Route*," *Journal of American Studies* 44.1 (2010): 1; Wood 9.

39 | Angelou 43. For months, Angelou refuses to visit Cape Coast. However, when she goes on a journey to the Ghanaian hinterland, she stops in this city to tank up. Thinking of her enslaved ancestors, she is overwhelmed by feelings of sorrow and pain. In her autobiographical narrative, this scene is constructed as a short and accidental interruption of her journey, not as an event that encourages her to rethink her view of Africa as a haven for black diasporic returnees. See Angelou 108-09.

40 | See also Tina M. Campt and Saidiya Hartman, "A Future Beyond Empire: An Introduction," *Small Axe* 13.1 (2009): 20.

emerges as a protest narrative that centralizes the unfulfilled dream of black emancipation and liberation:[41] "I was loitering in a slave dungeon less because I hoped to discover what really happened here than because of what lived on from this history. Why else begin an autobiography in a graveyard?" (LYM 130).

RE-NEGOTIATING THE BLACK ATLANTIC: *LOSE YOUR MOTHER* AND THE NOTION OF DIFFERENCE

By exploring the intricate relationship between black Americans and Africans—between black individuals in the diaspora and in the "homeland"—*Lose Your Mother* deals with a topic that has received relatively little attention in African diaspora studies.[42] Initially, Hartman privileged a view of the black world based on commonality and solidarity, assuming that different black communities are linked by "a thread of connection or a common chord of memory" (LYM 73). Like Gilroy in *The Black Atlantic*, she argued that the experience of suffering and oppression binds together black individuals and groups: "Dispossession was our history. [...] The solidarity I felt with other black people depended largely on this history" (LYM 74). For Hartman, the event of slavery and its afterlife are the defining moments of black life.

As *Lose Your Mother* shows, in Ghana, however, Hartman is forced to rethink her understanding of the black world as an intercultural and transnational formation united by common historical experiences. Hoping "to find a community in which—and with which—to grieve the losses borne from slavery,"[43] to quote Harvey Neptune, Hartman discovers that the majority of her interlocutors try to avoid any discussions about the history of the slave trade. Especially those whose ancestors collaborated with European and African slave raiders and traders are reluctant to acknowledge this fact or take recourse to legitimization strategies; but even for the Ghanaian descendants of enslaved Africans, these slave origins are too shameful to reveal. Also, confronted with poverty and unemployment, most Ghanaians have too many everyday problems to dig into the past (LYM 71-73). Given this strong reluctance or outright refusal to talk about slavery, Hartman's journey through Ghana proves to be, as Patricia J. Saunders puts it, "an experience of failed expectations, from day one."[44]

---

41 | Hartman, "Venus in Two Acts" 4. See also Holsey 156.
42 | Mayer 110-11; Zeleza 37. See also chapter 1, "The Concept of the African Diaspora and the Notion of Difference," in this study.
43 | Harvey Neptune, "Loving Through Loss: Reading Saidiya Hartman's History of Black Hurt," *Anthurium: A Caribbean Studies Journal* 6.1 (2008): 3.
44 | Patricia J. Saunders, "Fugitive Dreams of Diaspora: Conversations with Saidiya Hartman," *Anthurium* 6.1 (2008): 10.

Her conversation with Kofi, a Ghanaian assistant curator at the Elmina Castle Museum, represents one of those defining moments in which Hartman realizes that there can be no unitary black identity based on a common history. For Hartman, the system of slavery is closely connected with disturbing scenes of horror. When reflecting on what her great-grandfather Moses calls *"the dark days"* (LYM 10; italics in the original), she thinks of burning villages, inhuman slave auctions and violent masters. These images show that, to use an expression taken from Hartman's *Scenes of Subjection*, "to be a slave is to be under the brutal power and authority of another."[45] For Kofi, however, slavery cannot be solely interpreted as a horrible crime. As the grandson of a former slave owner, he is equipped with a completely different attitude towards the past than the slave descendent Hartman. Emphasizing that enslaved Africans were treated with respect and dignity within his family, he relegates the violence of slavery exclusively to the American continent (LYM 72). In other words, Kofi refuses to accept any historical responsibility for the crimes of the past. Drawing on legitimization strategies, he seeks to whitewash his country's history, to portray slavery in Africa as a benign institution and to absolve the African slave trader and master from guilt.

Lose Your Mother represents this confrontation with a sanitized version of slavery as an extremely disturbing and shocking experience for Hartman. Talking to local black residents like Kofi, she is forced to discover a painful familiarity, i.e., crucial similarities between Ghanaian and white American discourses on slavery and racial subjugation: In the United States, slaveholders and masters sought to offer moral and religious justifications of slavery, depicting it as a benign system, civilizing force and paternalistic institution in which enslaved women and men were happy and satisfied. As the historian Nathan I. Huggins explains, an influential pro-slavery statement was that slaves were better off than their white owners "because they were unfettered by responsibilities for subsistence or family."[46] For centuries, white Americans avoided to acknowledge the fact that the nation's ideals of democracy, equality, progress and liberty existed side by side with slavery and racial oppression. In public contexts and most academic works, until the 1960s, slavery was regarded as a historical aberration and disorder rather than as an integral component of American history and culture.[47] To this day, many stereotypical views about slavery and plantation life in North America continue to influence discussions about and attitudes towards the past. "Generally," the historian James Oliver Horton contends,

---

45 | Hartman, *Scenes of Subjection* 3.
46 | Huggins xlix.
47 | Ibid. xi-xxiii.

"Americans believe that slavery was a southern phenomenon, date it from the antebellum period, and do not think of it as central to the American story."[48]

What comes as a shock to Hartman is the insight that similar self-legitimizing discourses proliferate in contemporary Ghanaian society: On both sides of the Atlantic, there are attempts to present and justify slavery as a benevolent institution, to avoid questions of guilt and responsibility, to ignore the past altogether or to deny the enduring effects of slavery on contemporary black life. During the transatlantic slave trade, the African slave trader/owner felt connected to the white trader/master, not to the black victim. In other words, the dividing line here is not between black and white but between those who claimed the right to own human property and those who were reduced to objects; between the master's narrative (and the memory constructions of his descendants) and the slave's story (and the perspective of her descendants). This legacy, Hartman comes to understand, continues to shape contemporary interactions between African Americans and Ghanaians, destroying any hope for black solidarity across national and cultural borders.

Hartman's depiction of her encounter with Phyllis confirms this point: As a student at a prestigious private school, the Ghanaian teenager belongs to a higher social class in Ghana. Unlike many African Americans who are eager to connect to their roots in Africa, she is representative of those (educated) local residents intent upon "finding routes outside of their country,"[49] to use Holsey's words. When visiting Cape Coast Castle, Phyllis reveals her dream of studying in the United States but avoids any serious confrontation with the castle's dreadful history. For Phyllis, roots tourism offers a chance to socialize with Americans, to talk about American culture and to earn some money as a tour guide; however, she refuses to explore her country's past and its effects on contemporary Ghanaian society and black life, and nothing in her culture encourages her to do otherwise.

Influenced by contemporary popular representations of African Americans as successful and affluent individuals, many Ghanaians like Phyllis grow up with myths of the United States as a country of unlimited possibilities and opportunities, even for black people.[50] Struggling with inequality, poverty and oppression in Africa, some tend to emphasize the "positive" aspects of the history of the transatlantic slave trade and American racial slavery, assuming, as Holsey contends, "that slaves were simply low-status individuals in the New World, [...] and that their descendants ultimately benefited from their ability to be absorbed into a first world nation."[51] In other words, they are not familiar

---

48 | Horton 21. See also my introduction to *Transnational Black Dialogues*.
49 | Holsey 215.
50 | Ibid. 218.
51 | Ibid.

with or seek to trivialize the devastating effects of American chattel slavery as a dehumanizing "system of *thingification*."[52] Instead of acknowledging the brutality of "New World" slavery, they draw on the past only to highlight contemporary social inequalities and hierarchical structures between Ghanaian and African American communities based on different political, social and economic developments in the U.S. and Africa.

By putting her African experience at the center of *Lose Your Mother* and focusing on the perspectives of individuals in the "homeland," Hartman contributes to a rethinking of Gilroy's concept of the black Atlantic that is primarily concerned with African American society, history and culture.[53] What emerges from Hartman's encounters with Ghanaians like Kofi and Phyllis is the insight that there are essential differences in the experiences, memory constructions and attitudes of blacks in the diaspora and Africans at "home." African Americans and Ghanaians are not linked by a common history of oppression/dispossession and view of slavery. The granddaughters and grandsons of slave owners like Kofi invent completely different readings and discourses of the past than slave descendants like Hartman. Directing our attention to the heterogeneity and diversity of black life and inequalities and hierarchies within the black world, *Lose Your Mother* moves beyond conceptions of similarity that, Campt reminds us in *Other Germans*, "often anchor dominant modes of theorizing the diaspora and *its relations*."[54] Difference, Hartman comes to understand, is the defining feature of interactions and relations between blacks in Africa and in the United States.

While Ghanaians and diasporic subjects cannot possibly share the same notion of home and view of the past, the concept of diaspora, Holsey argues, "can be mobilized in quite conscious ways in order to form a transnational relationship that might have certain kinds of benefits."[55] In fact, since the early 1990s, on the part of the Ghanaian government, there have been attempts to forge links between local residents and diasporic tourists, to build a bridge between Africa and its diaspora. Driven by economic interests and, in particular, the fear of losing the enormously profitable roots tourists, since 1991, the Ministry of Tourism has initiated several (cultural) projects centered on the history of the transatlantic slave trade to continue to attract African Ameri-

---

52 | Broeck, "Enslavement as Regime of Western Modernity" 37; italics in the original.
53 | See chapter 1, "The Concept of the African Diaspora and the Notion of Difference," in this study.
54 | Campt, *Other Germans* 23; emphasis added.
55 | Tina M. Campt and Deborah A. Thomas, "Diasporic Hegemonies: Slavery, Memory, and Genealogies of Diaspora: Dialogue Participants: Jacqueline Nassy Brown and Bayo Holsey," *Transforming Anthropology* 14.2 (2006): 165.

can visitors.[56] By privileging diasporic narratives of loss, grief and mourning rather than return, reunion and recovery, Hartman contests this discourse of diaspora tourism in Ghana.

LOSS, GRIEF AND MOURNING: CHALLENGING THE DISCOURSE OF ROOTS TOURISM IN GHANA

Evoking the loss of family members and (African) origins, the title of Hartman's travelogue has a double meaning: Not only does it deconstruct myths of Africa as a welcoming home for black diasporic subjects;[57] it also refers to the fact that, during the era of the transatlantic slave trade, African, American and European slave owners and masters tried to erase the African past of the enslaved, to destroy the captive's memories of her life before bondage: "A slave without a past had no life to avenge. No time was wasted yearning for home, no recollections of a distant country slowed her down as she tilled the soil, no image of her mother came to mind when she looked into the face of her child" (LYM 155). Today, within the framework of diaspora or roots tourism in Ghana, slave descendants around the world are urged to do the opposite and to remember their African ancestors; they are encouraged not to forget their "mothers" (LYM 162)—as if that were possible through an act of will.

Every year, Ghanaian guides take thousands of black Americans and other members of the African diaspora to and through former slave dungeons and the castles in Elmina and Cape Coast, suggesting that it is possible to experience the pain and sorrow of their enslaved forebears. Moreover, there are regular festivals, such as "Panafest," intended to revitalize the bonds between Africa and its diaspora. In other words, whereas in everyday life, many Ghanaians hesitate or refuse to discuss this past defined by slavery, the history of the slave trade and slavery, however devoid of the African guilt issue, now is made to play a prominent part within the (public) performance sphere of tourism.[58] Drawing on Gilroy's discussion of the exchange of concepts and practices between different black groups, Holsey reads the emergence of roots tourism in Ghana as the result of a "black Atlantic conversation,"[59] as the product of a transnational discussion between Africans and African Americans "in which various notions of connection are regularly mobilized."[60] Exploiting and perverting myths of unity and solidarity, diaspora tourism is reconceptualized to

---

56 | Holsey 156-64.
57 | See also Broeck, "Enslavement as Regime of Western Modernity" 37.
58 | Holsey 1-14.
59 | Ibid. 152.
60 | Ibid.

create the illusion that the differences and gaps between Ghanaians and black diasporic subjects can be overcome.

Hartman, however, documents that Ghana's political decision to remember, stage and memorialize the transatlantic slave trade is primarily motivated by financial interests: "Every town or village had an atrocity to promote—a mass grave, an auction block, a slave river, a massacre. It was Ghana's equivalent to a fried chicken franchise" (LYM 163). *Lose Your Mother* shows that it is a shocking and painful experience for Hartman to discover that there are cruel similarities between the commemoration of slavery in Ghana and North America: In the U.S., historic plantation sites and living history museums have become popular tourist destinations. Created to engage, educate and, most crucially, to entertain the public, these places are notorious for offering sensationalized stories or presenting a sanitized view of slavery. In Colonial Williamsburg in Virginia, a highly commercialized tourist attraction and one of the most famous living history museums in the country, large numbers of visitors are drawn by highly problematic reenactments, guided tours about slavery and reconstructed slave quarters. Since the late 1970s, there have been bitter controversies about the way slavery is represented by historians and costumed interpreters. In 1994, for instance, a mock slave auction depicting the separation of a black family attracted an enormous amount of criticism.[61] Many black Americans, in particular members of the NAACP, were outraged at "the trivialization and degradation of African American history,"[62] as Dan Eggen explains in a 1991 article in the *Washington Post*.

In addition to denouncing this commercialization of the past, Hartman criticizes that, in Ghana, the history of slavery is exclusively constructed as an African American narrative. While the return of black Americans to Africa is celebrated with festivals, ceremonies and rituals, there is no public debate about the participation of African royals, elites, merchants and common folk in the slave trade or about the experiences of those Africans who managed to escape captivity and enslavement. For many Ghanaians, diaspora tourism offers a chance to improve their living conditions, by giving them jobs and attracting affluent visitors from all over the world. But most local residents refuse to explore their connections to the African diaspora, examine their country's history of slavery or reflect on internal tensions and differences based on class, ethnic-

---

61 | See Dan Eggen, "In Williamsburg, the Painful Reality of Slavery," *Washington Post* 7 July 1991: A1; Horton 30-31; Eric Gable, Richard Handler and Anna Lawson, "On the Uses of Relativism: Fact, Conjecture, and Black and White Histories at Colonial Williamsburg," *American Ethnologist* 19.4 (1992): 791-805; Michael Janofsky, "Mock Auction of Slaves: Education or Outrage?" *New York Times* 8 Oct. 1994, 17 Apr. 2014 http://www.nytimes.com/1994/10/08/us/mock-auction-of-slaves-education-or-outrage.html.
62 | Eggen A1.

ity, gender and region (LYM 162-65). Although thousands of African American root seekers continue to travel to Ghana to discover their African ancestry, the discourse of diaspora tourism cannot serve to unite the black world, Hartman argues: "What each community made of slavery and how they understood it provided little ground for solidarity" (LYM 164).

A couple of years ago, the Ghanaian government initiated an advertising campaign asking local residents to avoid using the term *obruni* and to embrace black Americans as beloved family members (LYM 164).[63] In *Lose Your Mother* and in her 2002 essay "The Time of Slavery," Hartman offers a critical reflection on the impossibility of reunion between tourists and Ghanaians: In front of Elmina Castle, she encounters a group of teenagers, who welcome her return to Africa, address her as "sister" and urge her to stay in touch as pen pals. Emphasizing their common ancestry as people of African descent, the boys give her three, rather stilted, letters focused on the notion of familial bonds between black women and men in the diaspora and in Africa. While Hartman is drawn "by the lure of filial devotion extended by these budding amorists,"[64] she stresses the impossibility of recovering the loss caused by the horror and brutality of slavery. In her view, the boys' letters serve as "a pretend cure for an irreparable injury"[65] rather than as a bridge between Africans and black diasporic subjects.

By directing our attention to the crucial role of grief, loss and mourning in black diasporic life, Hartman's *Lose Your Mother* challenges dominant narratives of roots tourism in Ghana that center on the success of black liberation and the end of slavery.[66] In her conversation with Khalid, an Atlanta-based filmmaker, she discards the idea of return and spiritual renewal. Khalid, by contrast, constructs his journey to Ghana as powerfully redemptive: "'All the folks taken across the waters are returning home through me,' he said with absolute earnestness" (LYM 108). In "The Time of Slavery," Hartman explicitly argues against such interpretations that depict African American tourists as victorious survivors and "vessels" for their dead ancestors' return to Africa. In her view, the yawning gap caused by the Middle Passage cannot be closed by the captives' descendants.[67] Instead of celebrating the slave's redemption, in her discussion with Khalid, she reveals her feelings of loneliness in Ghana and begins to cry. Within the travelogue, this expression of grief directs our attention to a moment of utter disillusionment and despair in Hartman's life in Ghana. For her, roots tourism cannot serve to transform the violence of slavery into a story of recovery, to translate the past of defeat and dispossession into "a history

---

63 | See also Polgreen, "Ghana's Uneasy Embrace of Slavery's Diaspora" A1+.
64 | Hartman, "The Time of Slavery" 761.
65 | Ibid. 762.
66 | Ibid. 758; see also Holsey 233.
67 | Hartman, "The Time of Slavery" 768.

of progress."[68] Like Morrison in *A Mercy* and Christiansë in *Unconfessed*, Hartman explores the destructive nature of slavery as "thingification" to reflect on the enduring effects of this history on black life, "to illuminate the intimacy of our experience with the lives of the dead."[69]

BRIDGING THE GAP: "THE FUGITIVE'S DREAM" AND THE AFRICAN DIASPORA

Contrary to what many (twentieth-century) studies suggest, during the time of the transatlantic slave trade, African individuals and groups whose lives were impacted or threatened by the trade did not passively and silently submit to enslavement, subjugation and forced migration. Rather, they developed a wide variety of violent and non-violent strategies to resist enslavement and to stay free. While some African communities managed to protect and defend themselves against slave-raiding by migrating to distant and unknown places and building walls around their villages and towns, other groups actively participated in slave rebellions or attacks on slave depots. Despite this long and vibrant history of black struggles against enslavement in Africa, for long, scholars in the field of slave trade studies have primarily shed light on the crushing power of the slave system or forms of (commercial) cooperation between African and European slave traders. In many academic works, the historian Sylviane A. Diouf observes, Africans are only seen as passive commodities or treacherous collaborators but not as active agents in the fight against the slave trade.[70]

By exploring the history of refugees and warriors in the Ghanaian village of Gwolu, Hartman's *Lose Your Mother* deconstructs notions of black passivity towards enslavement in Africa. In the heyday of the slave trade, Gwolu was a place of refuge for those Africans fleeing from freebooters, soldiers and slave raiders, a remote village in the northwestern hinterland where fugitives and runaways came together, hoping to avoid kidnapping and deportation. Having migrated from different regions, these refugees, who became known as "the Sisala," had neither a common language, ancestry, ethnicity nor history. What united them, however, was "the danger that had driven them" (LYM 225) to leave their familiar homes and cross the savanna—as well as a determination to stay free.

While they were filled with feelings of loss, they were ready to start a new life, to forge bonds of love, friendship and solidarity with other villagers and to share their traditions, customs and religious values. In short, they started to

---

68 | Ibid.
69 | Hartman, "Venus in Two Acts" 4.
70 | Sylviane A. Diouf, "Introduction," *Fighting the Slave Trade: West African Strategies* (Athens: Ohio UP, 2003) ix-xxvii.

Rethinking the African Diaspora: Saidiya Hartman's *Lose Your Mother* (2007)

reinvent themselves, creating a new home and community not based on kin and ethnic affiliations but on the hope for freedom: "'We' was the collectivity they built from the ground up, not one they had inherited, not one that others had imposed" (LYM 225). In Gwolu, strangers were welcomed as allies as long as they helped to defend the town and accepted that "there would be no masters" (LYM 225). Threatened by foreign troops and warriors, the villagers knew that they were still in danger of being attacked, captured and sold as property. Like other African groups of runaways in other places, they decided to build a barricade around their settlement, a high defense wall whose remains are still there.[71]

In *Lose Your Mother*, Hartman's trip to Gwolu marks the end of her journey through Ghana; it is her last chance to encounter and reconstruct stories about the defeated and dispossessed, "to discover the signpost that pointed the way to those on the opposite shore of the Atlantic" (LYM 231). Contrary to her expectations, however, in the northwestern area of Ghana, "in the heartland of slavery" (LYM 232), nobody talks about slaves. Unlike Hartman and other African Americans, the local residents of Gwolu do not define themselves through narratives of captivity, loss and enslavement. For the descendants of "the Sisala," the past of racial slavery is not a matter of suffering, sorrow and pain "but rather a source of pride" (LYM 233), a story of triumph over powerful hostile communities, aggressive states and predatory troops.

What follows from Hartman's reflections on the history of Gwolu is, again, an emphasis on difference as a constitutive element of the black world: In the Ghanaian hinterland, she comes to the insight that the complex history of the transatlantic slave trade cannot be restricted to the experiences of those African women and men kidnapped in villages and towns, violently taken to the West African coast, shipped across the Atlantic Ocean and forced to work in the Americas.[72] Listening to the residents of Gwolu, she realizes that the past of slavery cannot be read solely through the lens of African America. It is not only about captives, orphans and coerced laborers but also about fugitives, runaways

---

71 | This section on the history of Gwolu is based on Hartman's account in *Lose Your Mother*; see LYM 219-35.

72 | In *Routes of Remembrance: Refashioning the Slave Trade in Ghana*, the cultural anthropologist Bayo Holsey reaches a similar conclusion, arguing that the transatlantic "slave trade has never been solely the history of those who were captured from their homes, placed in chains, carried across the sea, and forced to toil on plantations. It is also the history of those in the bondage of the global system of oppression that emerged at the moment of this forced migration. This interpretation provides then a different vision of black Atlantic community that might be a stronger basis for connection than those based on overcoming the divide between those who were enslaved and those who remained." Holsey 237.

and fighters—about African individuals and communities who managed to escape enslavement.

"The fugitive's dream" (LYM 233), the story of those Africans who left behind their old lives and came together to protect themselves and fight against the slave trade, has an inspiring, empowering and transformational effect on Hartman. Reconstructing the experiences of "the Sisala," she discovers a past that is not only about loss, dispossession and grief but also, and essentially, about reinvention, resistance, cooperation and solidarity. In particular, she embraces the runaway's idea of "home as making"[73] rather than as heritage, the refugees' concept of community not grounded on common ancestral ties but on shared goals. Emphasizing the interrelation between local contexts and global structures and between the past and the present, she draws a connection between the history of Gwolu and the current formation of the African diaspora, the narrative of fugitives and rebels in Ghana during the period of the slave trade and the dream of contemporary black people in Africa and elsewhere.[74]

For Hartman, the struggle against racial oppression, the fight against "slavery in all of its myriad forms" (LYM 234), serves as a transnational link between black communities and individuals marked by different ethnic origins, languages, traditions, cultural values, experiences and histories: "The bridge between the people of Gwolu and me wasn't what we had suffered or what we had endured but the aspirations that fueled flight and the yearning for freedom" (LYM 234). Gwolu, *Lose Your Mother* insists, is connected to any other place around the world where black people come together to resist white supremacy and anti-black racism.

Reflecting on the relation between towns like Gwolu and the African diaspora, Hartman engages in and contributes to a re-negotiation of diaspora theory. In an interview with Patricia J. Saunders, she points out that there are essential similarities between freedom communities, such as the group of fugitives in Gwolu, and diasporic formations: They are shaped by experiences of dislocation as well as by processes of arrival and settlement.[75] Living far away from their ancestors' places of origins, these groups try to produce "conditions that make dwelling possible,"[76] to quote Hartman. This view echoes Campt's understanding of diaspora as a concept that is "quite fundamentally about dwelling and staying put."[77]

---

73 | Saunders, "Fugitive Dreams of Diaspora: Conversations with Saidiya Hartman" 13.
74 | See also Diedrich, "'As if Freedom Were a City Waiting for Them in the Distance'" 98.
75 | Saunders, "Fugitive Dreams of Diaspora: Conversations with Saidiya Hartman" 13.
76 | Ibid.
77 | Campt, *Image Matters* 25.

While Hartman emphasizes the significance of local contexts for black diasporic identity formation, she also focuses on the dialogic nature of the African diaspora: the possibility and necessity to enter into a conversation with other black groups, to exchange and compare different experiences and to position yourself in relation to other black people. Highlighting the construction and ongoing negotiation of black diasporic identity, this is a dynamic view of diaspora privileged by scholars like Campt, who has recently argued:

> I can't understand diaspora through only African-Americans—there's no way I can do that. I can only understand diaspora by understanding my own location in relationship to other communities, how they struggle with, and actually thrive, under circumstances of racial oppression. So to me [...] diaspora is what happens when you're in one place and still have to connect to and utilise the resources of other black communities to make sense of your own.[78]

In *Lose Your Mother*, Hartman tries to make sense of diaspora by exploring the connection between black Americans and the inhabitants of Gwolu. While they do not share the same experiences of suffering, both communities are linked by common political goals to end oppression. Listening to the story of fugitives and freedom fighters, Hartman embraces her identity as an *African* American: "Africa wasn't dead to me, nor was it just a grave. My future was entangled with it, just as it was entangled with every other place on the globe where people were struggling to live and hoping to thrive" (LYM 233).

"CRITICAL FABULATION:"
WRITING WITH AND AGAINST THE *DEAD BOOK*

In *Lose Your Mother*, Hartman directs the reader's attention to a photo included in a Ghanaian tourist brochure. The picture shows a group of Ghanaian schoolchildren engaged in an attempt to re-enact the past. Crowded together in the dungeon of Cape Coast Castle, the boys and girls are costumed as enslaved Africans; some of them are in chains. This scene parallels the cruel (and highly profitable) spectacle of historical reenactments in the United States in places like Colonial Williamsburg, where costumed slave interpreters attract thousands of visitors by offering a sanitized version of slavery. Assuming that a bridge between the past and the present can be built, the photograph in the tourist brochure claims that the painful experiences of African captives can be reconstructed and captured, that the slaves can be rescued from oblivion (LYM 133-35). In her analysis of the picture, Hartman emphasizes the moral and

---

78 | Campt, "Imagining Ourselves."

ethical risks of this visual representation of slavery: "By providing the anonymous with faces, the image succeeded only in killing the dead a second time by replacing them with stand-ins. The loss that the photo struggled to articulate was at cross-purposes with the gaggle of children huddled in the dungeon" (LYM 134-35).

Without doubt, these reflections on the dangers inherent in re-imagining the history of the slave trade and slavery are not specific to the medium of photography; they are as well relevant to the field of literature. In writing about slavery from twenty-first-century perspectives, contemporary authors of neo-slave narratives are faced with the challenge of finding an appropriate form to represent the past. In a chapter called "The Dead Book," Hartman reflects on the hazards and ultimate impossibility of recovering and telling the story of an eighteenth-century enslaved African woman who was murdered during the Middle Passage, on a British slave vessel known as the *Recovery*. As the ship's surgeon Thomas Dowling later testified, the young woman was tied up, severely beaten, whipped, mutilated and eventually killed by Captain John Kimber. In 1792, the abolitionist William Wilberforce gave a speech before the House of Commons to campaign for the abolition of the transatlantic slave trade. In his talk, he referred to the incidents on board the *Recovery*, highlighting the woman's suffering, degradation and sexual abuse as well as the captain's cruelty. When the case came to trial in Britain, Kimber was accused of murder but a jury absolved him of the charge (LYM 136-49).[79] What the anonymous black woman has in common with other female captives is the fact that there is hardly any information on her experiences in Africa and aboard the slave ship. This paucity of sources especially about black women, Hortense J. Spillers contends, characterizes much of the historiography of the transatlantic slave trade: "At any rate, we get very little notion in the written record of the life of women, children, and infants in 'Middle Passage.'"[80]

In fact, the only text about the female captive on board the *Recovery* is a trial transcript, a musty document in the archive of slavery reducing her to the acts of (sexual) violence committed against her.[81] It consists only of the statements of white men, including the ship's surgeon, the third mate and Captain Kimber. In the transcript, the woman's voice is absent. The scandalous and shocking depictions of her body's violation, "are the only defense of her existence," Hartman observes, "the only barrier against her disappearance; and these words killed her a second time and consigned her to the bottom of the Atlantic" (LYM 138).

---

79 | See also Hartman, "Venus in Two Acts" 7-8.
80 | Spillers, "Mama's Baby, Papa's Maybe: An American Grammar Book" 73.
81 | See also Hartman, "Venus in Two Acts" 2.

While the trial against Captain Kimber attracted considerable public attention in the eighteenth century, the woman's terrible story on board the *Recovery* is largely forgotten today (LYM 138). In *Lose Your Mother*, Hartman seeks to rescue the female slave from oblivion and to deconstruct the horrible stories told about her. Based on the conviction that narratives can be seen "as a form of compensation,"[82] Hartman's goal is to create a black counter-history of the slave trade that does not depict the enslaved as a number, a value unit, a human commodity or an object of voyeuristic desire. In her 2008 essay "Venus in Two Acts," she directs our attention to the ethical risks of her project: Since it is only possible to explore the woman's life through the eyes of white masters and captors, there is the danger of repeating and re-articulating the humiliations, atrocities and obscene phrases of the archive and to expose the enslaved to a second act of victimization and violence.[83]

As Sabine Broeck has shown in "Enslavement as Regime of Western Modernity: Re-Reading Gender Studies Epistemology through Black Feminist Critique" (2008), Hartman is highly influenced by the literary and theoretical writings of Toni Morrison and Hortense J. Spillers. Like Morrison's *Beloved*, *Lose Your Mother* is not only marked by a strong determination to revisit the past of the slave trade and slavery but also by a painful reflection on the limits of this endeavor. "In *Beloved*," Broeck contends, "it is the very void of story which gestures towards an ethically, and linguistically impossible representation"[84] of the Middle Passage. In *Lose Your Mother*, Hartman explicitly and repeatedly refers to the impossibility of reconstructing and articulating the slave's experience onboard the *Recovery*.[85] Focusing on acts of (sexual) violence directed against the black female body, Hartman knows that her attempt to represent the past necessarily "translates into a potential for pornotroping."[86] In her landmark essay "Mama's Baby, Papa's Maybe: An American Grammar Book" (1987), Spillers introduces the term "pornotroping" to describe processes in which enslaved black women were violently mutilated and sexually mistreated, reduced to flesh

---

82 | Ibid. 4.
83 | Ibid. 2-5.
84 | Broeck, "Enslavement as Regime of Western Modernity" 35.
85 | Ibid. 34-51.
86 | Spillers, "Mama's Baby, Papa's Maybe" 67. In an interview, Hartman explicitly refers to the influence of Spillers's writings on her own work: "Indebtedness is the word that comes to mind that I would use to describe my relation to Hortense's work. That's how I would summarize it. I mean I am still struggling with the problematic terms that 'Mama's Baby, Papa's Maybe' has generated." See Hortense Spillers, Saidiya Hartman, Farah Jasmine Griffin, Shelly Eversley and Jennifer L. Morgan, "'Watcha Gonna Do?'—Revisiting 'Mama's Baby, Papa's Maybe: An American Grammar Book,'" *Women's Studies Quarterly* 35.1/2 (2007): 300.

and then, in abolitionist discourse, exposed to a (white) audience.[87] As Michael A. Chaney puts it in his reading of Spillers's concept, "pornotroping" is an act that is about "satisfying voyeuristic desire by reinforcing the viewer's self-perception of bodily integrity."[88] It refers to the widespread and highly problematic circulation of shocking images and sensationalized narratives of black suffering by white abolitionists who sought to illustrate and prove the cruelty of the transatlantic slave trade.

Determined to minimize the risk of "pornotroping," Hartman uses a narrative and aesthetic strategy "best described as critical fabulation."[89] This practice of writing is based on the conviction that, as Hayden White's work has shown, the traditional differentiation between history and fiction, in which history is regarded "as the representation of the actual" and literature "as the representation of the imaginable,"[90] is untenable. On the one hand, "critical fabulation" is grounded on a careful analysis and critical incorporation of archival documents, which represent "the building blocks of the narrative."[91] On the other hand, a writer drawing on this narrative strategy is required to confront the silences and omissions in the archive. The goal is to discuss and portray the complexity of the slave's life, while acknowledging and commenting on the fact that there are certain aspects of history that cannot and must not be recovered and articulated. In other words, it requires a self-reflexive and critical examination of the value and the limits of digging into the past and representing the captive's experiences of (sexual) violation.[92] Marked by ambiguity and uncertainty and a refusal to offer narrative closure, it is a strategy that involves writing "with and against the archive,"[93] as Hartman puts it.

An analysis of "The Dead Book" illustrates Hartman's complex project: Blurring the line between what has been conventionally perceived as fact and fiction, she incorporates "authentic" voices into this chapter. Taken from eighteenth-century documents, these are the statements of white men, such

---

87 | Spillers, "Mama's Baby, Papa's Maybe" 67-68. See also Alexander G. Weheliye, "Pornotropes," *Journal of Visual Culture* 7.1 (2008): 71-72; Michael A. Chaney, *Fugitive Vision: Slave Image and Black Identity in Antebellum Narrative* (Bloomington: Indiana UP, 2008) 63.
88 | Chaney 63.
89 | Hartman, "Venus in Two Acts" 11.
90 | Hayden White, "The Historical Text as Literary Artifact," *The Northern Anthology of Theory and Criticism*, ed. Vincent B. Leitch (1978; New York: Norton, 2001) 1727.
91 | As Hartman explains, the term "fabula" refers to "the basic elements of story, the building blocks of the narrative." Hartman, "Venus in Two Acts" 11.
92 | Ibid. 11-12. See also Broeck, "Enslavement as Regime of Western Modernity" 34-51.
93 | Hartman, "Venus in Two Acts" 12.

as the judge of the Admiralty Court, who chaired the trial against Kimber in 1792, the ship's surgeon Dowling or the insurance expert John Weskett. In their utterances, they construct the enslaved as a non-human being or justify the captain's violent actions on board the *Recovery* as a means to prevent slave rebellions. In addition to these original phrases from the archive of slavery, Hartman presents sentences that might have been uttered and acts that might have been performed, telling the story from the points of view of the captain, the surgeon and the third mate. While all of them claim the authority to tell the truth, each character offers a different version of the incident on the slave vessel. By reconstructing the same narrative—the captain's brutal flogging of the woman and the slave's death—from contradictory perspectives, Hartman manages to deprive the white men of their authority and to deconstruct the "received or authorized account."[94] For the reader, it is a challenging task to piece together the episodes and to identify and distinguish between the different speakers and the narrator of the story.[95] As Hartman explains, by dividing the plot into different parts, she seeks "to illuminate the contested character of history, narrative, event and fact."[96]

While the trial transcript only gives voice to white captors, Hartman's reconstruction of the past ends with a sequence presented from the perspective of the female victim. This passage not only highlights the black woman's traumatic experiences on board the *Recovery* but also sheds light on her strong determination to resist the captain's control over her. Without losing sight of the horror of the Middle Passage, in Hartman's narrative, the woman's spirit returns home to her family and friends in Africa. What follows, however, is a short self-reflexive part, in which Hartman addresses the limits of her project to salvage the female captive. Like Morrison in *A Mercy* and Christiansë in *Unconfessed*, Hartman challenges the naïve idea of the liberating and reconciliatory power of slavery fiction: She resists the temptation to provide narrative closure and to transform the slave woman's story of (sexual) violence and despair into a triumphant account of redemption:

If the story ended there, I could feel a small measure of comfort. I could hold on to this instant of possibility. I could find a salutary lesson in the girl's suffering and pretend a story was enough to save her from oblivion. I could sigh with relief and say, "It all happened so long ago." Then I could wade into the Atlantic and not think of the *dead book*. (LYM 153; italics in the original)

---

94 | Ibid. 11.
95 | Ibid. 11-12.
96 | Ibid. 12.

The black woman's fate still has relevance today, *Lose Your Mother* insists, drawing attention to the enduring and destructive effects of the Middle Passage and slavery on twenty-first-century black life—to what Campt and Hartman describe as "[t]he tragic entanglement of our era with that of the Atlantic slave trade, the weight of dead generations upon the present."[97] For Hartman, it is impossible to reconstruct, recreate and rescue the life of the eighteenth-century slave woman who was murdered on board the *Recovery* but not too late to imagine a different future for black individuals around the world.[98]

In recent years, Hartman and other Afro-pessimists have been criticized for concentrating exclusively on the crushing power of chattel slavery; for reading slavery and blackness as a condition of "social death" (Orlando Patterson);[99] for ignoring the agency of the enslaved; for interpreting dispossession, alienation and despair as defining elements of black life in the past and in the present. In his 2009 essay "Social Death and Political Life in the Study of Slavery," the historian Vincent Brown argues that Hartman "remains so focused on her own commemorations that her text makes little space for a consideration of how the enslaved struggled with alienation and the fragility of belonging, or of the mourning rites they used to confront their condition."[100] According to Brown, Hartman's view of slavery as a form of social death "precludes her from describing the ways that violence, dislocation, and death actually generate culture, politics, and consequential action by the enslaved."[101]

This failure, Brown contends, is especially noticeable in Hartman's representation of the Middle Passage in "The Dead Book:"

Hartman discerns a convincing subject position for all of the participants in the events surrounding the death of the girl, except for the other slaves who watched the woman die and carried the memory with them to the Americas, presumably to tell others [...], who must have drawn from such stories a basic perspective on the history of the Atlantic world.[102]

---

97 | Campt and Hartman, "A Future Beyond Empire" 20.
98 | Hartman, "Venus in Two Acts" 13-14.
99 | In his 1982 work *Slavery and Social Death: A Comparative Study*, Orlando Patterson defines slavery as *"the permanent, violent domination of natally alienated and generally dishonored persons."* Orlando Patterson, *Slavery and Social Death: A Comparative Study* (Cambridge, MA: Harvard UP, 1982) 13; italics in the original.
100 | Vincent Brown, "Social Death and Political Life in the Study of Slavery," *American Historical Review* 114.5 (2009): 1239.
101 | Ibid.
102 | Ibid. 1240.

Significantly, Brown does not take into account that Hartman strategically decides not to adopt the perspective of Venus, another female captive on board the *Recovery*, who possibly witnessed the slave woman's death: "Initially I thought I wanted to represent the affiliations severed and remade in the hollow of the slave ship by imagining the two girls as friends, by giving them one another. But in the end I was forced to admit that I wanted to console myself,"[103] Hartman explains in "Venus in Two Acts." *Lose Your Mother*, I argue, never denies the possibility and existence of black agency under slavery, yet refrains from evoking the social power of friendship and mourning rites in slave women's lives: "In a free state," as Hartman points out, "it would have been possible for the girls to attend to the death of a friend and shed tears for the loss, but a slave ship made no allowance for grief and when detected the instruments of torture were employed to eradicate it."[104]

Conclusion

Crossing the borders of different genres such as travelogue, autobiography and historical writing, Hartman's second-generation neo-slave narrative *Lose Your Mother* contributes to a critical re-negotiation of the concept of the African diaspora. Focusing on experiences of loss and estrangement, Hartman stresses the impossibility not only of going back to an "authentic" ancestral village; she powerfully challenges the myth of "mother Africa" as a welcoming home for black diasporic subjects.[105] Hartman reconstructs her time in Ghana as a process of disenchantment: She comes to understand that black communities and individuals around the world are not necessarily linked by common historical experiences of suffering and interpretations of the transatlantic slave trade and racial slavery. Drawing on her encounters with local black residents during her Fulbright year in Ghana, she highlights differences, gaps and hierarchical structures between African Americans and Africans and among Africans, thus countering dominant narratives of black relations based on similarity.

Hartman depicts her time in Gwolu as a turning point of her journey through Ghana: In this village in the northwestern hinterland, she realizes that the experience of the slave trade cannot be read solely through the eyes of captives transported to the Americas. Inspired by the stories of fugitives and rebels, she engages in a rethinking of her identity as an *African* American woman and the global formation of the black world. For Hartman, the fight against racial oppression serves as a transnational link between black commu-

---

103 | Hartman, "Venus in Two Acts" 9.
104 | Ibid. 8.
105 | See also Broeck, "Enslavement as Regime of Western Modernity" 37.

nities around the world: "The legacy that I chose to claim was articulated in the ongoing struggle to escape, stand down, and defeat slavery in all of its myriad forms. It was the fugitive's legacy" (LYM 234). Hartman's view, however, excludes large segments of the Ghanaian population descended from African slave owners and slave traders from this inheritance.

Published exactly twenty years after *Beloved*, *Lose Your Mother* cannot be read without considering its complex intertextual relationship to Morrison's 1987 masterpiece. In "The Dead Book," Hartman struggles to give an account of the Middle Passage from a black female perspective "without committing further violence in [her] own act of narration."[106] Like Morrison, Hartman employs a sophisticated narrative strategy marked by self-reflexivity and ambiguity: Based on archival material and white voices, she seeks to reconstruct the young woman's life on board the *Recovery* by drawing on a variety of (contradictory) perspectives, while simultaneously emphasizing the obligation and urge to bear witness to the past and the impossibility of writing slavery and recovering the captive's voice.

In a way similar to Morrison's *A Mercy* and Christiansë's *Unconfessed*, Hartman offers an intertextual counter-discourse to "kitsch" interpretations of *Beloved*. Deconstructing the idea of history as progress, *Lose Your Mother* explicitly directs the reader's attention to the persistent legacy of slavery and black abjection, or what Hartman describes as the "future created by" slavery (LYM 133). For her, representing the experiences of the forgotten and dispossessed is not at all an attempt to close the wounds of the past but to excavate them to examine "what lived on from this history" (LYM 130).

---

106 | Hartman, "Venus in Two Acts" 2.

4 "Hertseer:" Re-Imagining Cape Slavery in Yvette Christiansë's *Unconfessed* (2006)

INTRODUCTION

Over the last years, in the vast and diverse realm of South African literature, numerous black and white authors (such as Zakes Mda, Zoë Wicomb, Rachel Zadok, Marlene van Niekerk, Troy Blacklaws and Michiel Heyns) have chosen to turn their attention to the past, addressing the injustice, violence and cruelty of apartheid and the struggle against racial segregation and discrimination in South Africa. These novelists enter into a dialogue with internationally recognized white writers like Nadine Gordimer and André Brink, who, since the 1950s, have been at the forefront of exploring and highlighting the racist nature of the apartheid system; and who have been "authorized" by white publishers and publishing houses to write about this period and to "speak for"[1] the oppressed.

While South Africa's relatively recent past is a key theme of many contemporary black novels, there are also a growing number of literary texts by nonwhite authors (e.g. Rayda Jacob's 1998 *The Slave Book* and Therese Benadé's 2004 *Kites of Good Fortune*) that deal with the institution of chattel slavery from the seventeenth to the nineteenth centuries (1652-1834).[2] In this study, I focus

---

1 | For a theoretical discussion of "the problem of speaking for others" (Linda Alcoff), see chapter 5, "Transnational Diasporic Journeys in Lawrence Hill's *The Book of Negroes* (2007)," in this study.

2 | See Crystal Warren, "South Africa: Introduction," *The Journal of Commonwealth Literature* 41.4 (2006): 181; Ena Jansen, "Slavery and Its Literary Afterlife in South Africa and on Curaçao," *Shifting the Compass: Pluricontinental Connections in Dutch Colonial and Postcolonial Literature*, eds. Jeroen Dewulf, Olf Praamstra and Michiel van Kempen (Newcastle: Cambridge Scholars Publishing, 2013) 171; Margaret Stead, "A Better Connection," *Guardian* 29 Oct. 2005, 28 Aug. 2014 http://www.theguardian.com/books/2005/oct/29/featuresreviews.guardianreview27; Marita Wenzel, "Cross-on Yvette Christiansë's *Unconfessed* (2006)—a critically acclaimed novel about the hardships of black motherhood in the Cape Colony in the early nineteenth century—for the following reason: *Unconfessed* engages in an intertextual discussion with both twentieth-century neo-slave narratives like *Beloved* and twenty-first-century literary representations of slavery like *A Mercy* and *Lose Your Mother*, while simultaneously contributing to a critical rewriting of South African history from a black feminist perspective.

In an interview published as an appendix to her novel, Christiansë, who was born in South Africa in 1954, refers to the significance of racial slavery in South African history and culture, highlighting its enduring legacy and impact on (twentieth-century) black life:

Slavery in the Cape Colony, and in almost all places where Europeans had instituted slavery, was racially determined. As someone who grew up under apartheid, I am acutely aware of this history and its relationship to the founding of what would become the Republic of South Africa.[3]

Faced with racial discrimination, as a young adult, Christiansë (and her family) left the country to escape from apartheid, moving to Swaziland and later to Australia, where she earned her PhD in English at the University of Sydney. An expert on postcolonial and African American literature and theory, she has held numerous distinguished positions at universities in the United States and South Africa and is currently professor at Barnard College.[4] Like Hartman and Morrison and other contemporary authors of neo-slave narratives, Christiansë thus has achieved considerable acclaim as a writer and scholar; and she has been "appropriated" by U.S.-American academia.

In her sophisticated study *Toni Morrison: An Ethical Poetics* (2013), she focuses particularly on the discourses of witnessing, testimony and trauma and the representation of slavery in texts like *Beloved* and *A Mercy*. While Morrison seeks to challenge dominant white versions of American history and to tell stories that have been neglected, suppressed or marginalized, her novels are not written with the primary intention of closing the gaps of the historical record, Christiansë contends. In fact, "the narrators of Morrison's fictions often refuse such easy consolations and do not offer themselves in the mode of the wit-

---

ing Spatial and Temporal Boundaries: Three Women in Search of a Future," *Literator* 21.3 (2000): 23-25.
3 | Yvette Christiansë, "A Conversation with Yvette Christiansë," *Unconfessed: A Novel* (New York: Other Press, 2006) 351-53.
4 | Liesl Jobson, "Yvette Christiansë," *Poetry International Rotterdam* 1 Dec. 2009, 28 Aug. 2014 http://www.poetryinternationalweb.net/pi/site/poet/item/15564/10/yvette-christianse. See also https://barnard.edu/profiles/yvette-christianse.

ness whose storytelling will stand in where official history failed."⁵ According to Christiansë, Morrison's literary texts (characterized by fragmented narrative structures, opacities, silences and highly self-reflexive passages) thematize the ultimate impossibility of bearing witness to slavery and of healing the wounds of the past with the help of fiction.⁶ In this regard, there are crucial similarities between Christiansë's interpretation of Morrison's work in *An Ethical Poetics* and my reading of *A Mercy* in chapter 2 of this study.

Unlike many other Morrison scholars, Christiansë refuses to offer what Sabine Broeck would call a "kitsch"⁷ interpretation of texts like *Beloved* and *A Mercy*. Arguably, Christiansë's reading of Morrison's work strongly influences her own literary projects: In a way similar to Morrison's *A Mercy* and Hartman's *Lose Your Mother*, *Unconfessed* not only self-reflexively highlights the intricacies and inherent dangers of articulating the experiences of the enslaved and dispossessed; it also accentuates the impossibility of working through and overcoming the trauma of slavery.

In *Unconfessed*, Christiansë unfolds the story of Sila, a nineteenth-century black woman kidnapped from Mozambique as a child and shipped to the Cape Colony, where she and her children are repeatedly mistreated and (sexually) exploited by different masters. In response to an extremely brutal attack by the slave owner Jacobus van der Wat, Sila takes the life of her nine-year-old child Baro, desperately wishing to protect him from further violence. Written on the basis of fragmented archival material composed by the colonial authorities, *Unconfessed* seeks to deconstruct the received and racist representation of Sila as a murderer and piece of property. In Christiansë's fictional (re-)appropriation of the archive of slavery, the enslaved woman is re-imagined as a complex person plagued by ambivalent feelings. At the same time, marked by a sophisticated narrative structure, the novel directs our attention to the limits and ethical dangers of giving an account of Sila's life and the impossibility of recovering her voice from the existing documents.

Published first in the United States (by Other Press in New York City in 2006) and then in South Africa (by Kwela Books in Cape Town in 2007),⁸ *Unconfessed* has to be read as a border-crossing novel: One the one hand, as a novel about chattel slavery in the Cape Colony, it makes a crucial contribution to contemporary cultural and political discourse in South Africa, seeking to explore a history that was repressed, ignored and marginalized in the apartheid era. By

---

5 | Christiansë, *Toni Morrison* 35.
6 | See ibid. 28-75.
7 | Broeck, "Trauma, Agency, Kitsch and the Excesses of the Real" 247.
8 | Christiansë's decision to publish her novel first in New York was certainly based on commercial considerations, i.e., the desire to attract a large readership in the United States.

critically engaging with the colonial archive and trying to present the forgotten story of a female captive who is treated as an object and subjected to extreme cruelty, Christiansë draws not only attention to the brutality and violence of slavery at the Cape and, in particular, the slave woman's plight in a racist and sexist society but also reflects on the new violation contained in this telling. Drawing on fragments of information about Sila's life, *Unconfessed* is firmly "rooted" in a specific region and historical context, i.e. the Cape Colony in the 1820s, several years after the second British occupation.

On the other hand, as a scholar who is strongly influenced by the work of (African) American literary/cultural theorists and writers, Christiansë deliberately writes herself into the vibrant and commercially successful African American literary tradition of neo-slave narratives. Given its non-linear structure, fragmented character and lyrical tone,[9] its refusal to fill in the gaps and silences of the historical record and, last but not least, its thematic focus on infanticide committed by a female slave, Christiansë's text stands in an intertextual relationship to *Beloved*. As in Morrison's highly acclaimed novel, there is the determination to revisit the past from a black feminist perspective as well as the insight that certain experiences cannot be reconstructed and should not be put into words. Like *Beloved*, *Unconfessed* focuses on the interior life of a slave mother who is willing to do everything to protect her children from violence and, in a state of utmost despair, decides to commit infanticide. Rather than describing the actual violent act, Christiansë's text highlights the circumstances and events in Sila's life that lead to the killing, including the slave woman's unsuccessful attempt to convince the local authorities and her different masters of her legal status as a manumitted slave. Directing the reader's attention to Sila's feelings and thoughts, Christiansë finds a way to avoid repeating the racist descriptions that can be found in the archive.

The significance of Christiansë's work, I argue, lies not only in its critical re-writing of the historical record and exploration of the history of slavery in South Africa from a black feminist perspective but also in its complex reflection on the aesthetics and ethics of writing slavery. I read Christiansë's intertextual engagement with *Beloved* not simply as a commercial strategy to enter into the best-selling tradition of female-authored neo-slave narratives. For Christiansë, one of the most prominent Morrison scholars, it is primarily an act of respect towards and a gesture of appreciation of Morrison's theoretical and literary work. At the same time, *Unconfessed* offers a counter-discourse to "kitsch" interpretations of *Beloved* by resisting the temptation to transform Sila's story into a narrative of overcoming, to construct an "optimistic ending."

---

9 | In this context, it is worth noting that Christiansë has received wide critical acclaim as a poet. She has written two books of poems: *Castaway* (1999) and *Imprendehora* (2009).

In this chapter, first of all, I will give a brief historical account of slavery in the Cape Colony, focusing on specific characteristics (e.g. the slave's legal status as chattel and the oppression of slave women) and developments (e.g. the British takeover of the Cape and the period of "amelioration" in the 1820s and 1830s). Drawing on the writings of revisionist historians like Nigel Worden, I will challenge the widespread notion—and legitimizing myth created by white South African historiography—that Cape slaves were treated with dignity and kindness. In a next step, the chapter will examine Christiansë's critical exploration and (re-)appropriation of the archive of slavery, highlighting the ways she reflects upon the challenges and limits inherent in her ambitious project to reconstruct Sila's life. I will demonstrate that Christiansë employs specific narrative and aesthetic devices to refer to the fragmented character of the archive, to depict the protagonist's experiences of despair and loss and to emphasize the impossibility of healing the wounds of the past. Finally, drawing on diaspora studies, this chapter will shed light on Christiansë's representation of the complex interconnections between race, class and gender at the Cape and the meaning Christiansë attributes to acts of humiliations and violence within the slave community.

HISTORICAL CONTEXT: RACE-BASED CHATTEL SLAVERY IN THE CAPE COLONY

For a long time, research within the fields of slavery and African diaspora studies was primarily concerned with the history of the transatlantic slave trade and the experience of racial slavery in the "New World," in particular in mainland North America and the Caribbean. This focus on the Atlantic world reflects the avant-garde role as well as the enormous influence and dominance of African American and black British texts and theories in contemporary academic discussions about black diasporic life and slavery.[10] More recently, however, a number of scholars have begun to move beyond the framework of the Atlantic. Determined to explore the global nature of the African diaspora, they have started to analyze the complex history of the slave trade and slavery in the Mediterranean and in the Indian Ocean, within Africa and in other parts of the world.[11] In particular, one topic that has received increasing attention over the last decades is slavery in South Africa under Dutch and British rule.

---

10 | See also my introduction to *Transnational Black Dialogues*.
11 | Gwyn Campbell, "Slavery and Other Forms of Unfree Labour in the Indian Ocean World," *The Structure of Slavery in Indian Ocean Africa and Asia*, ed. Campbell (London: Frank Cass, 2004) vii-ix; Zeleza 35-68; Isabel Hofmeyr, "The Black Atlantic Meets the Indian Ocean: Forging New Paradigms of Transnationalism for the Global South – Liter-

As the historians Kerry Ward and Nigel Worden point out in their 1998 essay "Commemorating, Suppressing, and Invoking Cape Slavery," in South Africa, this history was systematically ignored, suppressed or misrepresented during the apartheid era. For instance, in public museums, such as the South African Cultural History Museum in Cape Town, the nation's past was constructed as exclusively white.[12] In South Africa's school curriculum, the issue of slavery was largely suppressed, aiming to "present a favourable view of white Cape colonists as brave pioneers and bringers of civilization, rather than exploiters of slave labour."[13] In those few school texts in which Cape slavery was discussed, it was depicted as a paternal and benign institution not comparable to the large-scale and brutal plantation systems of the Americas.[14] "A sub-text here," Ward and Worden contend, "was the oft-repeated statement of apartheid apologists that racial discrimination and genocide had been considerably worse in countries then critical of South Africa, such as the United States."[15]

Likewise, at least until the 1980s, most historians ignored the centrality of slavery to the economic, cultural, social and political development of South Africa, concentrating instead on the history of the Cape frontier in the eighteenth century or the industrial revolution in the late nineteenth century. Moreover, in academic works, a widespread assumption was "that in the fair Cape, with its production of the more genteel crops of wheat and wine, slavery was somehow 'mild.'"[16] According to this myth, under Dutch and British rule, enslaved individuals in South Africa were treated with respect and kindness and, unlike in places such as Jamaica or Brazil, did not participate in slave revolts; in the 1830s, slavery at the Cape ended without much protest and without a violent war.[17] These attempts to downplay or deny the brutality and cruelty of South African slavery remind us of similar pro-slavery and self-legitimizing discourses in the United States, where (early) twentieth-century historians like Ulrich Phillips

---

ary and Cultural Perspectives," *Social Dynamics* 33.2 (2007): 3-32. See also chapter 1, "The Concept of the African Diaspora and the Notion of Difference," in this study.
12 | Kerry Ward and Nigel Worden, "Commemorating, Suppressing, and Invoking Cape Slavery," *Negotiating the Past: The Making of Memory in South Africa*, eds. Sarah Nuttall and Carli Coetzee, 2nd ed. (Oxford: Oxford UP, 1999) 202.
13 | Ibid. 201-02.
14 | Ibid.
15 | Ibid. 202.
16 | Nigel Worden and Clifton Crais, "Introduction," *Breaking the Chains: Slavery and Its Legacy in the Nineteenth-Century Cape Colony*, eds. Worden and Crais (Johannesburg: Witwatersrand UP, 1994) 2.
17 | Ibid. 1-2.

interpreted, defined and justified racial slavery as a paternalistic and civilizing system that offered support and protection for African women and men.[18]

In South Africa, since the 1980s, scholars such as Nigel Worden have contributed to a radical transformation of the historiography of Cape slavery. Unlike their predecessors, they have begun to highlight the violence of Dutch and British rule, the Cape slave's legal status as chattel, the slave woman's (sexual) victimization, as well as forms of black resistance against colonial control. In the following, based on the work of these revisionist historians, I will offer a short overview of specific historical developments and characteristics of slavery at the Cape that help contextualize Christiansë's novel *Unconfessed*.

In 1652, the occupation of the Cape by the Dutch East India Company (VOC) marked the beginning of race-based chattel slavery in South Africa. Soon after arriving in the colony, the Dutch commander Jan van Riebeeck criticized "the inability of the small garrison to produce sufficient fruit, vegetables and grain to feed itself as well as to supply passing ships."[19] As a solution, he proposed the importation and use of slaves to work on the recently established settler farms and in the Company's Lodge in Cape Town. The VOC fully supported van Riebeeck's plan to introduce slavery as the dominant labor system: In the course of the seventeenth and eighteenth centuries, thousands of women and men were violently taken from a great variety of places in Africa and the Indian Ocean world, in particular from Madagascar, Mozambique, India and Indonesia, and brought to the Cape on Dutch, French, Portuguese and British ships. Over the decades, the Dutch enclave changed from a small settlement and refreshment station for VOC ships traveling between Europe and Asia into an influential trading center, a profitable agriculturally oriented colony and a brutal slave society based on the subjugation and racial discrimination of enslaved individuals and indigenous communities.[20]

Contrary to what seventeenth- and eighteenth-century European colonists and white visitors to the Cape Colony claimed and most twentieth-century historians continued to argue, slavery in Dutch South Africa was not at all benign and benevolent. Under VOC rule (1652-1795), enslaved women and men were legally defined and treated as chattel, as objects that could be bought, loaned and sold like an animal or a piece of furniture. They were not allowed "to marry, had no rights of *potestas* over their children, and were unable to make legal

---
18 | Huggins xxi.
19 | Nigel Worden, *Slavery in Dutch South Africa* (1985; Cambridge: Cambridge UP, 2010) 6.
20 | Robert C.-H. Shell, *Children of Bondage: A Social History of the Slave Society at the Cape of Good Hope, 1652-1838* (Hanover, NH: Wesleyan UP, 1994) xxx; Worden, *Slavery in Dutch South Africa* 3-9, 41-46; Wayne Dooling, *Slavery, Emancipation and Colonial Rule in South Africa* (Scottsville: U of KwaZulu-Natal P, 2007) 3-4.

contracts, acquire property or leave wills."[21] As in other slave societies, such as those in the Americas, violence was used as a means to maintain and control the labor force, to demonstrate the master's authority and power and to prevent slave uprisings and escapes. In urban and rural areas alike, house and field slaves were regularly exposed to extreme forms of exploitation, discrimination and punishment. For instance, they were severely whipped and beaten for working too slowly or trying to run away.[22] As Worden points out, female captives at the Cape were particularly vulnerable to abuse. In many cases, they "were obliged to submit to their owner's sexual appetites if so ordered, and risked beatings if they refused."[23]

In theory, the colony's law (known as Roman-Dutch law) provided Cape slaves with the right to approach the Company's authorities to complain about mistreatment and assaults committed by their masters. Moreover, they were allowed to testify in court against whites, including their owners. In that respect, Cape slavery differed—at least on the surface, in theory—from slavery in the United States. Among farmers and government officials, this resulted in the self-legitimizing view that enslaved women and men in Dutch South Africa were better off than those in other parts of the world.[24] In practice, however, the law clearly supported and protected the interests of slave owners to ensure "that control over slaves was effectively maintained and that sufficient produce was extracted from their labour to keep the colony self-sufficient and to provide the necessary surplus for Company and burgher requirements."[25] In court, the slave's testimony was treated with utmost suspicion or completely dismissed as unreliable. In general, slaves were extremely afraid to accuse their owners of abuse because they knew they had to return to them after the trials.[26]

Like their counterparts in the Atlantic world, enslaved women and men at the Cape did not passively accept their fate. While there were no collective slave uprisings in the seventeenth and eighteenth centuries, Cape slaves engaged in various forms of individual resistance to challenge the masters' authority and break the chains of bondage. As archival court records indicate, many slaves tried to escape to the colony's hinterland or the mountains near Cape Town, where some of them joined maroon communities. In many cases, however, fugitive slaves were not able to hide and stay free forever because "there was no permanent point of refuge in the western Cape after the expansion of the sett-

---

21 | Worden, *Slavery in Dutch South Africa* 115; italics in the original.
22 | Ibid. 101-18; see also Dooling, *Slavery, Emancipation and Colonial Rule* 40-41.
23 | Worden, *Slavery in Dutch South Africa* 105.
24 | Ibid. 110-16; see also Dooling, *Slavery, Emancipation and Colonial Rule* 41-42.
25 | Worden, *Slavery in Dutch South Africa* 110.
26 | Ibid. 111-16; see also Dooling, *Slavery, Emancipation and Colonial Rule* 42.

ler farming region."[27] In addition to escape attempts, slaves offered resistance by slowing their work pace, attacking their owners or overseers, setting fire to the masters' houses or poisoning their food, participating in underground networks and, tragically, by committing suicide and infanticide.[28]

As the historian Wayne Dooling points out, the beginning of the nineteenth century (the time in which Christiansë's novel *Unconfessed* is set) was a period of transformations and "considerable flux in the colony, primarily stemming from the replacement of the moribund VOC at the end of the eighteenth century by a British colonial government."[29] One of the primary goals of the new administration was to create and ensure political, social and economic stability in South Africa. Shortly after the first British occupation of the Cape in 1795, some of the new local authorities recognized the need to address and improve the situation of the enslaved population in order to reduce the risk of unrest and rebellion.[30] Certainly, this debate was influenced by recent slave revolts in British colonies such as Jamaica and, most notably, by the Haitian Revolution (1791-1804)—which, as Iyunolu Folayan Osagie puts it, "symbolized the vigor of slave resistance in the New World."[31] Ultimately, however, the British reform plans at the Cape were not put into practice, primarily because Cape slaveholders and settlers strongly defended their rights and privileges.[32]

In the 1820s, more than a decade after the second conquest of the Cape in 1806 and the legal abolition of the transoceanic slave trade in 1808, the British colonial authorities started to pursue "an official policy of 'amelioration'"[33] in South Africa, intended to improve the slave's legal position. As a result of this new initiative insistently demanded by abolitionists in Great Britain, during the 1820s and 1830s, enslaved individuals were given the right to marry, the slave's working hours were reduced and "[t]he sale in separate lots of husbands,

---

27 | Worden, *Slavery in Dutch South Africa* 125.
28 | Ibid. 119-37.
29 | Wayne Dooling, "'The Good Opinions of Others': Law, Slavery & Community in the Cape Colony, c.1760-1830," *Breaking the Chains: Slavery and Its Legacy in the Nineteenth-Century Cape Colony*, eds. Nigel Worden and Clifton Crais (Johannesburg: Witwatersrand UP, 1994) 25.
30 | Dooling, *Slavery, Emancipation and Colonial Rule* 72-73.
31 | Iyunolu F. Osagie, *The Amistad Revolt: Memory, Slavery and the Politics of Identity in the United States and Sierra Leone* (Athens, GA: U of Georgia P, 2000) 29. For more information on slave revolts in eighteenth-century Jamaica as well as on the Haitian Revolution, see chapter 6, "A Vicious Circle of Violence: Revisiting Jamaican Slavery in Marlon James's *The Book of Night Women* (2009)," in this study.
32 | Dooling, *Slavery, Emancipation and Colonial Rule* 72-73.
33 | Ibid. 84.

wives, and children under the age of ten was prohibited."³⁴ In case of maltreatment, slaves could turn to local authorities (so-called "Assistant Guardians"), who were required to carry out investigations and provide legal assistance and representation in court. Moreover, the Dutch masters and farmers were obliged "to keep record books of punishments inflicted and these were to be submitted to the Slave Protectors biannually."³⁵

In practice, however, these measures did not change the slave's status as chattel or ameliorate her living and working conditions. In several rural districts, slave owners strongly, and at times violently, protested against the new policy. Not willing to cooperate with the office of the "Protector of Slaves," they refused to fill out the required documents and continued to subject their slaves to sexual assaults and mistreatment. In the 1820s and 1830s, a large number of slaves actually went to the courts to complain about their owners, hoping to escape from further violence. Yet, in many cases, they were forced to realize that their charges were not taken into account and their masters were not punished.³⁶ "Colonial policy was deliberately aimed at arriving at 'amicable' settlements in conflicts between masters and slaves," Dooling explains. "For the most part, this consisted of the withdrawal of slave complaints."³⁷

(RE-)APPROPRIATING THE ARCHIVE OF SLAVERY: GOALS, CHALLENGES AND LIMITS

The *landdrost* said, is it true that on the twenty-fourth of December last ... *Hai.* What could I say that would be answer enough for us all? [...] *Speak, Sila van den Kaap. You have committed a heinous crime.* [...] I told him, *hertseer.* It is like wind blowing against a closed door.³⁸

In this key passage taken from Christiansë's *Unconfessed*, the novel's protagonist Sila, an enslaved woman in early nineteenth-century South Africa, recalls the day she was brought to court and condemned to death for infanticide: Her trial takes place in 1823, seventeen years after the second British occupation of the Cape. Despite the ameliorative measures introduced by the new colonial go-

---

34 | Ibid. 85.
35 | Dooling, "'The Good Opinions of Others'" 31; see also Dooling, *Slavery, Emancipation and Colonial Rule* 84-86.
36 | Dooling, *Slavery, Emancipation and Colonial Rule* 86-89.
37 | Ibid. 89.
38 | Yvette Christiansë, *Unconfessed: A Novel* (New York: Other Press, 2006) 231-34; italics and first ellipsis in the original. All further references to this novel (U) will be cited in the text and will refer to this edition.

vernment to reform the colony's slave law, the situation of the enslaved in South Africa has not significantly improved. In most legal proceedings, the slave's testimony is either ignored or dismissed as unreliable and untrustworthy.[39] In *Unconfessed*, Sila is aware of the fact that her tragic story will not be heard by the colonial authorities. Thus, when asked by the local magistrate, Van der Riet, to confess the killing of her nine-year-old son Baro, "in response to the law's demand for corroboration of what it already claims to know,"[40] Sila refuses to give a detailed account of the crime and her motives. Knowing that her master will probably not be punished, she does not explain that she and her children were routinely exposed to mistreatment and (sexual) abuse by Van der Wat. Instead of answering the magistrate's question in a direct way and confessing the infanticide (the novel's title alludes to this fact), she only says: *hertseer*.[41] For the reader of *Unconfessed*, this utterance provides (partial) insight into Sila's complex emotional state as a slave mother who, driven by extreme sorrow and utmost despair, decides to take the life of her child in order to protect him from further pain and harm.

Outside the fictional realm of the novel, the term *hertseer* refers to Christiansë's exploration and critical (re-)appropriation of the colonial archive. As she explains in her author's note and a detailed accompanying essay called "'Heartsore': The Melancholy Archive of Cape Colony Slavery" (2009), *Unconfessed* is based on historical documents found at the Cape Town Archive and other institutions that, from the colonizer's perspective, reveal the case of Sila van de Kaap, a female slave accused of slitting the throat of her child. Her name occurs in various forms like Siela, Silia or Drusilla in a number of white-authored sources, including the will of her first mistress Hendrina Jansen, court and prison records and a decree by King George IV, composed in 1827. In these texts, Sila is defined as chattel and reduced to a criminal without history. Based on these documents, it is impossible to gain insight into her feelings and thoughts or to discover the circumstances surrounding her son's death.[42] As Christiansë puts it, "Of her life, we know almost nothing. [...] To the extent that she remains visible to us now, it is as a shadow figure [...]."[43]

---

39 | See, for instance, Dooling, *Slavery, Emancipation and Colonial Rule* 89.
40 | Yvette Christiansë, "'Heartsore': The Melancholy Archive of Cape Colony Slavery," *S&F Online* 7.2 (2009): 10.
41 | In the novel's glossary, this Dutch term is translated as "[a]nguish; sore of heart (heartsore); distress." Yvette Christiansë, "Glossary," *Unconfessed: A Novel* (New York: Other Press, 2006) 344.
42 | Christiansë, "'Heartsore'" 2.
43 | Ibid. 1.

What can be reconstructed from the archival material is the following account of events, which forms the basis of the plot in *Unconfessed*:[44] In the Cape Colony, Sila was apparently first owned by a widow called Hendrina Jansen, who died in 1806. In her testament, Jansen directed that Sila and her other slaves be manumitted after her death. In order to earn money to compensate Jansen's son Theron, the slaves should be hired out to other masters. Contrary to what her mistress had stated in her will, however, Sila did not obtain her freedom. Rather, four years later, she was sold to Carl Hancke in Cape Town, where she gave birth to Carolina, Camies and Baro. In 1817, after a heated legal dispute between Theron and Hancke over the ownership of the slave woman, Sila and her children were transported to a farm in Plettenberg Bay.

At this place, Sila and Baro were repeatedly whipped and flogged by their new owners, Jacobus van der Wat and his wife; Carolina and Camies were sold to another farmer. In December 1822, after a terrible beating that left Baro with serious injuries, Sila killed her son with a knife. Then, she escaped from the farm to turn to her neighbor, a militia officer named Witte Drift, where she confessed the crime. Complaining about her master's cruelty and brutality, she was examined by the district's surgeon, who discovered a number of bruises on Sila's body and confirmed her story of mistreatment. A couple of months later, in March 1823, the slave woman was brought to trial for *kindermoord*. In court, her fellow slave Jephta was asked by Sila's lawyer to testify against Van der Wat. Instead of corroborating Sila's version of events, Jephta called her a drunkard and described his master as a kind and good-natured man. "The fact that he was obliged to return to Van der Wat's farm after his testimony—and that this might have had some bearing upon his claims—went unchallenged,"[45] Christiansë observes.

As the official (court) records show, Sila was found guilty of killing her child and, despite the surgeon's notes, of falsely accusing her owners of mistreatment of their slaves. As a result, she was sentenced to death and taken to the prison in Cape Town. However, since Sila was with child and the law forbade the execution of pregnant women, the punishment was not carried out. In 1826, a number of years after the trial, the new superintendent of police, de Laurentz, became aware of the fact that Sila was still imprisoned and exploited as a prostitute. After obtaining a royal pardon from the king of England, her death sentence was changed to a fourteen-year imprisonment on Robben Island,[46] where she was forced to work in a quarry. As one of the few women

---

44 | The following paragraphs focusing on the archival account of Sila's life are based on Christiansë, "'Heartsore'" 2-6.
45 | Ibid. 5.
46 | As Harriet Deacon explains: "Robben Island has been used for many different purposes and held various contrasting meanings for South Africans during the course of

living on the island, she was again repeatedly subjected to sexual abuse. What is striking is that her name does not appear in any records after 1830; it might be that Sila was transported back to the prison in Cape Town a year after the official ending of slavery in 1834. But it is impossible to say if "she survived or not."[47]

In her author's note, Christiansë reflects on her motivation for exploring Sila's life and telling her story, after discovering the slave's name in several historical documents in South Africa and England:

My own questions were straightforward: Who was she? What did it take for someone, a slave, a woman, to survive a death sentence, and for three years? Trying to answer these questions took years of summers and any other times I could get in the Cape Town archives, the British Library, and the Public Records Office in Kew. What pulled me? It was that trace, the word that all of the official documents seemed unable to resist—that single Dutch word, *hertseer*, which the English translated directly into "heartsore." Not "grieving" or "griefstruck," but this forceful, corporeal, "heartsore." I believed it to be one real world she uttered when the prosecutor outlined and demanded that she confirm her act.[48]

Inspired by this archival source, in *Unconfessed*, Christiansë seeks to write against the one-sided representation of Sila as a criminal within the colonial record, presenting her as a complex woman and loving mother with fears, hopes and dreams as well as a strong desire to protect her children. Focusing on everyday practices, experiences and relations of domination and subordination, Christiansë's primary goal is "to recover, to the extent possible, some sense of the life and conditions Sila lived in and from which she attempted to speak."[49] Like Hartman in "The Dead Book," she is faced with the ethical and aesthetic challenge of finding an appropriate way to engage with the archive and deal with its silences and gaps, racist depictions and "pornotroping" characteristics. To repeat an important point raised in my chapter on *Lose Your Mother*: Dependent on the information contained in white-authored sources, Christian-

---

its history. [...] During the eighteenth century the island became a place of detention for those defined as the worst criminals and most dangerous opponents of the Dutch East India Company." Harriet Deacon, "Remembering Tragedy, Constructing Modernity: Robben Island as a National Monument," *Negotiating the Past: The Making of Memory in South Africa*, eds. Sarah Nuttall and Carli Coetzee, 2nd ed. (Oxford: Oxford UP, 1999) 162.
47 | Christiansë, "'Heartsore'" 6.
48 | Yvette Christiansë, "Author's Note," *Unconfessed: A Novel* (New York: Other Press, 2006) 350; italics in the original.
49 | Christiansë, "'Heartsore'" 2.

së's difficult task is to write about scenes of oppression, rape and humiliation without "reinforcing the authority of these documents even as [she tries] to use them for contrary purposes"[50] and without subjecting the female captive to a further act of violation.

Like Hartman and Morrison, Christiansë is fully aware of the limits of her project to explore and articulate the experiences of enslaved women: While she attempts to challenge the dominant white account of the past, she points out that it is impossible to reconstruct Sila's life or to recover her voice from the material available. Legally defined as chattel, in court, Sila was only allowed to answer to questions asked by members of the colonizing group. Without support and protection, she could not give an account of the cruelty of the slave system and her traumatic experiences as a slave mother.[51] Drawing on Gayatri Chakravorty Spivak's work and her landmark essay "Can the Subaltern Speak?" (1988), Christiansë argues that, in the archive, "Sila is structurally muted in that, although we have words from her, the state never granted her full subjectivity, and her utterances remained, for them, utterly illegible."[52] Although she had the opportunity to speak, she knew that her voice would not be heard by the colonial authorities.

For Christiansë (and any other contemporary author dealing with this subject), the attempt to explore the history of slavery in South Africa from the slave's point of view is complicated by "the absence of generic forms for slave self-articulation in the Cape Colony."[53] In contrast to the United States and other countries in the Americas, there are virtually no autobiographical texts written by (former) Cape slaves. As Christiansë explains, the primary reason for this dearth of first-person accounts of slavery in South Africa was the lack of abolitionist groups supporting the writing and publication of slave narratives. While British abolitionists like William Wilberforce also drew attention to the terrible conditions for Cape slaves and the high rate of infanticide among slave mothers in South Africa, "little effective abolitionist activity occurred in the Cape itself."[54] As a result, for enslaved individuals like Sila, there was no public space for self-representation. Today, confronted with silences, gaps and fragments of information, the novelist's task is

---

50 | Hartman, *Scenes of Subjection* 10-11.
51 | Christiansë, "'Heartsore'" 10-11.
52 | Ibid. 1. See also Gayatri Chakravorty Spivak, "Can the Subaltern Speak?" *Marxism and the Interpretation of Culture*, eds. Cary Nelson and Lawrence Grossberg (Urbana: U of Illinois P, 1988) 271-313.
53 | Christiansë, "'Heartsore'" 9.
54 | Ibid.

to listen to echoes of subjects for whom one might not have an adequate language; one must also learn how to discern what they might have been trying to say within the statements attributed to them (but that could very well represent the redactions of colonial officials—notaries, court reporters).[55]

Most crucially, as a contemporary author who intends to bring to light the intricacies involved in recovering the forgotten story of a slave woman like Sila, Christiansë, like Hartman and Morrison, has to acknowledge and respect the fact that the archive's fragments cannot be pieced together to create a coherent picture of the past.[56]

FRAGMENTATION, NON-LINEARITY AND TEXTUAL BLANKS: AESTHETIC STRATEGIES IN *UNCONFESSED*

In *Toni Morrison: An Ethical Poetics*, Christiansë vigorously disagrees with and powerfully challenges "kitsch" interpretations of *Beloved* that conceptualize this novel as an ultimately triumphant narrative of overcoming and redemption.[57] On an intertextual level, I argue, Christiansë's neo-slave narrative *Unconfessed* presents an oppositional response to such reductive reconciliatory readings: By using an extremely complex, fragmented and non-linear narrative style that refers to Sila's painful experiences of loss and violence and that reflects the archive's omissions, contradictions and gaps, in a way similar to Morrison and Hartman, Christiansë discards the notion of slavery fiction as a form of therapy, healing and reconciliation.

As Christiansë argues, an aesthetic strategy of fragmentation is "the only form that would resist any narrative longing for a complete, consoling recuperation of the colonial record on [the novelist's] part and, perhaps, a reader's."[58] By drawing attention to the interiority of the slave experience and exploring Sila's state of mind—her contradictions, inner conflicts and struggles—Christiansë seeks to re-imagine the enslaved woman's tragic story in all its depth, complexity and ambiguity, avoiding "sentimentality and nostalgia that would want to make this life heroic or even representative, as a bearer of truth we might want to universalize."[59]

---

55 | Ibid. 2.
56 | See also Hartman, "Venus in Two Acts" 4.
57 | See Christiansë, *Toni Morrison* 34, 35, 46, 75.
58 | Christiansë, "Author's Note" 350.
59 | Yvette Christiansë, "A Freedom Stolen," *Dialogues Across Diasporas: Women Writers, Scholars, and Activists of Africana and Latina Descent in Conversation*, eds. Marion Rohrleitner and Sarah E. Ryan (Lanham, MD: Lexington Books, 2013) 104.

As a loving and caring slave mother, who is treated as chattel and (sexually) exploited by different masters, reduced to her reproductive capacities and separated from some of her daughters and sons, Sila is faced with the same dilemma as Sethe in *Beloved* and Florens's mother in *A Mercy*: How to protect her offspring and herself in this violent society that denies her the right to decide over her own body and the lives of her children? How to carry out her role and tasks as a mother in a world in which she and her children are registered as the property of white women and men? Focusing on the destructive psychological effects of slavery and colonial discourse on the female captive, *Unconfessed* offers no redemptive vision or easy solutions to Sila's predicament; ultimately, the novel's protagonist sees no other option but to commit infanticide to save her boy Baro from being beaten and mistreated by van der Wat. While Sila's deed could be interpreted as a strong act of black resistance against the colonizer, "the fact that Baro bears the full burden of this violence puts the brakes on any runaway 'triumphalism' of late twentieth-century readerly practice,"[60] Christiansë contends. In *Unconfessed*, as in *A Mercy* and *Lose Your Mother*, the main focus is on loss, grief and pain rather than on the celebration of resistance. Given Baro's death, for Christiansë, it is impossible to transform Sila's story into a narrative of overcoming and liberation.[61]

Like Hartman's attempt to reconstruct the slave's experience aboard the *Recovery* in "The Dead Book," Christiansë's text is based on the archive of slavery but also written against it.[62] In a third-person point of view, *Unconfessed* begins with a description of the new superintendent's visit to the prison in Cape Town in 1826, where he encounters Sila, a female slave "moved from master to master, farm to farm, from the district's prison, to the big town's prison" (U 12). In the following pages, in a non-chronological order and fragmentary manner, the reader is introduced to the tragic events of Sila's life, circling around her separation from her family and home in Mozambique and her terrible experiences in South Africa. After this introductory sequence, the narrative perspective shifts to the protagonist's point of view, which gives the reader insight into Sila's thoughts and feelings and highlights her "desire for speech resulting from the inability to be heard fully from within slavery's discourse."[63] Her decisive remark "*Out of my way!*" (U 34; italics in the original) is the prelude to a complex act of black self-representation and to a deep and extremely intense confrontation with her past. The rest of the novel "has the deep inner logic of the oral storyteller who relates to past events and characters in a different way than a chronicler, or even third person narrator," Christiansë contends. "Key

---

60 | Christiansë, "'Heartsore'" 12.
61 | Ibid.
62 | See Hartman, "Venus in Two Acts" 12.
63 | Christiansë, "'Heartsore'" 1.

moments taken from the archive provide the temporal ordering but they are set in an approaching claim to how Sila might have seen and heard."[64]

As in Toni Morrison's *Beloved*, it is the "unhomely"—"a paradigmatic colonial"[65] situation, to use Homi K. Bhabha's words—that causes the female protagonist to wrestle with memories that have been repressed or forgotten. On Robben Island, Sila encounters the spirit of her dead son Baro whose presence makes her feel stronger and forces her to re-experience traumatic events and feelings: "Now that you are back, my thoughts are like bees in a bottle. Days long ago are back, fresh and with them a pain that is sharp" (U 66). Unlike some of her fellow prisoners, Sila believes in the necessity to remember and, in a poetic and fragmented narrative that switches between times and places, she begins to dig into her past. However, what characterizes her internal speech—a sophisticated fusion of dreams, memories, flashbacks and visions—is a high level of self-reflexivity concerning the limits and dangers of her attempt to talk about her experiences. Put differently, in *Unconfessed*, there is an underlying voice emphasizing that certain aspects of Sila's life cannot (and should not) be articulated or represented. To use Sila's words: "Some things just cannot be told" (U 150).

As an enslaved black woman, Sila is categorically excluded "from the full and putatively universal subjecthood of 'free white male.'"[66] For the European colonizers, she is "that 'otherness' which is at once an object of desire and derision."[67] As mentioned before, on van der Vat's farm as well as in the Cape Town prison and on Robben Island, Sila becomes a rape victim. In her speech, she is torn between the wish to address her mistreatment and the refusal to recount it. In these passages, the novel enters into a discussion with contemporary theoretical explorations within the fields of African American and African diaspora studies that focus on the risks of representing slavery's violence. It is in this context that I will, once again, look at the work of Saidiya Hartman.

In *Scenes of Subjection*, Hartman justifies her decision not to incorporate Frederick Douglass's famous description of the violent act against Aunt Hester by arguing that she seeks to highlight "the ease with which such scenes are usually reiterated, the casualness with which they are circulated, and the consequences of this routine display of the slave's ravaged body."[68] As Hartman goes on to explain, in most cases, such accounts of violence do not evoke the reader's indignation but rather "reinforce the spectacular character of black suffering."[69]

---

64 | Christiansë, "A Freedom Stolen" 104-05.
65 | Homi K. Bhabha, *The Location of Culture* (London: Routledge, 1994) 13.
66 | Christiansë, "'Heartsore'" 2.
67 | Bhabha 96.
68 | Hartman, *Scenes of Subjection* 3.
69 | Ibid.

According to Hartman, writers dealing with the issue of slavery are faced with the challenge of bearing witness to the atrocities "without exacerbating the indifference to suffering that is the consequence of the benumbing spectacle."[70]

In *Unconfessed*, instead of satisfying a contemporary reader's thirst for violent entertainment and offering an account rich in detail,[71] Christiansë carefully employs specific narrative strategies to describe these scenes of humiliation and violence against the black female body. Sila's "Let us talk about the things these guards do. Let us not" (U 154), for instance, allows the protagonist to refer to her experience of being raped by the prison guards without having to narrate it. Here, Sila gives us a short glimpse into her tragic situation as one of the few female prisoners on Robben Island but, by refusing to talk about it, prevents us from becoming "voyeurs fascinated with and repelled by exhibitions of terror and sufferance."[72] When she recalls the events leading up to Baro's death, a single, onomatopoetic word depicts the beating of Sila by her master: "Van der Wat caught me when I came in. *Klap!*" (U 266; italics in the original). In this utterance, the brutal act is indicated but not explicitly told; it is up to the reader to imagine it or not. As Christiansë explains in an essay called "A Freedom Stolen" (2013), in *Unconfessed*, her goal "was to *not* show the violence in any descriptive detail. This was made easier by the fact that the novel becomes a first person narration. One does not 'write' a description of violence while experiencing it. Rather, a listener might hear a sound that tells everything."[73]

Built in a circular way around repetitions with a difference, the text slowly moves towards the novel's climax: the protagonist's act of infanticide. Again and again, Sila's reconstruction of the event is interrupted by textual blanks. At one point, signifying on Sethe's combination of mono-syllables in Morrison's *Beloved*,[74] Sila's train of thought suddenly stops in the middle of a sentence—after a clear, repeated "no" that expresses her refusal to confront her past: "That

---

70 | Ibid. 4.
71 | See also Maria Geusteyn, "The Art of Looking Sideways: Articulating Silence in Yvette Christiansë's *Unconfessed*," *Postamble: A Multidisciplinary Journal of African Studies* 7.1 (2011): 5.
72 | Hartman, *Scenes of Subjection* 3.
73 | Christiansë, "A Freedom Stolen" 110; italics in the original.
74 | Here, I am referring to Sethe's response to Schoolteacher's arrival at 124, "Simple: she [Sethe] was squatting in the garden and when she saw them coming and recognized schoolteacher's hat, she heard wings. Little hummingbirds stuck their needle beaks right through her headcloth into her hair and beat their wings. And if she thought anything, it was. No. No. Nono. Nonono. Simple." Toni Morrison, *Beloved* (1987; London: Vintage, 2007) 192. In her insightful reading of this scene, Sabine Broeck argues that "*Beloved* enacts the answerlessness, which I take to mean the impossibility to respond to a traumatic event with words, in the ultimate collapse of signification into the

day. Oh. No, nono. I do not want to go to that day. I should have [...]" (U 257). In this passage, Christiansë's text performs the difficulty and pain involved in the process of remembering the infanticide and talking/writing about it. Throughout *Unconfessed*, Sila uses euphemisms[75] to describe the *kindermoord* ("I sent him away from this world;" U 294) and, as illustrated in the quotation above, only refers to "that day." In a similar way as Morrison's *Beloved*, Christiansë's text seeks to shift the attention away from the actual act of infanticide (the crime that is centralized in the archive) to the circumstances that lead to the event, to the motives that lie behind the killing, to Sila's life with the killing.

POWER RELATIONS IN A RACIST AND SEXIST SOCIETY

In *Unconfessed*, Christiansë depicts a society profoundly marked by power inequalities and hierarchical structures based on race, class, gender and sexuality. To draw, once again, on the work of Avtar Brah, the Cape Colony can be described as a "diaspora space," in which various power struggles take place between diasporic and non-diasporic individuals. Written from a black woman's perspective, Christiansë's novel not only explores the intricate web of relationships that exist between the white male colonizers/slaveholders, the white women living in the Cape Colony and the enslaved community. Like Morrison's *A Mercy* and James's *The Book of Night Women*, it also sheds light on what Tina M. Campt and Deborah A. Thomas would describe as "intra-diasporic"[76] tensions, that is, on acts of oppression, betrayal and jealously within the black diasporic group. What emerges is a complex portrait of a violent and male-dominated world, in which black women like Sila are subject to both racism and sexism: They suffer not only from the same experiences of violence as male slaves; they are also exposed to forms of humiliation and abuse by black men, i.e. male fellow slaves.

A key theme that runs through the novel is Sila's desperate (and ultimately unsuccessful) attempt to gain manumission. As the historian Robert Shell points out in his 1994 study *Children of Bondage: A Social History of the Slave Society at the Cape of Good Hope, 1652-1838*, manumission was "a juridical act in which the property rights in the slave were surrendered by the owner and the slave assumed a new—but at the Cape, unfortunately not full—legal and civic

---

mono-syllable 'no,' strengthening its effect of denial by repetition, 'nonono.'" Broeck, *White Amnesia - Black Memory?* 37.

[75] | See also Jessica Murray, "Gender and Violence in Cape Slave Narratives and Post-Narratives," *South African Historical Journey* 62.3 (2010): 458.

[76] | Campt and Thomas, "Gendering Diaspora: Transnational Feminism, Diaspora and Its Hegemonies" 3.

status and responsibility as a 'free black.'"[77] In private households (in contrast to the Company's lodge), a large number of enslaved women and men "were manumitted by testamentary disposition after their owners died."[78] However, it was not uncommon that the slave owner's heirs went to court to contest their fathers' or mothers' will. Noteworthy, under Roman Dutch law, the children of manumitted slave mothers were also treated as free individuals. Therefore, for members of the ruling class, the manumission of an enslaved woman was a significant economic loss.[79] Not coincidentally, in the years following the abolition of the oceanic slave trade in 1808, the number of manumitted female captives rapidly declined because enslaved "women then became the main source of supply for all future slaves in the colony."[80]

As the archival material reveals, when the widow and Cape slave owner Hendrina Jansen died in 1806, her son Theron ignored his mother's instructions to offer manumission to her slaves, including Sila van de Kaap. For Theron, Sila was especially valuable because she was of childbearing age and already had several children, who could be rented out or sold to other farmers. Presumably, Jansen's son (and other masters) repeatedly changed Sila's name to conceal that she was, in fact, a free person. Their efforts were successful: While Sila believed that she "was working off the price of her freedom, as stipulated in Hendrina Jansen's will,"[81] she was actually transferred from master to master as chattel and never gained her freedom. Instead of intervening in this matter, the relevant colonial authorities did not question Theron's act.[82] Deprived of her freedom, Sila was forced to accept "that any children born to her would also be slaves, and therefore, property."[83] For the slave mother, this was certainly the most painful aspect of Theron's fraud.

In *Unconfessed*, Christiansë focuses our attention to Sila's (failed) efforts to enforce the will of her deceased mistress. Throughout the novel, the slave woman struggles to make her voice heard and assert her legal status as a manumitted slave. Exposed to abuse and sexual exploitation, her primary goal is to protect and liberate her children:[84] "When *Oumiesies* put me in her will, she meant for my children to be free too. That is how the law is. I know that. The children of a free woman are free. And when *Oumiesies* died I became free. Eighteen and oh-six" (U 65; italics in the original). However, Sila's predicament

---

77 | Shell 371-72.
78 | Ibid. 390.
79 | Ibid. 384, 390.
80 | Ibid. 384.
81 | Christiansë, "'Heartsore'" 3.
82 | Ibid. 3-4.
83 | Ibid. 3.
84 | See also Christiansë, "A Freedom Stolen" 109.

is that the colony's law provides no help or protection for free black women and men held as slaves. Living in a society in which her subjectivity is completely denied, Sila's cries for justice are systematically ignored. Except for friends like Lys, a fellow prisoner on Robben Island, nobody listens to her complaints or stands up for her rights. At the Cape, the master not only has the power to humiliate, beat and torture his slaves on a daily basis without being punished for it; he is also in a position to defy the law. Although the British authorities claim to be willing to improve the conditions of the enslaved, before the law and in court, Cape slaves are "never treated as the responsible authors of meaningful statements,"[85] to quote Christiansë.

In *Unconfessed*, Christiansë shows that the slaveholder's power over his slaves is nearly unlimited, which regularly leads to cruel and degrading treatment of those in bondage: At a certain point in the novel, van der Wat's daughter Susanna asks Sila to follow her into her father's office. A few hours after the painful separation from her children Carolina and Camies, Susanna attempts to humiliate Sila by reading from a book compiled by van der Wat; an inventory of his possessions that puts Sila and her daughters and sons on the same level as his animals: "She made my name come out of that book like a crazy thing lost in a big wind when everything is thrown up in the air and spins around. There we all were, the cows and you and me and Carolina and Camies and Pieter" (U 246).

This passage, which reminds us of a similar scene in Morrison's *Beloved*, where Schoolteacher evokes Sethe's supposed "animal" characteristics,[86] refers to the concept and colonial process of "thingification:"[87] the slaveholder's attempt and power to transform African captives into mere objects, destroying the slave's possibility of subjecthood. As shown before, this is also a central theme of Morrison's *A Mercy* and Hartman's *Lose Your Mother*. In *Unconfessed*, throughout her life, Sila is forced to work for masters who treat and (as van der Wat's book illustrates) represent her and her children as "things bought and sold" (U 299). Within the existing power structure of the colony, the slave holder's children have internalized their fathers' racist beliefs that white men and women are superior to black individuals. In this regard, van der Wat's daughter Susanna is representative.

In addition to exploring the relationship between white and black, *Unconfessed* offers striking examples of the complex power structure and conflicts between male and female slaves at the Cape. In her speech to her dead son, Sila recounts a series of incidents in October 1823, two months before the killing

---

85 | Christiansë, "'Heartsore'" 9.
86 | Morrison, *Beloved* 228.
87 | See also chapter 2, "From Human Bondage to Racial Slavery: Toni Morrison's *A Mercy* (2008)," in this study.

of Baro: Having lost his master's cattle, Jeptha, one of Sila's fellow slaves, finds himself in a precarious situation. His only chance to avoid being severely punished by van der Wat is to leave the farm and run away. As indicated before, flight was a widespread form of slave resistance in South Africa.[88] However, while many enslaved women and men in North America gained their freedom by traveling to regions and states where slavery was not allowed or practiced, "there was no 'outside' for slaves of the Cape Colony, no northern, nonslaving state to which a slave might escape."[89] Thus, given the colony's geographical location, in most cases, the attempt to escape was doomed to failure. And, quite often, recaptured Cape slaves were beaten or even whipped to death.[90] Despite these enormous risks, Sila expresses her strong wish to join Jeptha, together with her children, hoping to leave behind the violence she encounters on van der Wat's farm: "We can do it. I told him. My blood was coming back. My blood was running away. *My children* [...] But he said, that is not possible. They will slow us down" (U 251; italics in the original). While Sila believes in the power of black solidarity and responsibility in the face of slavery's horror, Jeptha is depicted as a cold and emotionless man who is only concerned about his own future and unable or unwilling to empathize with a black mother and fellow slave struggling to protect and care for her children.

In its depiction of Jeptha's cruel behavior towards Sila, this passage illustrates the fact that, as Christiansë puts it, "slave men, too, regarded women as beneath them."[91] In her insightful essay "'Strength of the Lion ... Arms Like Polished Iron': Embodying Black Masculinity in an Age of Slavery and Propertied Manhood" (2011), the historian Kathleen M. Brown argues that male slaves tried and managed to express their manhood in various ways: for instance, by running away from the master, starting fights with fellow slaves and whites, engaging in sexual relationships, participating in cultural activities or seeking to control and oppress black women.[92] "Subjected to a labor system and a legal context that attempted to strip them of their humanity," Brown contends, "enslaved men struggled to find space to be men."[93]

For Jeptha, the refusal to allow Sila to take her children with her provides him with the opportunity to dominate and exert power over a slave woman; it offers the chance to assert his manhood, restore some sense of self-esteem and

---

88 | Warden, *Slavery in Dutch South Africa* 123.
89 | Christiansë, "Author's Note" 351.
90 | Warden, *Slavery in Dutch South Africa* 125-27.
91 | Christiansë, "A Freedom Stolen" 109.
92 | Kathleen M. Brown, "'Strength of the Lion ... Arms Like Polished Iron': Embodying Black Masculinity in an Age of Slavery and Propertied Manhood," *New Men: Manliness in Early America*, ed. Thomas A. Foster (New York: New York UP, 2011) 172-80.
93 | Ibid. 174.

gain respect within the slave community—at the expense of Sila and the lives of her children. Focusing on intra-black violence in the Cape Colony, this scene parallels Morrison's representation of the Blacksmith's rejection of Florens in *A Mercy*: Both Morrison and Christiansë challenge static conceptualizations of black groups as homogeneous communities of victims and rebels and, therefore, move beyond a strict dichotomy between black victimhood/resistance and white guilt culture. Adopting a black feminist standpoint, they highlight the brutalizing impact of slavery on the dispossessed and explore the ways in which black men like Jeptha and the Blacksmith seek to gain or regain some form of power by oppressing black women and other fellow captives.

Instead of celebrating acts of kindness and cooperation within the black diasporic community, *Unconfessed* thus draws our attention to "the collusion between a slave owner and his male slave"[94] at the Cape. "At some point in their relation to women," Christiansë contends, "these men are in concert, even while they remain in their hierarchical relation to each other."[95] In fact, subordinated to van der Wat's will, Jeptha acts like his master when he tries to rape Sila, reducing her to a (sexual) object and destroying any sense of solidarity between enslaved women and men. As Jessica Murray shows in her essay "Gender and Violence in Cape Slave Narratives and Post-Narratives" (2010), *Unconfessed* sheds light on the black man's feelings of powerlessness, inferiority and bitterness, given the fact that he is unable to protect members of the black female community from being exposed to (sexual) abuse by white men. According to Murray, Christiansë's text shows "how this rage is projected onto the female victim of rape rather than being solely directed at the perpetrator/owner."[96]

On one of her first days on van der Wat's farm, Sila is terrible beaten although she is pregnant. While she hopes to get help from her fellow slaves, Jeptha offers no words of consolation but laughs and spits at Sila: "And she knew the men were jealous and ashamed, and that was why their eyes went dull with hatred when they looked at her. She knew there would be no Sunday afternoon dancing or singing with these people" (U 21).[97] Participating in a dialogue with Afro-pessimism about the utterly destructive nature of anti-blackness, *Unconfessed*, like *A Mercy*, examines the devastating effects of slavery as "thingification" on relationships within the black community, foregrounding violence, loss and despair as defining features of the female captive's life.

---

94 | Christiansë, "A Freedom Stolen" 109.
95 | Ibid.
96 | Murray 459.
97 | See also ibid.

Conclusion

In her essay "'This is Our Speech': Voice, Body and Poetic Form in Recent South African Writing" (2011), the South African poet and literary scholar Gabeba Baderoon analyzes the sophisticated use of lyrical language and poetic devices, such as repetitions and ellipses, in *Unconfessed*. According to Baderoon, Christiansë strategically employs these narrative and aesthetic strategies to address the cruelty of Cape slavery and acts of sexual violence against enslaved women without running the risk of "reproducing an intrusive gaze on their suffering."[98] The protagonist's highly poetic interior monologue, Baderoon contends, offers a powerful alternative to Sila's life as a prisoner and slave on Robben Island: In her private speech, the slave mother is able to communicate with her sons and daughters who are dead or have been sold, to recount her childhood in Mozambique, to swear at her cruel masters and to dream about freedom.[99] While Sila's story of abuse and violence is ignored or dismissed by members of the ruling class, her thoughts and utterances directed at Baro and friends like Johannes, "constitute the anguished but ultimately triumphant words of the novel,"[100] Baderoon concludes. Drawing our attention to Sila's private memories of her past as a free woman, her desires and hopes and her attempts to offer resistance against her masters, "the text emphatically conveys her powerful resilience and creation of intimacy and wholeness."[101]

Highlighting the novel's careful representation of (sexual) violence, Baderoon identifies and analyzes a crucial aspect of Christiansë's neo-slave narrative that is also addressed in this chapter. However, by reading Sila's private "confession" to her children and friends as an empowering narrative that allows the protagonist to find a new sense of wholeness, Baderoon's interpretation fails to take into account that Christiansë explicitly refuses to offer a triumphant reconstruction of the slave woman's life. As I have shown, *Unconfessed* is marked by contradictory tendencies: By focusing on the interiority of the slave's experience, Christiansë indeed writes against the one-sided and racist depiction of Sila within the archive of slavery. At the same time, however, the novel self-reflexively elaborates on the ultimate impossibility of reconstructing Sila's experiences; it refuses to fill in the silences of the historical record as it abstains from transforming the slave mother's story into a narrative of overcoming. Fiction, for Christiansë, cannot heal the wounds of slavery: "Confronted by such a figure as Sila," Christiansë explains, "a researcher must skirt a lon-

---

98 | Gabeba Baderoon, "'This is Our Speech:' Voice, Body and Poetic Form in Recent South African Writing," *Social Dynamics* 37.2 (2011): 214.
99 | Ibid. 219.
100 | Ibid. 220.
101 | Ibid.

ging for evidence of agency or escape."[102] The same is true for a writer trying to piece together the fragments of the past and to represent the tragic life of a slave woman exposed to extreme cruelty and violence.

Christiansë's refusal to engage in a therapeutic project and to provide narrative closure is particularly apparent at the end of the novel.[103] As mentioned before, the archival documents do not reveal any information about Sila's fate after 1830. We cannot know with certainty if Sila, like her fellow prisoners, had to leave Robben Island in 1835 and was taken to the town prison.[104] In *Unconfessed*, on the last page of the novel, in a third-person point of view, the narrator directly addresses the reader and refers to the impossibility to give an accurate account of the events in Sila's life after the end of slavery in the Cape Colony in 1834: "*You want to know. What happened to her? Well, some say she left the island, but there is no agreement on how*" (U 341; italics in the original). Written in a highly poetic style, the narrator offers five different versions of Sila's departure from the island. Among these stories is one narrative that deals with the slave woman's death. Thus, struggling with the unknown, Christiansë resists the temptation to construct an optimistic ending that would present a consoling and reconciliatory view of the past, in general, and Sila's life as a slave, in particular. While it is impossible to recover the voice of an enslaved woman like Sila, Christiansë's goal is to provide us with a "sense of the world that reduced such a person to traces."[105]

---

102 | Christiansë, "'Heartsore'" 11.
103 | See also Meg Samuelson, "'Lose Your Mother: Kill Your Child': The Passage of Slavery and Its Afterlife in Narratives by Yvette Christiansë and Saidiya Hartman," *English Studies in Africa* 51.2 (2008): 39.
104 | Christiansë, "'Heartsore'" 6.
105 | Christiansë, "A Conversation with Yvette Christiansë" 353.

5 Transnational Diasporic Journeys in Lawrence Hill's *The Book of Negroes* (2007)

INTRODUCTION

Born in Newmarket/Ontario in 1957 as the son of civil rights activists, Lawrence Hill is an African Canadian novelist, essayist, non-fiction writer and former journalist. With *The Book of Negroes* (2007), a novel about a free-born West African woman captured by slave raiders in 1756, shipped across the Atlantic Ocean and forced to work as a slave in South Carolina, Hill has written an extremely popular and commercially successful neo-slave narrative: As of February 2013, his novel has "sold more than 600,000 copies—over half a million—in Canada alone, where sales of 5,000 constitute a bestseller."[1] Moreover, it has been translated into several languages, including French, Dutch and German, and continues to attract the attention of readers from around the world.

Since the publication of *The Book of Negroes*, Hill has become one of Canada's most acclaimed and internationally recognized writers. Over the last years, he has received numerous prestigious awards, such as the "Commonwealth Writers' Prize for Best Book" in 2008 and the "Freedom to Read Award" by the Writers' Union of Canada in 2012.[2] Recently, Hill's best-selling neo-slave narrative was adapted into a six-part television miniseries that aired on CBC Television in Canada and BET (Black Entertainment Television) in the United States in January and February 2015. Directed by Clement Virgo and co-written by Lawrence Hill, the series was filmed in South Africa and Nova Scotia/Cana-

---

1 | Bishop, "Introduction" xiv.
2 | See ibid. xiv-xv; see also Katherine Ashenburg, "Seeing Black," *Toronto Life* Dec. 2009, 21. Jan 2015 http://lawrencehill.com/LawrenceHill.pdf 62-70.

da and features prominent actors and actresses, such as Aunjanue Ellis, Louis Gossett, Jr. and Cuba Gooding, Jr.[3]

Like Morrison, Hartman, Christiansë and other contemporary authors of neo-slave narratives, Hill seeks to explore aspects of black diasporic history that have been systematically ignored, suppressed or forgotten in both popular and academic discourses. In *The Book of Negroes*, his particular focus is on the complex experiences of African Americans during and after the American Revolutionary War (1775-1783): Adopting a black woman's perspective, the novel unfolds the story of those fugitive slaves who joined the British after Dunmore's proclamation of 1775, received their freedom for their faithful service and were relocated to Nova Scotia in 1783. Contrary to their hopes and expectations, in Canada, they were not treated as equal citizens but confronted with anti-black violence. In 1792, less than a decade after their arrival in Nova Scotia, more than one thousand black women and men left the British colony to move to West Africa, determined to create a new colony in Sierra Leone.[4]

Tracing the history of black refugees and self-liberators in late eighteenth-century North America, Hill contributes to a rewriting of the American Revolutionary War from a black perspective and powerfully deconstructs mythical conceptions of Canada as a "paradise" for blacks during the time of slavery: Today, within white (Canadian) mainstream discourses, there is a strong tendency to suppress the nation's history of slavery and racial segregation and to present an idealized view of Canada as a safe haven for American runaway slaves.[5] In fact, most discussions and debates about Canada's role in and relationship with slavery exclusively focus on the "Underground Railroad."[6] This term, Larry Gara explains, "refers to the assistance abolitionists provided fu-

---

3 | See, for instance, Taber, "How *The Book of Negroes*, a Profound Yet Unknown Canadian Story, Became a Miniseries;" Hill, "Adaptation: Rewriting *The Book of Negroes* For the Small Screen." See also my introduction to *Transnational Black Dialogues*.
4 | See also Lawrence Hill, "Freedom Bound," *The Beaver* Feb./Mar. 2007, 21 Jan. 2015 http://www.lawrencehill.com/freedom_bound.pdf 16-23; see also my following sub-chapter.
5 | See, for instance, Christian J. Krampe, "Inserting Trauma into the Canadian Collective Memory: Lawrence Hill's *The Book of Negroes* and Selected African-Canadian Poetry," *Zeitschrift für Kanada-Studien* 29.1 (2009): 62-83; George Elliott Clarke, "White Like Canada," *Transition* 73 (1997): 103; Siemerling 4-8, 182-85.
6 | See, for instance, Judith Misrahi-Barak, "Post-*Beloved* Writing: Review, Revitalize, Recalculate," *Black Studies Papers* 1.1 (2014): 44; Jutta Zimmermann, "From Roots to Routes: The Dialogic Relation between Alex Haley's *Roots* (1976) and Lawrence Hill's *The Book of Negroes* (2007)," *Cultural Circulation: Dialogues between Canada and the American South*, eds. Waldemar Zacharasiewicz and Christoph Irmscher (Wien: Verlag der Österreichischen Akademie der Wissenschaften, 2013) 119-20.

gitive slaves going through the northern states, usually on their way to Canada.[7] Since the nineteenth century, many scholars, intellectuals and politicians "have used the fact that a portion of Canada's black population had reached the country via the Underground Railroad to create the image of Canada as the 'better America,'"[8] as a place of refuge for black runaways and freedom seekers. In *The Book of Negroes*, Hill strongly challenges this self-legitimizing discourse and sanitized interpretation of Canada's past, directing the reader to the black protagonist's experiences of racial discrimination, violence and disillusionment in Nova Scotia.

As I will outline in the following sub-chapter, the novel's (Canadian) title refers to a 1783 British military ledger that, despite its historical significance, has received little scholarly or popular attention in Canada and elsewhere: Documenting the migration of black refugees to Nova Scotia, Great Britain and Germany in the late eighteenth century, it gives precise information "about the names, ages, places of origin, and personal situations of thousands of blacks who fled American slavery."[9] Significantly, shortly before the publication of the U.S.-American edition of *The Book of Negroes* in 2007, Hill was urged by his editor in New York City to change the novel's title. As he explains in a 2008 interview with Jessie Sagawa:

There were two reasons. The first is that the publisher, W.W. Norton & Company, felt that *The Book of Negroes* sounded to their ears like a work of non-fiction and felt they would have trouble selling it as a work of fiction. The second reason was that they thought the word "Negroes" would be so inflammatory to American readers that they wouldn't give the book a chance, even to discover that the title had a historical resonance and authenticity stemming from a British military ledger kept during the American Revolutionary War.[10]

Initially, the African Canadian author was infuriated by his editor's decision: "It was a frustrating exercise. I didn't like having the title changed on me," Hill explains, "but as time went on I came to appreciate that the word 'Negroes' has

---

7 | Larry Gara, "Underground Railroad," *Slavery in the United States: A Social, Political, and Historical Encyclopedia*, ed. Junius P. Rodriguez, vol. 1 (Santa Barbara, CA: ABC-CLIO, 2007) 487. Crucially, most enslaved women and men who tried to escape from their masters and hoped to find freedom in the North traveled without the help of abolitionists. See Gara 489.
8 | Zimmermann 120-21.
9 | Hill, "Freedom Bound" 17.
10 | Jessie Sagawa, "Projecting History Honestly: An Interview with Lawrence Hill," *Studies in Canadian Literature* 33.1 (2008): 319.

become offensive in American culture—particularly in Black urban culture, where its meaning has evolved over time."[11]

In the U.S., Hill's novel is called *Someone Knows My Name*, an intertextual reference to James Baldwin's "Nobody Knows My Name," published in his collection of essays of the same title (1961). In this text, Baldwin reflects on one of his first visits to the American South in the 1950s, in particular on his trips to Atlanta, Georgia, and Charlotte, North Carolina. Focusing on feelings of helplessness and bitterness caused by white racism, Baldwin highlights the devastating (psychological) effects of racial segregation on African American women and men in the first half of the twentieth century. Directing our attention to the hopelessness of the black struggle for recognition and equality in a white-controlled society, the essay's title captures Baldwin's emphasis on deprivation as a defining characteristic of black life.[12]

In striking contrast, by choosing *Someone Knows My Name* for the U.S.-American edition of his novel, Hill offers an empowering and consoling view of the past of slavery. The title is a quotation taken from "We Glide over the Unburied," a central chapter in Hill's neo-slave narrative about the trauma of the Middle Passage. Transforming a scene of oppression and utter humiliation into a narrative of affirmation, Hill particularly highlights the slave characters' attempts to resist the white power structure and to form relationships with other African captives: Reduced to objects, they call out each other's names, struggling to be recognized as human beings. On a meta-level, moving from victimization to empowerment, Hill's rewriting of Baldwin's title refers to a paradigm shift in the conceptualization of African American history and culture.

Like other neo-slave narratives discussed in this study, *The Book of Negroes* thus actively participates in contemporary discourses on the nature and history of the African diaspora. At the heart of Hill's novel is an exploration of the meaning of home for those black women and men who were violently kidnapped from their native villages in West Africa, exposed to the brutality of the Middle Passage, sold into American slavery and reduced to objects. Focusing on various forms of black agency and resistance and dynamic processes of diasporic self-invention, "the entire point of the novel," Hill contends, "was to offer dignity, depth and dimensionality to a person whose very humanity would have been assaulted as a slave."[13] In fact, Aminata Diallo, the novel's protagonist, is depicted as an extremely resilient female character driven by the overwhelming desire to escape from slavery and return to her place of birth.

---

11 | Lawrence Hill, *Dear Sir, I Intend to Burn Your Book: An Anatomy of a Book Burning* (Edmonton: U of Alberta P, 2013) 7.
12 | See James Baldwin, *Nobody Knows My Name: More Notes of a Native Son* (1961; New York: Vintage International, 1993).
13 | Hill, *Dear Sir, I Intend to Burn Your Book* 6.

In exploring the past from the perspective of a female character, Hill, I argue, seeks to enter into the best-selling tradition of female-authored neo-slave narratives that unfold the stories of enslaved women. Moreover, in a self-legitimizing move, he intends to justify his decision to depict violence against female slaves. Employing a first-person narrator who gives an eyewitness account of her struggle for freedom and explicitly refers to her act of writing about slavery, Hill not only claims to create "authenticity" but also tries to encourage the reader's identification with his protagonist.[14] Without doubt, much of the novel's enormous popularity is due to this strategy of identification and its narrative of overcoming, healing and reconciliation.

Written in an easily accessible way, *The Book of Negroes*, unlike *A Mercy, Lose Your Mother* and *Unconfessed*, never reflects on the risks of writing slavery and the ethical implications of appropriating a female slave's voice. Rather, it directs the reader's attention to the transformative power of literature as a tool in the fight against racial oppression. What makes the novel extremely problematic from a black feminist or Afro-pessimistic perspective is its melodramatic narrative structure and strong emphasis on the possibility of consolation: By incorporating "fairy-tale" elements into his narrative, Hill trivializes the horrors of the slave trade and slavery. Furthermore, he fails to explore the true implications of being a slave woman and to articulate the full meaning of chattel slavery as an utterly dehumanizing experience of "thingification." Thus, I argue, *The Book of Negroes* exposes the captives to what Hartman would call a second act of victimization.[15]

Focusing on specific historical developments and events on which Hill's novel is based, this chapter begins with a brief overview of the experiences of black Americans during and after the American Revolutionary War. In a next step, I will demonstrate that Hill's novel offers a dynamic perspective on the meaning of home for African diasporic subjects: While *The Book of Negroes* sheds light on Aminata's strong emotional attachment to her ancestral village, it also directs our attention to complex processes of black self-invention, dwelling and *"diasporic home-making,"*[16] to use Tina M. Campt's words, in late eighteenth-century/early nineteenth-century North America, West Africa and England. In a way similar to Hartman's *Lose Your Mother*, it emphasizes the impossibility to restore the past and to reconnect with an African origin. Paying particular attention to the novel's triumphant ending as well as to the representation of the Middle Passage, the chapter's last part critically examines Hill's narrative and aesthetic strategies as well as his ethical self-positioning and theoretical conception of slavery.

---

14 | See also Siemerling 25.
15 | See Hartman, "Venus in Two Acts" 5.
16 | Campt, *Image Matters* 52; italics in the original.

STRUGGLING FOR FREEDOM: AFRICAN AMERICANS AND THE REVOLUTIONARY WAR

When the African American historian Benjamin Quarles published his groundbreaking study *The Negro in the American Revolution* (1961),[17] he presented what Gary B. Nash describes as "the first full-scale, document-based history of the black revolutionary experience."[18] Over the last decades, Quarles's work has inspired several historians, such as Graham Russell Hodges, Leslie M. Harris, Ira Berlin, Simon Schama and Douglas R. Egerton, to examine the history of African Americans during and after the Revolutionary War.[19] Drawing on this scholarship, the following part gives an overview of specific historical developments in North America in the second half of the eighteenth century relevant for Hill's *The Book of Negroes*.

In early November 1775, a proclamation by Virginia's last royal governor John Murray, fourth Earl of Dunmore, marked a significant moment in the history of the American Revolutionary War. Suffering from a shortage of soldiers, Dunmore promised freedom to enslaved black men and white indentured servants who managed to run away from Patriot farms and plantations and were willing to fight for the British Crown.[20] As Schama and Egerton have shown, this offer of freedom was neither motivated by humanitarian considerations nor based on abolitionist principles; it was solely a military decision. Seeking to destabilize the enemy and put an end to the American rebellion, the British governor intended to increase the number of Loyalist soldiers, to damage the economy of the southern colonies and to encourage slave resistance. His goal was not, however, to abolish the institution of slavery.[21]

---

17 | Benjamin Quarles, *The Negro in the American Revolution* (1961; Chapel Hill: U of North Carolina P, 1996).
18 | Gary Nash, "Introduction," *The Negro in the American Revolution*, by Benjamin Quarles (1961; Chapel Hill: U of North Carolina P, 1996) xx.
19 | Graham Russell Hodges, ed., *The Black Loyalist Directory: African Americans in Exile after the American Revolution* (New York: Garland, 1996); Harris, *In the Shadow of Slavery*; Berlin, *Generations of Captivity*; Simon Schama, *Rough Crossings: Britain, The Slaves and the American Revolution* (London: BBC Books, 2005); Douglas R. Egerton, *Death or Liberty: African Americans and Revolutionary America* (New York: Oxford UP, 2009).
20 | Hodges, *The Black Loyalist Directory* xii; Harris 54; Schama 15, 80, 108; Egerton 66, 70; Berlin, *Generations of Captivity* 112; Diedrich, "'As if Freedom Were a City Waiting for Them in the Distance'" 99.
21 | Egerton 195; Schama 15. See also Robin W. Winks, *The Blacks in Canada: A History*, 2nd ed. (Montreal: McGill-Queen's UP, 1997) 29; Diedrich "'As if Freedom Were a City Waiting for Them in the Distance'" 99; Christopher L. Brown, "John Murray, Fourth

Nevertheless, for many blacks in places like Virginia, South Carolina, Georgia, Maryland, New Jersey, Rhode Island and New York, Dunmore's promise was a source of great hope. In fact, not long after the British proclamation, hundreds of slaves answered the governor's call and decided to flee from their masters. Although they knew that re-captured slaves faced serious punishments, they risked their lives to join the royal forces or, later, also the Hessian troops under British command, hoping to gain freedom and protection. Infuriated by the British efforts to recruit slaves, masters and planters desperately tried to stop this black exodus, sending out patrols to track down runaways.[22] Moreover, as Schama explains, articles "appeared in the press (to be read to servants) that Dunmore's offer of freedom was a ruse to entrap slaves who would then be sold in the West Indies for his personal benefit."[23]

In 1779, four years after Dunmore's announcement, Sir Henry Clinton, then British commander-in-chief in North America, repeated the British promise, broadening "the definition of those entitled to liberty to black women and children."[24] As a result, until the war's end in 1783, tens of thousands of black refugees made their way to the British lines, where they were employed as soldiers, foragers, guides, guerrilla raiders, cooks, washerwomen and nurses. After arriving in British-controlled regions, many of them suffered from a shortage of food, unhygienic conditions and racial discrimination but most continued to support the British/Hessian troops because there were few alternatives. At the same time, a large number of slaves, especially in New England, chose to join the Patriots. Countless others used the chaos caused by the Revolutionary War and escaped from plantations without the intention of fighting for King George III or the American cause.[25] In fact, Egerton contends, "the majority of Africans and black Americans regarded themselves as neither Patriot nor Loyalist, but as independent actors in a drama that was largely written by white men of power on either side of the Atlantic."[26]

In 1782, British and American representatives began to conduct peace negotiations in Paris, discussing the withdrawal of British troops and debating the

---

Earl of Dunmore (1730-1809)," *Slavery in the United States: A Social, Political, and Historical Encyclopedia*, ed. Junius P. Rodriguez, vol. 1 (Santa Barbara, CA: ABC-CLIO, 2007) 269. This is also a central argument of Benjamin Quarles's 1961 *The Negro in the American Revolution*. For a critical discussion of Quarles's work, see Nash xiii-xxvi.
22 | Schama 80-82; Diedrich "'As if Freedom Were a City Waiting for Them in the Distance'" 100.
23 | Schama 81.
24 | Ibid. 16.
25 | Harris 55; Egerton 6, 84-89; Schama 107-11; Diedrich "'As if Freedom Were a City Waiting for Them in the Distance'" 100; Hill "Freedom Bound" 18.
26 | Egerton 88.

fate of American fugitive slaves. In cities like Charleston, Savannah and New York City, thousands of black runaways hoped to obtain the freedom promised by Dunmore and Clinton. In several cases, they were bitterly betrayed by the British and other individual profiteers, who sold them into Caribbean slavery. Most American farmers and plantation owners demanded that their former slaves be returned to them. However, the British commander-in-chief, Sir Guy Carleton, was determined to protect any black refugee who had served the British Crown for a year or more during the American Revolutionary War.[27] In 1783, "Carleton ordered his officers to inspect all blacks who wished to leave New York and, most importantly, to register those who could prove their service to the British in the *Book of Negroes*."[28] This handwritten military document, Hill contends, "was the first massive public record of blacks in North America."[29]

For many fugitives faced with the threat of re-enslavement, Carleton's decision to keep the British promise of liberty marked a significant moment in their lives: Between April and late November 1873, approximately 3,000 black freedom seekers (whose names had been recorded in the *Book of Negroes*) embarked on British ships in New York Harbor. While most travelled to Nova Scotia/Canada or other British colonies, some went with the British troops to England or with the Hessian forces to Germany. However, several other blacks, especially younger refugees and single women, did not receive certificates of freedom and were left behind.[30]

Today, (excerpts from/transcriptions of) the *Book of Negroes* can be found, for instance, "in the Nova Scotia Public Archives, the National Archives of the United States and in the National Archives (Public Records Office) in Kew, England"[31] as well as in Graham R. Hodges's *The Black Loyalist Directory* (1996).[32] Like other white-authored documents in the archive of slavery (such as court and plantation records, bills or captains' diaries) that reduce enslaved women and men to silent objects, the *Book of Negroes* does not include black voic-

---

27 | Berlin, *The Making of African America* 94; Schama 134-40; Hill "Freedom Bound" 22; Hodges xvi.
28 | Hill, "Freedom Bound" 22; italics in the original.
29 | Ibid. 18.
30 | Berlin, *The Making of African America* 94-95; Hill, "Freedom Bound" 22; Maria I. Diedrich, "From American Slaves to Hessian Subjects: Silenced Black Narratives of the American Revolution," *Germany and the Black Diaspora: Points of Contact, 1250-1914*, eds. Mischa Honeck, Martin Klimke and Anne Kuhlmann (New York: Berghahn Books, 2013) 102; Diedrich, "'As if Freedom Were a City Waiting for Them in the Distance'" 107-110; Egerton 205-06.
31 | Lawrence Hill, "A Word about History," *Someone Knows My Name* (New York: Norton, 2007) 472.
32 | Hodges 1-214.

es. However, as a research resource, Hill argues, it provides us with valuable insights into the complex but largely forgotten history of black refugees and self-liberators in late eighteenth-century North America: In addition to listing the names of those black individuals who departed from New York in 1783, "it gives a description of each person, information about how he or she escaped, his or her military record, names of former slave masters, and the names of white masters in cases where the blacks remained enslaved or indentured."[33]

Those black refugees who migrated to Nova Scotia, hoping to start a new life as free women and men, soon became bitterly disillusioned: Upon arriving in Canada, they were forced to realize that only a few of them "received the promised land grants, and the plots turned out to be substantially smaller than the parcels awarded to white Loyalists."[34] Moreover, in the British colony, they were not allowed to vote, faced racial segregation and were exposed to anti-black violence. For instance, in July 1784, a mob of white disbanded soldiers attacked the black community of Birchtown, destroying several houses. In other words, for black women and men who had escaped American slavery, Nova Scotia was anything but a promised land.[35] The fact that there was "a small number of slaves in the province served as yet one more painful reminder that for His Majesty's government, their liberation had been but a means to a military end, not a moral goal in itself,"[36] as Egerton puts it.

Treated as second-class citizens in a racist society, almost 1,200 blacks decided to leave Nova Scotia in January 1792: Struggling for political autonomy and racial justice, they accepted the offer by the newly formed Sierra Leone Company to cross the Atlantic Ocean, aiming to establish a new colony in West Africa. Some of them had been kidnapped from Africa and sold into American slavery decades earlier; in 1792, they returned to their ancestral homeland as free women and men. Contrary to their expectations, however, in Sierra Leone, they were again subjected to racial discrimination, oppression and humiliation.[37] Although they had been granted free land by Lieutenant John Clarkson, the company's authorities in London "demanded a quitrent—a payment from landholders in lieu of services—of two shillings per acre from each settler."[38] This political decision caused enormous anger and frustration among the former American slaves; some of them rose in rebellion in 1800:[39] "Denied the

---

33 | Hill, "Freedom Bound" 22.
34 | Egerton 207.
35 | Hill, "Freedom Bound" 23; Egerton 206-09; Winks 35-9; Hodges xxi-xxviii.
36 | Egerton 207.
37 | Winks 61-78; Egerton 214-21.
38 | Egerton 218.
39 | Winks 68.

right to govern themselves, the freedmen regarded land ownership as the antithesis of their former condition,"[40] Egerton explains.

THE LOSS OF HOME AND THE HOPE OF RETURN

Like Hartman's genre-defying *Lose Your Mother*, Hill's novel enters into a fruitful dialogue with contemporary discourses on the African diaspora revolving around issues of home, forced displacement, return, loss and resistance.[41] Focusing on a slave woman's experiences of capture, enslavement, self-liberation and migration in the eighteenth-century transatlantic world, *The Book of Negroes*, Hill contends, particularly explores the following questions: "What is home? Does it exist once you have left it? Can you ever go back once you have been taken away?"[42]

Examining the intricate relationship between "roots" and "routes,"[43] *The Book of Negroes* not only directs our attention to the black protagonist's strong determination, overwhelming desire and constant attempts to escape from her captors and masters and to return to her ancestral village. Deconstructing static and essentialist concepts of black diasporic identity based on the idea of continuity, Hill's text also highlights the impossibility of going back to any "authentic" place of origin in West Africa. Moreover, and crucially, it addresses Aminata's attempts to create a new sense of belonging and feeling of home in the diaspora, emphasizing the possibility of black self-invention and solidarity in the "New World."

What emerges from Aminata's first-person account is a highly ambivalent depiction of Bayo, the place of her birth and childhood in West Africa. Raised by loving parents in Bayo, Aminata learns to develop such values as respect, responsibility and tolerance and is trained early on to assist her mother as a midwife. In London in 1802, decades after the violent separation from her parents and her deportation from Africa, she looks back nostalgically on this childhood and life before enslavement, constructing her native village as a place of stability and comfort: "In those days, I felt free and happy, and the very idea of safety never intruded on my thoughts."[44]

---

40 | Egerton 218.
41 | See also Zimmermann 119-33.
42 | Sagawa, "Projecting History Honestly: An Interview with Lawrence Hill" 311.
43 | See chapter 1, "The Concept of the African Diaspora and the Notion of Difference," in this study. See also Zimmermann 119-33.
44 | Lawrence Hill, *Someone Knows My Name* (New York: Norton, 2007) 2. All further references to Hill's novel *Someone Knows My Name/The Book of Negroes* (BoN) will be cited in the text and will refer to the 2007 U.S.-American edition.

At the same time, and this is a significant point, *The Book of Negroes* deconstructs this idealized view of Bayo and eighteenth-century life in West Africa. Throughout the novel, Hill strategically incorporates a number of elements into his text that challenge Aminata's nostalgic reminiscences of her childhood and highlight the ugly reality of Bayo. In a chapter called "Small Hands Were Good," which is set in Aminata's village between 1745 and 1756, Hill emphasizes the cruelty and inhumanity of domestic African slavery, directing our attention to forms of violence and abuse suffered by Fomba, the village chief's slave. Exploring Aminata's experiences as a child, *The Book of Negroes* also sheds light on acts of gender discrimination: In Bayo, young women are exposed to the harmful practice of female circumcision[45] and denied access to education. Breaking the village's rules, Aminata's father secretly teaches his daughter to read and write Arabic:[46] "So, in the privacy of our home, with nobody but my mother as a witness," Aminata recalls, "I was shown how to use a reed, dyed water and parchment" (BoN 11). Hill shows that Aminata suffers from the oppressive nature of a patriarchal and sexist society, having no chance to lead a self-determined and independent life in Bayo: On board the slave ship bound for America, she is shocked to hear that her mother and father have sold her to the village chief to become his next wife, without informing her about it. Via these plot elements, Hill deconstructs his protagonist's nostalgic memories of Bayo as her childhood paradise, while at the same time legitimizing and qualifying them as elements vital for Aminata's survival under slavery and anti-black racism.

In addition to directing the reader's attention to forms of gender-related oppression, Hill's novel depicts the devastating effects of the transatlantic slave trade and the practice of slave raiding on African communities like Bayo. In a way similar to *Lose Your Mother*, it not only highlights the complicity of Africans in the slave trade but also refers to a variety of strategies employed by African women and men to defend themselves against predatory troops and hostile groups, to protect their families and villages and to resist enslavement: "People were disappearing, and villagers were so concerned about falling into the hands of kidnappers that new alliances were forming among neighbouring villages. Hunters and fishermen travelled in groups. Men spent days at a time building walls around towns and villages" (BoN 11). Thus, like Hartman in "Fugitive Dreams," Hill challenges the myth of black passivity during the period of the slave trade: Focusing on forms of solidarity and cooperation between Afri-

---

45 | See also Zimmermann 129-30.
46 | See also Siemerling 172.

can groups with different ethnic backgrounds, *The Book of Negroes* represents blacks as active agents in the struggle against enslavement and deportation.[47]

Although Hill constructs Bayo as a place of patriarchal domination, *The Book of Negroes* emphasizes Aminata's strong attachment to her home and her family. Therefore, unsurprisingly, the violent capture by African slave raiders is depicted as a traumatic turning point in Aminata's life. Crucially, Hill has his protagonist suffer from extreme humiliation and violence on the forced march to the Atlantic coast: "We had no head scarves or wraps for our body, or anything to cover our private parts. We had not even sandals for our feet. We had no more clothing than goats, and nakedness marked us as captives wherever we went" (BoN 29). Soon after their capture and separation from their ancestral land, *The Book of Negroes* insists, African women and men are exposed to the process of "thingification" while still on the African continent. Having lost their freedom, they are denied the status of human beings and reduced to mere objects.

This passage provides invaluable insight into Hill's approach to writing and theorizing slavery: While *The Book of Negroes* repeatedly illustrates the disturbing effects of processes of "thingification" on the enslaved, unlike Morrison, Hartman and Christiansë, Hill does not engage in a radical rewriting of the past from an Afro-pessimistic and/or black feminist perspective. Creating an affirmative and empowering narrative of a slave woman's life, his primary goal is to depict and celebrate forms of black agency, cooperation, solidarity and cultural innovation, highlighting the slaves' efforts to resist the dehumanizing nature of the slave trade and slavery. Texts like *A Mercy*, *Lose Your Mother* and *Unconfessed* put a strong emphasis on loss and dispossession as constitutive elements of black life in order to reflect on the devastating logic of anti-blackness, to explore the misery of slave women and to emphasize the impossibility of working through and overcoming the traumatic past. In stark contrast, *The Book of Negroes* focuses on survival and the triumph over slavery, suggesting that it is possible to heal the wounds caused by "the transatlantic system of *thingification*,"[48] to use Sabine Broeck's phrase. Thus, in his chapter on Aminata's terrible march to the coast, Hill not only gives voice to Aminata's experiences of oppression, loss and pain but also calls attention to her longing and strong determination to run away from her captors and, most importantly, to go back to her place of birth—although she knows that her native village has been destroyed and her parents have been killed by slave raiders: "Surely I would get free. Surely this would end. Surely I would find a way to flee into the woods and

---

47 | For a critical discussion of strategies used by African women and men in the fight against enslavement in Africa, see also Diouf ix-xxvii.

48 | Broeck, "Enslavement as Regime of Western Modernity" 37; italics in the original.

to make my way home" (BoN 31). At this point of her life, Aminata clings to an idealized vision of Bayo, wishing to restore the past.

In these passages, *The Book of Negroes* engages in an intertextual dialogue with contemporary theories of diaspora. As shown in chapter 1 of this study, in recent scholarship, there are divergent conceptualizations of (the African) diaspora based on different understandings and constructions of home.[49] As the political scientist Safran contends, members of a diaspora community are not only united by traumatic experiences/collective memories of displacement from their homeland and feelings of loss and uprootedness but also, and essentially, by the desire to go back to their ancestral country.[50] In other words, this view of diaspora, which is closely associated with rootedness, continuity, tradition and authenticity and the metaphor of roots, "depends on attachments to a former home, and typically, on a fantasy of return,"[51] as Marianne Hirsch and Nancy K. Miller put it. Scholars like Campt and Edwards, on the other hand, argue for a vibrant understanding of the African diaspora: Exploring the complex interplay between "roots" and "routes," their works focus on transnational exchanges and relations between black diasporic communities, hierarchical power structures and processes of arrival and home-making in specific local environments outside the original homeland.[52]

In his neo-slave narrative, Hill explores the meaning of the "fantasy of return" for African women and men abducted from villages and treated as objects: Given the brutality of the slave trade and forced migration to the coast, Aminata's yearning to find her way back to her roots in Bayo is presented as a powerful survival strategy, helping the young African woman to cope with loss, oppression and utter humiliation. In fact, in the course of the novel, in situations of hopelessness, despair and suffering, Aminata begins to engage in imaginary dialogues with her dead parents[53] and repeatedly indulges in nostalgic memories of her childhood in Bayo. *The Book of* Negroes presents the dream to go back to a native African village as a source of hope and consolation in the face of violence and death for enslaved Africans like Aminata, while at the same time highlighting the impossibility of return.

---

49 | See chapter 1, "The Concept of the African Diaspora and the Notion of Difference," in this study. See also footnote 21 in chapter 1.
50 | See Safran 83-99.
51 | Hirsch and Miller, "Introduction" 3.
52 | See chapter 1, "The Concept of the African Diaspora and the Notion of Difference," in this study.
53 | See Krampe, "Inserting Trauma" 68.

PROCESSES OF MOVEMENT, ARRIVAL AND HOME-MAKING IN THE AFRICAN DIASPORA

Hill's text elaborates on the loss of home and family in Africa; even more vital to the novel's agenda is the way it directs our attention to complex processes of black self-invention, dwelling and *"diasporic home-making"*[54] in North America and elsewhere: In 1757, after having survived the horrors of the Middle Passage, Aminata is bought by Robinson Appleby, a plantation owner on St. Helena Island in South Carolina. Separated from family members and friends, Appleby's slaves take every opportunity to exchange messages with black women and men from other farms and plantations, hoping to find or get information about their lost loved ones. This secret network of communication is called "the fishnet" (BoN 121). As Georgia, one of the female slaves on Appleby's plantation, explains in a conversation with her adopted daughter Aminata: "Our words swim the rivers, all the way from Savannah to St. Helena to Charles Town and farther up. I done hear of our words swimming all the way to Virginia and back. Our words swim farther than a man can walk" (BoN 141). Although they live in different places, Georgia and her fellow slaves manage to create a strong sense of community that transcends borders. For them, home is not a specific geographical location (in West Africa or elsewhere) but "a fluid, vibrant and frequently changing set of cultural interactions."[55] In other words, Hill represents black diasporic formations in eighteenth-century North America as dynamic groups that are not "spatially bounded,"[56] to use an expression taken from Arjun Appadurai's work on deterritorialization and diaspora.

Although, in North America, Aminata never abandons her dream of returning to Bayo, she participates in dynamic processes of home-making in the diaspora. The following scene—which is set in April 1775, shortly after the outbreak of the American War of Independence and a few months before Dunmore's proclamation—illustrates this point: Hill shows how Aminata takes advantage of the revolution's chaos in New York City and manages to run away from her owner, the indigo inspector Solomon Lindo. On the next morning, she encounters a heterogeneous group of black women and men who are about to bury a child. Some of these blacks are enslaved; others are free. Although they do not share the same language, cultural background and ethnic identity, they welcome Aminata as a community member: "They took me into their dancing, and did not ask where I came from, for all they had to do was look at me and hear my own sobs in my maternal tongue and they knew that I was one

---

54 | Campt, *Image Matters* 52; italics in the original.
55 | Cohen 123.
56 | Arjun Appadurai, *Modernity at Large: Cultural Dimensions of Globalization* (Minneapolis: U of Minnesota P, 1996) 48.

of them" (BoN 256). In other words, what unites these black women and men is not a common African origin but a common history of anti-black violence, oppression, exploitation and resistance. Like the refugees and freedom seekers in the Ghanaian village of Gwolu, whose story Hartman tells in "Fugitive Dreams," they create a powerful sense of home not based on ethnic affiliations but on black solidarity and cooperation.[57] By focusing on the fusion of different (African) cultures and the complex relationship between tradition and innovation, Hill offers a dynamic and anti-essentialist view of black diasporic identity as "a matter of 'becoming' as well as of 'being,'"[58] to use Stuart Hall's words.[59]

The Book of Negroes presents dwelling and movement as key features of Aminata's diasporic experience: During the American Revolutionary War, after escaping from her master, Aminata joins the British forces and works as a midwife and nurse in New York City. Like many other black fugitives serving the British Crown as soldiers, cooks or washerwomen, she hopes to be officially freed at the end of the war, as promised by Dunmore in 1775 and Clinton in 1779. Since she is literate and knows English and several African languages, Aminata is employed as a scribe in 1783. Her task is to register in the *Book of Negroes* all blacks who have worked for the British Army and are allowed to leave for Europe, Canada and other British colonies. Threatened with re-enslavement, Aminata accepts the British offer to relocate to Nova Scotia, hoping to escape anti-black racism and violence and to start a new life in Canada.

Challenging myths of Canada as a "paradise" for black women and men during the period of the transatlantic slave trade and slavery, Hill constructs Aminata's time in Nova Scotia (from 1783 to 1792) as an experience of utter disillusionment.[60] Highlighting the precariousness of black life, the novel calls attention to the existence of slaves in the British colony and to the hardships of

---

57 | See chapter 3, "Rethinking the African Diaspora: Saidiya Hartman's *Lose Your Mother* (2007)," in this study.
58 | Hall, "Cultural Identity and Diaspora" 225.
59 | See also Zimmermann 119-34.
60 | For similar interpretations of Hill's representation of Aminata's experience in Nova Scotia, see also, Christian J. Krampe, *The Past is Present: The African-Canadian Experience in Lawrence Hill's Fiction* (Frankfurt a.M.: Peter Lang, 2012) 170-78; Krampe, "Visualizing Invisibility, Reversing Anonymity: A Case Study in African-Canadian Literature," *Slavery in Art and Literature: Approaches to Trauma, Memory and Visuality*, eds. Birgit Haehnel and Melanie Ulz (Berlin: Frank & Timme, 2010) 301-40; Krampe, "Inserting Trauma" 62-83; Zimmermann 119-34; Hans Bak, "Flights to Canada: Jacob Lawrence, Ishmael Reed, and Lawrence Hill," *Cultural Circulation: Dialogues between Canada and the American South*, eds. Waldemar Zacharasiewicz and Christoph Irmscher (Wien: Verlag der Österreichischen Akademie der Wissenschaften, 2013) 135-53; Siemerling 182-85.

the black community of Birchtown: Reduced to the status of second-class citizens, Aminata and the other black local residents are confronted with the ugly reality of segregation, poverty and white supremacy. Not long after her arrival in Canada, Aminata is exposed to the horrors of a race riot, witnessing the killing of two black men and the destruction of several black homes by a white mob.[61] Consequently, what emerges from Hill's construction of Aminata's experience in eighteenth-century Nova Scotia is the insight that enslaved and free black women and men are faced with the ever-present threat of death and racial violence in both the United States and Canada. Drawing on the biblical story of the Egyptian captivity, in his reading of *The Book of Negroes*, Hans Bak argues that, for Hill's black protagonist, "Canada has turned from a promised land into another land of bondage, from a New Jerusalem into another Egypt."[62]

For Aminata, the most traumatic event in Nova Scotia is the kidnapping of her daughter May by a white Loyalist family, the Witherspoons. Although she is no longer enslaved, Aminata is deprived of the right to live with and to care for her children. "Conditions of life in Canada under British rule turn out to be uncannily similar to (if not worse than) those in America,"[63] to quote Bak once more. Again, however, Hill not only refers to Aminata's painful experience of loss and despair but also foregrounds her ability to find a way to deal with her extremely difficult situation: "But I kept going," Aminata recalls, "Somehow, I just kept going" (BoN 351). This passage is another revealing example of Hill's strategic goal to highlight the slave woman's resilience in the face of enormous adversity. His affirmative approach to writing and theorizing slavery differs intrinsically from Morrison's project in *A Mercy*: Employing a radical black feminist perspective, Morrison illuminates the complexity of black motherhood under slavery and the impossibility of overcoming the pain caused by the separation of slave families. In *A Mercy*, in sharp contrast to *The Book of Negroes*, the main focus is on deprivation and destruction rather than on black self-invention and renewal. While writers like Morrison, Hartman and Christiansë explore the full meaning of slavery as an utterly dehumanizing system based on "thingification,"[64] Hill offers a triumphant and, ultimately, "kitsch" narrative about a black woman's heroic fight against slavery, failing to show the true implications of being a black female captive.

Driven by the overwhelming desire to return to the place of her childhood, Aminata decides to board the Sierra Leone Company's vessels and to emigrate

---

61 | See also Siemerling 182-85.
62 | Bak 148.
63 | Ibid.
64 | For a similar interpretation of Hartman's *Lose Your Mother*, see Diedrich, "'As if Freedom Were a City Waiting for Them in the Distance'" 98; Broeck, "Enslavement as Regime of Western Modernity" 34-51.

from Canada to Freetown in 1792, taking part in "the first 'back to Africa' exodus in the history of the Americas."[65] Tracing Aminata's journeys from Bayo to South Carolina, New York City, Nova Scotia and then Sierra Leone, Hill presents a distinct transnational story of black life in the eighteenth-century transatlantic world, while at the same time paying attention to the specificity of local histories and contexts: By focusing on Aminata's experiences of disenchantment, segregation and anti-black violence in Nova Scotia, Hill writes against a sanitized vision of Canada's past that ignores the country's role in the history of slavery and racism.[66]

A STRANGER AT HOME: AMINATA'S AFRICAN EXPERIENCE

Throughout her life, in South Carolina, New York City and Nova Scotia, Aminata clings to an idealized notion of home in Africa, struggling to cope with her feelings of grief and pain caused by the slave trade and slavery. Emphasizing the impossibility to restore the past, to go back to an ancestral village and to reclaim an "authentic" African identity, Hill depicts Aminata's return to West Africa as another experience of disillusionment. Thus, in a way similar to Hartman, he challenges interpretations of the African diaspora that focus exclusively on cultural continuity, a diasporic attachment to ethnic roots and authenticity.[67]

In Sierra Leone, Aminata is forced to experience that the black Nova Scotians are betrayed by the British, who refuse to give them free land and political autonomy; moreover, it is a shock to discover that they are faced with the constant threat of re-enslavement by African slave traders: "Personally," Aminata writes, "I concluded that no place in the world was entirely safe for an African, and that for many of us, survival depended on perpetual migration" (BoN 385). In his chapters on Aminata's experience in Sierra Leone, Hill particularly sheds light on power negotiations and tensions between different African ethnic groups, deconstructing the notion of a single African identity or culture: What really troubles Aminata is the fact that she is treated as a stranger rather than as a beloved family member by the Temne people; they do not believe her story of forced migration to America and return to Africa. Like Hartman in *Lose Your Mother*, Hill draws the reader's attention to difference as a defining characteristic of the black world: Aminata and the local Temne people she encounters not only have different languages and cultural traditions; they are also not linked by a common history of transatlantic migration and enslavement.

---

65 | Hill, "Freedom Bound" 23.
66 | See also Bak 150-51; Siemerling 182-85.
67 | For a similar interpretation, see also Zimmermann 119-34.

Given her experiences of exclusion, betrayal and violence, for Aminata, Freetown is "nothing more than a stepping stone" (BoN 387). Searching for a true home, in 1800, she decides to accompany the local Fula slave trader Alassane on a journey inland, hoping to find her way back to Bayo. Focusing, once again, on the precariousness of black life during the period of the slave trade and the oppressiveness and cruelty of a patriarchal society, Hill challenges the idea of a static identification with an ancestral territory. Exposed to Alassane's cruelty, Aminata critically reflects on the treatment of women in her homeland, giving up her idealized picture of Bayo: "I didn't like the way Alassane issued orders. It made me wonder if men would try to speak to me like that when I got home, and if all my time of living independently had made me unfit for village life in Bayo" (BoN 434). To put it differently, Hill shows how Aminata's experiences of migration have transformed her into a self-confident woman who is not willing to submit to a white or black man's tyranny and domination—neither in Freetown nor in Bayo.[68]

Discovering Alassane's plans to sell her, Aminata is forced to abandon her idea of return to her native village, emphasizing that freedom is the most essential value: "Bayo, I could live without. But for freedom, I would die" (BoN 443). Therefore, what results from Aminata's reflection on the impossibility to restore the past and the necessity for an African woman to fight for self-determination and freedom is a dynamic understanding of home based on discontinuity and change. "Whatever 'home' she may find," Bak argues, "is no longer to be recuperated in a geographical or national space or territory, but in a de-territorialized, hybridized sense of self in a perpetual process of migration."[69] Also, and even more importantly: Home as a definer of her life is replaced by (the struggle for) freedom. Like the fugitives in Gwolu in *Lose Your Mother*, Aminata comes to realize that "home is where freedom is."[70]

RE-IMAGINING THE HORRORS OF SLAVERY: HILL'S AESTHETIC STRATEGIES

Over the last decades, there have been fierce debates among writers and scholars (in fields such as African American, feminist, ethnic and postcolonial studies) about the ethical challenges, implications and dangers of speaking and theorizing for—and about—the racial, sexual, gendered and/or cultural "other." These discussions center on various (interrelated) issues, such as the silencing and appropriation of women's voices by men; the misrepresentation of African

---

68 | See also Bak 150.
69 | Ibid.
70 | Diedrich, "'As if Freedom Were a City Waiting for Them in the Distance'" 98.

American culture and history by white authors like William Styron; "the problem of the muted subject of the subaltern woman" (Gayatri C. Spivak); and the phenomenon of "ethnic ventriloquism" (Mita Banerjee).[71]

In a 1991 essay, the feminist philosopher Linda Alcoff contends that "there is a growing recognition that where one speaks from affects the meaning and truth of what one says, and thus that one cannot assume an ability to transcend one's location."[72] According to Alcoff, "the practice of privileged persons speaking for or on behalf of less privileged persons has actually resulted (in many cases) in increasing or reinforcing the oppression of the group spoken for."[73] Following Spivak, she argues for a "'speaking to,' in which the intellectual neither abnegates his or her discursive role nor presumes an authenticity of the oppressed but still allows for the possibility that the oppressed will produce a 'countersentence' that can then suggest a new historical narrative."[74]

In *The Book of Negroes*, Hill, I argue, strategically adopts a black woman's perspective, trying to cash in on the commercial success of female-authored neo-slave narratives that feature a female protagonist. However, he fails to critically elaborate on what Alcoff calls "the problem of speaking for others,"[75] i.e., the intricacies and challenges involved in appropriating a black woman's voice as a black male writer. Seeking to create "authenticity," Hill employs a first-person narrator who offers an eyewitness account of the past and reflects on her task and identity as a writer. What characterizes the novel's metafictional parts, which are mainly set in London at the beginning of the nineteenth century, is a strong emphasis on the transformative power and political potential of literature.[76] For Aminata, writing is her way to address the horrors she has experienced and witnessed as a slave, to support the abolitionist campaign and to give a voice to all those black women and men whose stories are not heard; most importantly, it gives meaning to her life: "I have my life to tell, my own private

---

71 | See, for instance, María C. Lugones and Elizabeth V. Spelman, "Have We Got a Theory for You! Feminist Theory, Cultural Imperialism and the Demand For 'The Woman's Voice,'" *Women's Studies Int. Forum* 6.6 (1983): 573-81; Alcoff 5-32; Henry Louis Gates, Jr., "Introduction," *Reading Black, Reading Feminist: A Critical Anthology*, ed. Henry Louis Gates, Jr. (New York: Penguin, 1990) 1-17; Rushdy, *Neo-Slave Narratives* 54-95; Spivak, "Can the Subaltern Speak?" 295; Mita Banerjee, *Ethnic Ventriloquism: Literary Minstrelsy in Nineteenth-Century American Literature* (Heidelberg: Winter, 2008). As Banerjee puts it, "[e]thnic ventriloquilism represents the strategy of a white subject looking at itself through—presumably—ethnic eyes." Banerjee 16.
72 | Alcoff 6.
73 | Ibid. 7.
74 | Ibid. 23.
75 | Ibid. 8.
76 | See also Siemerling 175.

ghost story, and what purpose would there be to this life I have lived, if I could not take this opportunity to relate it?" (BoN 7).

Aminata's story in *The Book of Negroes* is told in a linear fashion and from one single perspective. Written in a vivid and clear style, the message that the text conveys is that it is legitimate and possible to offer a coherent account of the slave's life. Whereas, in *A Mercy*, Florens reflects on the painfulness of writing about her traumatic experiences in the Puritan village and the Blacksmith's cabin, for Aminata, it is not a challenging, or even impossible, task to reconstruct her life and write about the slave trade and slavery: "My hand cramps after a while, and sometimes my back or neck aches when I have sat for too long at the table, but this writing business demands little. After the life I have lived, it goes down as easy as sausages and gravy" (BoN 7). In other words, in Aminata's account, there is no critical exploration of the limits and risks of rendering anti-black violence but, rather, a strong focus on the liberating effects of the act of testifying and writing.

The Book of Negroes represents Aminata as an incredibly resilient and strong-minded woman who uses every opportunity to resist slavery's dehumanizing effects. By giving deep insight into her inner emotional state and tracing her life from early childhood in West Africa through slavery and self-liberation to her final years in London, Hill tries to foster the reader's identification with Aminata.[77] What is extremely disturbing is the novel's highly melodramatic plot structure and, in particular, its "happy ending." While Morrison, Hartman and Christiansë vehemently refuse to present a narrative of liberation to foreground the impossibility of healing the trauma of slavery, Hill deliberately incorporates a number of sentimental, "fairy-tale" elements into his text to celebrate forms of black agency and to highlight the possibility of overcoming the past.

This is most apparent in the novel's last chapter, in which Hill gives voice to Aminata's experiences of estrangement and despair in London, depicting her struggle with British abolitionists and members of the parliamentary committee. "Despite my life of losses," Aminata writes, "the loneliness I felt in London rivalled anything I had felt before" (BoN 452). Although she knows that she cannot restore the past and that the vision of her native village is idealized, she continues to dream of her childhood in West Africa. Like in a fairy-tale or a sentimental novel, however, the novel's deserving protagonist is somehow "rewarded" for her suffering: Shortly after Aminata's audience with King George III and Queen Charlotte, her lost daughter May enters her room: "She stepped forward and threw herself into me with such vigour that she nearly knocked me over. It was the embrace for which I had been praying for fifteen years" (BoN 465). On the plot level, this reunion is presented as a truly triumphant moment: Near the end of her life, after many Atlantic crossings, Aminata finally finds

---

77 | See also ibid. 25.

a new sense of belonging, wholeness and fulfillment, re-inventing herself as a storyteller in a school in London. Moreover, to her great delight, her daughter tells her that she will become a grandmother. In other words, unlike *A Mercy*, *Lose Your Mother* and *Unconfessed*, *The Book of Negroes* is a narrative with a "happy ending," emphasizing the possibility to forget and overcome the traumatic past, to leave behind what Hartman describes as "the ghost of slavery."[78]

Arguably, a large part of the novel's popularity lies precisely in this evocation of "slavery as a closed chapter in American history:"[79] Like Haley's international best-seller *Roots*, *The Book of Negroes* tells a teleological story of redemption, reconciliation, rebirth and healing, without encouraging its readers to critically reflect on slavery's persistent legacies,[80] i.e., the systemic oppression and devaluation of blacks in our contemporary societies. To put it differently, both *Roots* and *The Book of Negroes* have found such a large readership because they offer an "empowering yet nonthreatening view of slavery"[81] as a phenomenon firmly situated in the past.

Hill's representation of Aminata's reunion with May not only "stretches the bounds of the probable,"[82] as Sarah Churchwell puts it in her 2009 book review for *The Guardian*, but also trivializes the complexity and painful reality of the black diasporic female experience in the eighteenth century: Focusing on May's successful escape from the Witherspoons and happy reunion with her mother, *The Book of Negroes* naively celebrates the possibility to challenge the existing white power structure and to sustain or restore familial bonds. In the last chapter, Hill's novel turns the reader's attention away from the black woman's plight in a white male-controlled society to Aminata's triumph over slavery and white supremacy. Thus, by drawing on what Hartman would call "the language of romance,"[83] Hill runs the risk of playing down and relativizing the core meaning of American chattel slavery as "thingification."

In stark contrast, in *A Mercy*, taking into account the complex (epistemological) insights of black feminist theory, Morrison offers a thorough, and excruciatingly painful, reflection on a slave mother's moral dilemma in the early colonial period:[84] Desperately wishing to protect her beloved daughter from rape on D'Ortega's plantation, Florens's mother is forced to give away

---

78 | Hartman, "The Time of Slavery" 763.
79 | Holsey 167-68.
80 | See also ibid. 155-56.
81 | Ibid. 156.
82 | Sarah Churchwell, "Bought and Sold," *Guardian* 24 Jan. 2009, 21 Jan. 2015 http://www.guardian.co.uk/books/2009/jan/24/lawrence-hill-book-ofnegroes.
83 | Hartman, "Venus in Two Acts" 6.
84 | See chapter 2, "From Human Bondage to Racial Slavery: Toni Morrison's *A Mercy* (2008)," in this study.

her daughter, without getting a chance to explain her behavior; at the same time, she knows that it is impossible to save her child from slavery. Throughout the novel, Florens is deeply traumatized by this abandonment because she is not familiar with her mother's story and cannot understand her motives. For Florens, the pain and suffering caused by the separation from her mother will never go away; even her writing thus cannot be an act of liberation, only a desperate attempt to articulate the horrors of her life. Written from a black feminist standpoint, *A Mercy* engages in a dialogue with theoretical debates about the meaning of black motherhood under slavery as she challenges the "kitsch" vision of redemption that is at the heart of texts like *The Book of Negroes*: Unlike Aminata, Florens's mother will never see her daughter again; what remains is a deep sense of loss and a last glimmer of hope that her child will find a way to live without her. Unlike *The Book of Negroes*, *A Mercy* radically counters the notion that it is possible to overcome the trauma of slavery.

Like other writers of neo-slave narratives, Hill is faced with the challenge of representing a female slave's experience on board a slave vessel on its way from West Africa to North America. Whereas texts like *Beloved* and *Lose Your Mother* offer incredibly complex, self-reflexive, highly fragmented and multi-perspective reflections on the terrible journey to highlight the painful limits of their attempt to revisit the past, Hill's "We Glide over the Unburied" is written in the extremely accessible, first-person narrative style characteristic of the whole novel. Unlike in Morrison's key chapters in *Beloved* and in Hartman's "The Dead Book," there are no silences, textual blanks or narrative ambiguities that would require an active reader willing to reflect on the ethical implications of writing and reading the Middle Passage.

In her first-person account of her journey across the Atlantic, Aminata sheds light on a wide variety of experiences and incidents: On the slave ship's deck, the African captives engage in dynamic cultural activities, singing African songs and calling out each other's names. Determined to resist their subjugation, some of them start a slave uprising but are overpowered by the ship's crew. *The Book of Negroes* centralizes such acts of black agency and resistance, while also illustrating the incredible brutality and inhumanity of the Middle Passage. Aminata is forced to witness how her fellow slaves are whipped by their white oppressors and subjected to utterly dehumanizing treatment in the ship's hold. Deeply traumatized by her experience of deportation, one of the female captives kills her own baby and another woman's child; black women and men who are wounded or weakened by the journey are thrown overboard.

Significantly, Hill has made sure that his protagonist is in an exceptional position on board the slave ship: "A series of coincidences saved my life during the ocean crossing," Aminata recalls. "It helped to be among the last persons from my homeland to be loaded onto that vessel. It also helped to be a child. A child had certain advantages on a slave vessel. Nobody rushed to kill a child"

(BoN 56). Problematically, by giving in to the temptation to create a consoling account of Aminata's experience of the Middle Passage, Hill domesticates the traumatic effects of this event: His chapter evokes the possibility of benevolence and kindness on the part of the white captors; in stark contrast to *A Mercy*, it suggests that female slaves might find a way to escape (sexual) violence. This reconciliatory depiction is, to draw on Hartman's insightful 2008 essay "Venus in Two Acts," utterly "at odds with the annihilating violence of the slave ship."[85]

In an interview, Hill gives the following explanation for his strategic decision to focus not only on the brutality of the slave trade but also on what Hartman would describe as "the instant of possibility:"[86]

One of the most difficult parts was writing the scenes in which Aminata is abducted and sent across the ocean in a slave vessel. How do you represent such human atrocity and not turn off the reader? If you depicted it in its full horror, who would want to keep reading? So somehow you have to shine enough of a light on the story that a reader has a reason, emotionally, to keep going, has to believe that his character Aminata will somehow survive, will carry on.[87]

Obviously, Hill's main concern is to create a story that captures the cruelty of the slave trade and slavery but that is, nevertheless and paradoxically, easy to digest; his primary goal is not to lose the reader's attention, even in those passages that deal with one of the darkest chapters of modern Western history, i.e. the Middle Passage. Of course, this narrative strategy is highly questionable: By putting Aminata in an exceptional position on board the slave ship, Hill trivializes the black female experience in the period of the slave trade and slavery, exposing the African captive to a second act of victimization.[88] Even more problematic, especially from an Afro-pessimistic and black feminist perspective: Hill refuses to acknowledge the full meaning of racial slavery as a dehumanizing institution of "thingification," to articulate the true implications of what it means to be a slave woman.

---

85 | Hartman, "Venus in Two Acts" 8-9.
86 | Ibid. 8.
87 | Sagawa, "Projecting History Honestly: An Interview with Lawrence Hill" 318.
88 | Hartman, "Venus in Two Acts" 5.

Conclusion

The Book of Negroes offers a transnational perspective on racial slavery and black life in the eighteenth century, challenging essentialist views of black culture and identity and static constructions of home as a geographically fixed place.[89] In Aminata, Hill invents a protagonist for whom the diaspora experience is not only about memories of the past, forms of migration and dreams of return but also about acts of home-making and struggles for freedom and equality in places outside the original homeland. Moving beyond what Brent Hayes Edwards would call "an obsession with origins"[90] and roots, Hill's novel presents a vibrant interpretation of the concept of the African diaspora; in this regard, there are significant similarities between Hartman's *Lose Your Mother* and *The Book of Negroes*.

Hill's novel makes a crucial contribution to the genre of neo-slave narratives: Set on three different continents (i.e., Africa, North America and Europe), it explores the interplay between local and global structures of enslavement and anti-blackness; moreover, it reconstructs important historical events, processes and developments that have been largely ignored or silenced in (twentieth-century) academic and popular discussions about the African diaspora and the transatlantic world: the complicity of Africans in the slave trade; the role of African Americans in the American Revolutionary War; the history of slavery and segregation in Canada and the black Nova Scotians' experiences of estrangement and disillusionment in Sierra Leone. Written in a vivid and accessible style, Hill's novel has reached a wide international audience; as a result, the history of American fugitive slaves in the time of the American Revolution is not only known to a handful of scholars but to a large number of readers in Canada as well as in other parts of the world.

Unlike Morrison, Hartman and Christiansë, Hill constructs an empowering and, ultimately, triumphant story of a slave woman's life. Having lost her home, Aminata eventually regains her freedom, re-invents herself as a writer, and, most importantly, is reunited with her kidnapped daughter. This teleological conception of history is not convincing: By offering narrative closure, using melodramatic devices and putting Aminata in an exceptional position on board the slave ship, Hill runs the risk of playing down the horrors of slavery and the hardships of black womanhood and motherhood.

While Morrison, Hartman and Christiansë engage in an Afro-pessimistic and black feminist rewriting of history and the archive of slavery in order to illustrate the impossibility of narration and/as healing, Hill's novel conveys the

---

89 | See also Krampe, "Visualizing Invisibility, Reversing Anonymity" 302; Bak 150-51; Zimmermann 119-34.
90 | Edwards 63.

message that it is possible to transform the history of slavery into a reconciliatory narrative of overcoming. "I am not wallowing in slavery, and this novel isn't really just about slavery," Hill contends in an interview. "It's a novel about liberation; it's a novel about human courage; and it's a novel about the triumph of the human spirit in conditions of adversity."[91]

Strikingly, Hill's use of narrative form and style reflects his decision to offer a triumphant reconstruction of the past: Unlike *A Mercy*, *Lose Your Mother* and *Unconfessed*, *The Book of Negroes* celebrates the healing power of literature, giving a first-person account of the slave's life without reflecting on the limits and risks of the attempt to re-imagine slavery from a twenty-first-century perspective.

---

[91] | Sagawa, "Projecting History Honestly: An Interview with Lawrence Hill" 317.

6 A Vicious Circle of Violence: Revisiting Jamaican Slavery in Marlon James's *The Book of Night Women* (2009)

INTRODUCTION

"I am more interested in darker subjects than brighter ones," the Jamaican author Marlon James contends in a 2006 interview, "because somewhere in that shadow is a story."[1] Highlighting the extreme brutality of slavery and British colonial rule in late eighteenth-century Jamaica, his prize-winning novel *The Book of Night Women* (2009) explores one of the darkest and most painful chapters of Caribbean and modern transatlantic history. Set between 1784 and 1801, James's text focuses on the fate of Lilith, the daughter of a slave woman—who dies giving birth to her child—and a tyrannical and sadistic white overseer, Jack Wilkins.

Growing up on Montpelier Estate, a large sugar plantation in eastern Jamaica, Lilith is constantly faced with cruel and gratuitous acts of violence committed not only by her white owners but also by fellow male slaves: As a fourteen-year-old girl, she is attacked and humiliated by a black overseer who tries to rape her; in an act of self-defense, she kills the man. This incident attracts the attention of the night women, a group of female slaves who secretly meet at night to prepare an uprising against their brutal oppressors. Homer, the rebel's leader, invites Lilith to take part in their conspiracy. However, the young black woman is sent to another estate, where she is again confronted with scenes of incredible horror. After witnessing her friend's murder, Lilith kills her master and his family, sets the house on fire and returns to Montpelier, where the night women start a massive but unsuccessful slave revolt. As becomes appar-

---

1 | Felicia Pride, "What Does It Take? An Interview with Marlon James (2006)," *To Create: Black Writers, Filmmakers, Storytellers, Artists, and Media-Makers Riff on Art, Careers, Life, and the Beautiful Mess in Between* (Chicago: Agathe Publishing, 2012) E-book. n. pag.

ent in a short metafictional passage at the end of the novel, the story is told from the perspective of Lilith's daughter.

The Book of Night Women deals with a variety of themes: the slaves' experience of being trapped in a vicious circle of oppression, counter-violence and retaliation; the brutalizing effects of slavery; intra-black violence and the slave woman's misery; the (potentially) transformative, yet also destructive power of black (counter-)violence.

Like Hill's *The Book of Negroes*, James's neo-slave narrative has received widespread critical acclaim as well as several prestigious awards, including, most notably, the 2010 Dayton Literary Peace Prize for Fiction. In reviews, *The Book of Night Women* has been enthusiastically hailed for its exploration of the complex history of slavery and white colonial rule in Jamaica, its attempt to capture the horrific violence of eighteenth-century plantation life, its vivid depiction of a strong black female protagonist as well as its artistic use of Jamaican patois.[2] However, there are also critical discussions of James's narrative approach: For instance, in a 2009 review for the *Los Angeles Times*, Susan Straight points out that "the novel can be unrelentingly violent, and the litany of terror, torture and revenge is long and horrifically detailed."[3]

Drawing on the work of black feminist critics such as Deborah E. McDowell, Angela Davis and Hartman, I will argue in this chapter that James's novel exposes the enslaved to a further act of violence[4] by presenting the (female) slave's experience of humiliation and sexual exploitation in an explicit, even pornographic, way. Unlike neo-slave narratives like Morrison's *A Mercy*, Hartman's *Lose Your Mother* and Christiansë's *Unconfessed*, *The Book of Night Women* offers no reflection whatsoever on the risks inherent in writing about slavery's violence. Rather, James's detailed renderings of acts of torture and execution "reinforce the spectacular character of black suffering,"[5] to use Hart-

---

2 | See Kaiama L. Glover, "Womanchild in the Oppressive Land," *New York Times Book Review* 26 Feb. 2009, 20 Feb. 2015 http://www.nytimes.com/2009/03/01/books/review/Glover-t.html; Suzanne Marie Hopcroft, "A Heartbreaking History," *Small Axe Salon* 27 Oct. 2010, 20 Feb. 2015 http://smallaxe.net/wordpress3/reviews/category/contributor/suzanne-hopcroft/; Michiko Kakutani, "Jamaica via a Sea of Voices: Marlon James's 'A Brief History of Seven Killings,'" *New York Times* 21 Sept. 2014, 20 Feb. 2015 http://www.nytimes.com/2014/09/22/books/marlon-jamess-a-brief-history-of-seven-killings.html?_r=0.
3 | Susan Straight, "'The Book of Night Women' by Marlon James," *Los Angeles Times* 8 Mar. 2009, 20 Feb. 2015 http://articles.latimes.com/2009/mar/08/entertainment/ca-marlon-james8.
4 | See Hartman, "Venus in Two Acts" 5.
5 | Hartman, *Scenes of Subjection* 3.

man's phrase from her 1997 study *Scenes of Subjection*, and, thus, potentially satisfy a reader's desire for violent entertainment.

This chapter opens with a short historical overview of slavery in (late) eighteenth-century Jamaica, focusing particularly on the (female) slaves' various forms of resistance to European rule; a theme that plays a crucial role in *The Book of Night Women*. In a next step, I will argue that one of the novel's main goals is to explore the intricate relations between masters, overseers, slaves and maroons in the "diaspora space" of eighteenth-century Jamaica and to highlight the slave woman's vulnerability to (sexual) abuse by both black and white men. As this chapter will demonstrate, *The Book of Night Women* examines different forms of black agency and resistance, yet ultimately directs our attention to the impossibility to break free from the chains of bondage and to escape racial violence. Focusing on James's conceptualization of counter-violence, I will show that *The Book of Night Women* enters into a dynamic intertextual relationship with Frantz Fanon's work as well as with African American male literary texts, in particular with Richard Wright's famous novel *Native Son* (1940). In a way similar to Wright, James explores both the liberating effect of violence on oppressed subjects and the disruptive nature of violent action. Throughout this chapter, I will offer a critical examination of James's narrative and aesthetic strategies and his theoretical reflections on slavery.

MASTERS, SLAVES AND BLACK RESISTANCE IN EIGHTEENTH-CENTURY JAMAICA

In his 1999 essay "Slavery and Emancipation in Caribbean History," the historian Francisco A. Scarano draws our attention to the centrality of slavery to Caribbean historiography, arguing that the enormous scholarly and popular interest in this topic "clearly mirrors the institution's overall historical significance and weight:"[6]

For nearly four centuries after the European conquest, the vast majority of the Caribbean's residents were slaves. Even now [...] possibly more than half of the region's inhabitants are descended from these enslaved people. Moreover, the *quality* of the human experiences involved amply justifies slavery's centrality in historical writings about the region. The chattel slaves of the Caribbean and elsewhere endured an extreme victimization. By contemporary standards of civil and human rights, the bondage to which so

---

6 | Francisco A. Scarano, "Slavery and Emancipation in Caribbean History," *General History of the Caribbean: Methodology and Historiography of the Caribbean*, ed. B. W. Higman, vol. VI (London: Unesco Publishing, 1999) 233.

many people were subject was bizarre, as were the societies that were built upon the institution.[7]

Over the last decades, especially since the 1970s, numerous scholars have turned their attention to exploring the past of slavery and its enduring legacy in the Caribbean, in general, and Jamaica, in particular. Recent scholarship by historians such as Vincent Brown, Trevor Burnard, Barbara Bush, Demetrius L. Eudell, Herbert S. Klein and Ben Vinson III focuses on a variety of topics, including economic and social dimensions as well as comparative aspects of slavery; the complexity of black family life under Caribbean slavery; the specific experiences of slave women; slave resistance and rebellions; the history of maroons; European immigration into the Caribbean; and the emancipation process in the Caribbean and other parts of the Americas.[8] In the following, I will particularly shed light on the subject of black resistance in eighteenth-century Jamaica.

As scholars like Brown and Burnard point out, during the second half of the eighteenth century, when the sugar boom was at its height, Jamaica became Britain's most valuable and profitable colony, attracting thousands of white European immigrants and sojourners. Most of these newcomers to the West Indies were free young Englishmen, especially from urban areas, driven by the desire to gain influence and power, to make a fortune as soon as possible and then to return home to Europe as absentee planters. In Jamaica, Europeans worked as merchants, (sugar) planters, traders, bookkeepers, attorneys or slave overseers, creating an extremely violent and materialistic society whose wealth was based on the systematic exploitation of African slaves.[9]

According to Burnard, eighteenth-century Jamaica was a place of economic and social opportunities for white Europeans from all social classes: "Any man with a modicum of ambition and a measure of talent was in a very strong position to acquire a fortune superior to that possible anywhere else in Britain

---

7 | Ibid.; italics in the original.
8 | See, for instance, Vincent Brown, *The Reaper's Garden: Death and Power in the World of Atlantic Slavery* (Cambridge, MA: Harvard UP, 2008); Trevor Burnard, "European Migration to Jamaica: 1655-1780," *William and Mary Quarterly* 53.4 (1996): 769-96; Barbara Bush, *Slave Women in Caribbean Society: 1650-1838* (Bloomington: Indiana UP, 1990); Demetrius L. Eudell, *The Political Languages of Emancipation in the British Caribbean and the U.S. South* (Chapel Hill: U of North Carolina P, 2002); Herbert S. Klein and Ben Vinson III, *African Slavery in Latin America and the Caribbean*, 2nd ed. (New York: Oxford UP, 2007).
9 | Burnard, "European Migration to Jamaica" 789-96; Brown, *The Reaper's Garden* 13-24; Trevor Burnard, *Mastery, Tyranny, and Desire: Thomas Thistlewood and His Slaves in the Anglo-Jamaican World* (Chapel Hill: U of North Carolina P, 2004) 13-67.

and its empire (save perhaps British India)."[10] As in other European colonies in the tropics, however, the white mortality rate was incredibly high; many whites died of diseases such as malaria and yellow fever: "Through the middle decades of the eighteenth century, immigrants could not expect to survive more than thirteen years," Vincent Brown explains. "Those native-born whites (Creoles) who survived childhood were likely to die before they reached the age of forty."[11]

Nevertheless, throughout the eighteenth century, large waves of white Europeans continued to flock to Jamaica, determined to take advantage of the island's enormous economic growth. Unlike in the plantation colonies of eighteenth-century British North America, in Jamaica, native-born whites were heavily outnumbered by immigrants.[12] Significantly, numerous Jamaican plantation owners and slave masters were absentees, living in Great Britain and "visiting their West Indian estates only once or twice in their lives."[13] This had devastating effects on black and white Jamaicans alike: Absenteeism, Richard B. Sheridan contends, "tended to promote a careless, cruel, and extravagant management of plantations; it established conditions that led to slave insurrections; it drained away wealth and income that might otherwise have gone into public and private improvements."[14]

Jamaica's booming economy depended on the forced labor of large numbers of enslaved blacks: From the beginning of British rule in Jamaica in 1655 until the early nineteenth century, hundreds of thousands of black captives were violently taken from Africa, in particular from the Bight of Biafra and the Gold Coast, shipped across the Atlantic and brought to Jamaica as slaves.[15] "The result," Burnard contends, "was a slave population that grew dramatically, despite the fact that deaths constantly outnumbered births and despite exceptionally low female fertility."[16] In the middle of the eighteenth century, blacks constituted the overwhelming majority of Jamaica's population: In 1752, about 10,000 whites and more than 110,000 slaves lived in the colony. Approximately 75 percent of the slaves worked on sugar plantations, where conditions were incredibly harsh and inhumane. Suffering from malnutrition, disease and great brutality, the African captives were forced to perform arduous (and often dan-

---

10 | Burnard, *Mastery, Tyranny, and Desire* 42; see also Burnard, *Mastery, Tyranny, and Desire* 38-41.
11 | Brown, *The Reaper's Garden* 17.
12 | Ibid.; see also Burnard, "European Migration to Jamaica" 791.
13 | Michael Craton, *Testing the Chains: Resistance to Slavery in the British West Indies* (Ithaca, NY: Cornell UP, 1982) 36.
14 | Richard B. Sheridan, *Sugar and Slavery: An Economic History of the British West Indies* (1974; Kingston: Canoe Press, 2010) 386.
15 | Burnard, *Mastery, Tyranny, and Desire* 15-16; Brown, *The Reaper's Garden* 25-27.
16 | Burnard, *Mastery, Tyranny, and Desire* 15.

gerous) tasks, such as digging holes, cutting the cane and transporting it to the mill, cutting firewood as well as crushing and boiling the sugarcane.[17]

Living in a society in which whites were heavily outnumbered by blacks, eighteenth-century Jamaican slave masters, plantation owners and overseers were in a state of constant alert: Faced with the threat of slave rebellions, they resorted to extreme physical and psychological violence to control and intimidate their labor force. Determined to demonstrate the extent of their power, they whipped, branded, humiliated, tortured or killed their slaves in horrific ways. Female captives were especially vulnerable since, in addition to being exposed to the same dehumanizing conditions as male slaves, they became victims of sexual abuse by both white and black men, as Bush has amply documented.[18] In terms of the legal status of enslaved women and men in the British West Indies, there were crucial similarities to slavery in (eighteenth-century) mainland North America: Denied the status of human beings, "once acquired by their masters, slaves became their owner's private property, as was his horse or cow," Bush contends. "As chattel slaves, they could be sold for debts if other moveable assets were exhausted, and disposed of in accordance with the laws of inheritance of real estate."[19]

Written from a slave owner's perspective, Thomas Thistlewood's diaries give a meticulous, and highly shocking, description of slavery's violence in eighteenth-century Jamaica: In 1750, at age twenty-nine, Thistlewood left England to move to Jamaica, where he became a pen keeper, a landowner, a horticulturalist and, above all, an extremely ruthless and sadistic slave overseer and master. As Burnard explains, Thistlewood's diary entries reveal that he repeatedly raped black women and children and punished his slaves dreadfully:[20] "Thistlewood whipped slaves; rubbed salt, lemon juice, and urine into their wounds; made a slave defecate into the mouth of another slave and then gagged the unfortunate recipient of this gift; and chained slaves overnight in 'bilboes' or stocks."[21] Thistlewood's horrific crimes, Saidiya Hartman argues in "Venus in Two Acts," "offer a graphic account of the pleasures exacted from the destruc-

---

17 | Klein and Vinson 56; Burnard, *Mastery, Tyranny, and Desire* 16-17, 181-83; Brown, *The Reaper's Garden* 52; Bush, *Slave Women in Caribbean Society* 27.
18 | Bush, *Slave Women in Caribbean Society* 8, 23-27; see also Burnard, *Mastery, Tyranny, and Desire* 138-271.
19 | Bush, *Slave Women in Caribbean Society* 27.
20 | Burnard, *Mastery, Tyranny, and Desire* 1-35; see also Brown, *The Reaper's Garden* 23; Barbara Bush, "African Caribbean Slave Mothers and Children: Traumas of Dislocation and Enslavement across the Atlantic World," *Caribbean Quarterly* 56.1/2 (2010): 80-81; Hartman, "Venus in Two Acts" 6.
21 | Burnard, *Mastery, Tyranny, and Desire* 150.

tion and degradation of life and, at the same time, illuminate the difficulty of recovering enslaved lives from the annihilating force of such description."[22]

Subjected to abominable conditions but unwilling to accept their fate passively, West Indian slaves employed a variety of means to challenge the white racist power structure. As in other slave societies in the Americas, forms of black resistance ranged from individual acts of sabotage, disobedience or non-cooperation to organized violent uprisings.[23] Crucially, Bush contends, female captives "had as deep a commitment to 'putting down massa' and the continuing struggle for human dignity and freedom, as any of their male counterparts."[24] Even though they knew they risked serious punishment, enslaved women attempted to run away from their plantations, tried to poison their masters, mutilated themselves or feigned illness to avoid working. They also actively participated in slave rebellions.[25] Furthermore, to their masters' dismay, many Jamaican slaves engaged in West African spiritual and religious practices such as obeah: "Practitioners of this art, of whom a significant proportion were women, were believed by the whites to wield a great influence over their fellow slaves and were hence accused of many subversive activities including incitement to revolt,"[26] Bush argues.

In Jamaica (and in other Caribbean countries), the history of black resistance against white colonial rule is closely connected with the complex story of maroons, a term used to refer to groups of escaped slaves and black freedom fighters who created semi-autonomous, defensible communities, mostly in isolated mountainous regions. Most maroon societies developed complex networks of communication; they combined African, European and indigenous (military) traditions and operated as guerrilla bands, raiding farms and plantations and generating fear and anxiety among white local residents. Throughout the early decades of the eighteenth century, Jamaican maroon communities and white settlers were engaged in constant power struggles and violent battles, resulting in staggering losses on both sides.[27]

---

22 | Hartman, "Venus in Two Acts" 6.
23 | Craton 33; Bush, *Slave Women in Caribbean Society* 51-82.
24 | Bush, *Slave Women in Caribbean Society* 81-82.
25 | Ibid. 51-82.
26 | Ibid. 74. For more information about "obeah," see James D. Rice, "Obeah," *The Historical Encyclopedia of World Slavery*, ed. Junius P. Rodriguez, vol. 2 (Santa Barbara, CA: ABC-CLIO, 1997) 477.
27 | Craton 61-87; Burnard, *Mastery, Tyranny, and Desire* 22-23; Isaac Curtis, "Masterless People: Maroons, Pirates, and Commoners," *The Caribbean: A History of the Region and Its Peoples*, eds. Stephan Palmié and Francisco A. Scarano (Chicago: U of Chicago P, 2011) 150-52; Nicholas J. Saunders, *The Peoples of the Caribbean: An Encyclopedia*

In 1739, British colonial officials and the maroon leader Cudjoe signed a peace treaty officially ending the so-called First Maroon War (1729-1739): "By this treaty," Burnard explains, "Cudjoe and his band were granted a large freehold property in the northwestern interior where they were to have almost sovereign rights and from which whites were excluded. They were also given rights to trade with whites."[28] In exchange, the maroons were required to assist the white authorities in suppressing slave revolts, "to help defend Jamaica against foreign invasion and return any future runaway slaves to their owners."[29] As Isaac Curtis contends, the 1739 peace treaty had devastating consequences for the enslaved population: "By employing maroons in enforcing the boundaries of the plantation, Jamaican planters eliminated the logical base of future maroon support while establishing more complete control over their own work force."[30]

In the following decades, most Jamaican maroons cooperated with the white ruling class, putting down slave revolts and catching runaway slaves. Yet, in July 1795, a violent conflict broke out between the Trelawny Town maroons, the largest Jamaican maroon group, and British troops. Known as the Second Maroon War, it lasted until March 1796, when the maroons, who were heavily outnumbered by the British, were forced to surrender. Seeking to prevent further maroon revolts, Lord Balcarres, then Governor of Jamaica, decided to banish more than five hundreds Trelawny maroons from the island: They were transported to the British colony of Nova Scotia in June 1796.[31] As James D. Lockett explains, this decision "was based on the fact that in 1783, some 1,200 former American slaves who gained their freedom by fighting on the British side during the American Revolution were taken to Nova Scotia."[32] Suffering from hunger and harsh living conditions, many of the Trelawny maroons were desperate to leave Nova Scotia. Like those black Nova Scotians who, in 1792,

---

of Caribbean Archeology and Traditional Culture (Santa Barbara, CA: ABC-CLIO, 2005) 174-75.
28 | Burnard, *Mastery, Tyranny, and Desire* 23.
29 | Saunders, *The Peoples of the Caribbean* 175. See also Burnard, *Mastery, Tyranny, and Desire* 23; Curtis 158.
30 | Curtis 158.
31 | Ibid. 160; see also Burnard, *Mastery, Tyranny, and Desire* 145; Winks 78-80. For more information about the Second Maroon War, see Craton 211-23.
32 | James D. Lockett, "The Deportation of the Maroons of Trelawny Town to Nova Scotia, then Back to Africa," *Journal of Black Studies* 30.1 (1999): 11. See also chapter 5, "Transnational Diasporic Journeys in Lawrence Hill's *The Book of Negroes* (2007)," in this study.

had accepted the offer by the Sierra Leone Company to relocate to West Africa, hundreds of them eventually migrated to Freetown in 1800.[33]

"Jamaica was a brutal and volatile slave society, contentious and unstable in the best of times," Vincent Brown emphasizes. "Slave rebellions and conspiracies of varying magnitudes occurred almost once each decade between 1740 and 1834."[34] One of the most significant slave uprisings in eighteenth-century Jamaica was Tacky's revolt: In early April 1760, on Easter Sunday, more than fifty Coromantee slaves (Akan-speaking captives from Africa's Gold Coast) started an insurgency in St. Mary's parish, where the number of white residents was especially small. Led by a slave named Tacky, they seized weapons and gunpowder, killed several whites, set fire to the sugar canes and collected new recruits. Their goal was to put an end to British colonial rule, to drive all whites from the island and to build an independent black society. Soon, thousands of male and female slaves joined the insurgents, causing considerable panic among slaveholders and plantation owners in all parts of the island. Although Tacky was shot and decapitated shortly after the outbreak of the uprising, the slaves continued to wage a guerrilla war in western Jamaica; the rebellion was not completely suppressed until October 1761. In the course of Tacky's Revolt, approximately 500 blacks were executed, killed in fighting or committed suicide, hundreds of rebels were shipped to the Bay of Honduras and about 60 whites lost their lives.[35] As Brown explains, Jamaican planters and colonial authorities were extremely shocked and frightened, responding to the events "by tightening social control, updating their slave codes, and urging more vigilant enforcement of existing regulations."[36]

In the last decade of the eighteenth century, the Haitian Revolution shattered the world of white slave masters in the Americas in general and Jamaican slave owners in particular: In 1791, in the neighboring French colony of Saint-Domingue, where whites and free people of African descent were vastly outnumbered by (African-born) slaves, black rebels "gained control of the plain and the mountains around Le Cap, turning plantations into military camps,

---

33 | See Winks 80-95; Lockett 5-14; Curtis 222; Junius P. Rodriguez, "Trelawney Town Maroons," *Encyclopedia of Slave Resistance and Rebellion*, ed. Rodgriguez. vol. 2 (Westport, CT: Greenwood, 2007) 517-18.

34 | Brown, *The Reaper's Garden* 3.

35 | Craton 125-39; Burnard, *Mastery, Tyranny, and Desire* 170-71; Diana Paton, "Tacky's Rebellion (1760-1761)," *The Historical Encyclopedia of World Slavery*, ed. Junius P. Rodriguez, vol. 2 (Santa Barbara, CA: ABC-CLIO, 1997) 625; Junius P. Rodriguez, "Tacky's Rebellion (1760-1761)," *Encyclopedia of Slave Resistance and Rebellion*, ed. Rodgriguez, vol. 2 (Westport, CT: Greenwood, 2007) 497-98; Brown, *The Reaper's Garden* 148.

36 | Brown, *The Reaper's Garden* 148.

recruiting new followers, finding weapons, and consolidating their territorial control."[37] Led by former slaves such as Toussaint Louverture and Jean-Jacques Dessalines, the slave insurrection finally resulted in the abolition of slavery in Saint-Domingue in 1793 and the founding of Haiti, the first independent black nation in the so-called "New World," in 1804. A watershed event in modern (Western) history, the Haitian Revolution had enormous effects on black (enslaved) communities as well as on white groups in the Atlantic world and elsewhere:[38] As Iyunolu F. Osagie has argued, it "produced two narrative paradigms—that of terror among the slaveholders and of liberation among the slaves."[39]

In late December 1831, twenty-three years after the legal abolition of the transatlantic slave trade in 1808, tens of thousands of Jamaican slaves rose against their white masters, setting fire to sugar plantations and estates. The so-called "Christmas Uprising," which also became known as the "Baptist War" because many white Jamaicans believed that Baptist missionaries had been involved in the conspiracy, was one of the largest slave revolts in the history of the British West Indies.[40] Although the rebellion was violently suppressed in early January 1832, it played a significant role in the Caribbean slaves' struggle against enslavement as it "helped hasten the British Parliament to decide the monumental question of whether or not slavery should be maintained in the British colonial possessions."[41] Chattel slavery was formally abolished

---

37 | Laurent Dubois, "The Haitian Revolution," *The Caribbean: A History of the Region and Its Peoples*, eds. Stephan Palmié and Francisco A. Scarano (Chicago: U of Chicago P, 2011) 279.

38 | Dubois, "The Haitian Revolution" 273-87. For more information about the Haitian Revolution, see also Laurent Dubois, *Avengers of the New World: The Story of the Haitian Revolution* (Cambridge, MA: Harvard UP, 2004); C.L.R. James, *The Black Jacobins: Toussaint L'Ouverture and the San Domingo Revolution*, rev. ed. (1963; New York: Vintage, 1989).

39 | Osagie 29.

40 | See Jean Besson, "Missionaries, Planters, and Slaves in the Age of Abolition," *The Caribbean: A History of the Region and Its Peoples*, eds. Stephan Palmié and Francisco A. Scarano (Chicago: U of Chicago P, 2011) 321-24; Colleen A. Vasconcellos, "Abolition in Jamaica," *Encyclopedia of Emancipation and Abolition in the Transatlantic World*, ed. Junius P. Rodriguez, vol. 2 (2007; New York: Routledge, 2015) 310-12; Colleen A. Vasconcellos, "Emancipation in Jamaica," *Encyclopedia of Emancipation and Abolition in the Transatlantic World*, ed. Junius P. Rodriguez, vol. 2 (2007; New York: Routledge, 2015) 312-14; Junius P. Rodriguez, "Jamaica Rebellion (1831-1832)," *Encyclopedia of Emancipation and Abolition in the Transatlantic World*, ed. Rodriguez, vol. 2 (2007; New York: Routledge, 2015) 314-15.

41 | Rodriguez, "Jamaica Rebellion" 314.

throughout the British Empire in 1833, yet Jamaica's ex-slaves "were forced into a life of apprenticeship until their full emancipation in 1838."[42] In the years (and decades) after the passing of the Slavery Abolition Act in 1833, Jamaica's black population continued to suffer from racial oppression and discrimination as "the ex-slaveholders attempted to replicate the structure of social, cultural, and labor relations that had existed under slavery,"[43] to quote Eudell.

POWER RELATIONS AND INTRA-BLACK VIOLENCE IN *THE BOOK OF NIGHT WOMEN*

Diaspora, to paraphrase Avtar Brah and Tina M. Campt, is not only closely linked with terms and concepts like forced migration, displacement and mobility. Even more fundamentally, it also refers to experiences of arrival, settlement and dwelling as well as to intricate power struggles in specific local environments outside the original homelands.[44] As I have shown in chapter 5, Lawrence Hill's *The Book of Negroes* provides a transnational perspective on a wide variety of diasporic themes: the loss of home and family in West Africa, the forced deportation to the Americas, the impossibility of recuperating the past and going back to an ancestral village and, equally important, the practices of home-making in the diaspora.

Unlike Hill's novel, James's *The Book of Night Women* is not concerned with exploring what Marianne Hirsch and Nancy K. Miller describe as "the intensities and contradictory impulses of diasporic return."[45] Rather, James's main goal is to shed light on the complex web of relationships between masters, overseers, slaves and maroons and to examine the constitutive role of violence in the "diaspora space" of eighteenth-century Jamaica. In particular, *The Book of Night Women* focuses on what Campt and Thomas would call "the vexing tensions of difference and inequity that characterize the internal relations of diaspora."[46]

Reflecting on the heterogeneity and complexity of black life under slavery, James depicts a slave community that is marked by constant power struggles and clear hierarchical divisions between creole and African-born slaves, be-

---

42 | Vasconcellos, "Abolition in Jamaica" 312.
43 | Eudell 16.
44 | Campt, *Other Germans* 7; Campt, *Image Matters* 25, 54; Brah 178-210; see also chapter 1, "The Concept of the African Diaspora and the Notion of Difference," in this study.
45 | Hirsch and Miller 4.
46 | Campt and Thomas, "Gendering Diaspora: Transnational Feminism, Diaspora and Its Hegemonies" 1.

tween black women and men as well as between house slaves, artisans, drivers, field slaves and overseers. Crucially, James particularly highlights the specific vulnerability of female slaves within this social structure: In *The Book of Night Women*, black women like Lilith are subjected to the same forms of exploitation, oppression and violence as male slaves; in addition, they become victims of sexual abuse and harassment by both white and black men. Exploring the intricate theme of intra-black violence, James participates in a powerful intertextual dialogue with slave narratives: As Diedrich has shown, many African American authors in the antebellum period deliberately and strategically avoided writing about conflicts, tensions, violence and acts of betrayal within the black community. In their attempt to fight for the end of slavery and racial oppression, one of their common objectives was to stress the slaves' moral incorruptibility, integrity and superiority over their white oppressors. Therefore, most antebellum slave narrative authors prioritize black solidarity, unity and loyalty rather than intra-black violence and black disloyalty. Their texts create a strict division between black victims, on the one hand, and white perpetrators, on the other.[47]

In his neo-slave narrative, James powerfully deconstructs what the historian Jeff Forret describes as "overtly romantic interpretations of a harmonious and idyllic slave community virtually devoid of conflict."[48] In other words, *The Book of Night Women* not only demonstrates how the slaves on Montpelier Estate form bonds of friendship and love, how they cooperate in their struggle against their white oppressors and support each other in moments of danger and desperation. In order to draw attention to slavery's corrupting and brutalizing effect on blacks, James's novel also explicitly shows that the slaves fight against, exert control over and sometimes even kill each other. In particular, it explores the complex power relationship between black enslaved women and men.

As the historian Kathleen M. Brown argues, male slaves often "created a culture of male performance that offered some protections from violence, and opportunities to dominate fellow slaves, particularly women, in certain circumscribed contexts."[49] Unable to lead an independent life and to protect their children and wives, many male slaves resorted to violence to assert their manhood, to "channel the anger and frustration they repressed when around the master and liberate themselves temporarily from their powerlessness."[50] By exploring how the institution of chattel slavery perverts the slaves' moral values and how

---

47 | See Diedrich, *Ausbruch aus der Knechtschaft* 78-83.
48 | Jeff Forret, "Conflict and the 'Slave Community:' Violence among Slaves in Upcountry South Carolina," *Journal of Southern History* 74.3 (2008): 553.
49 | Brown, "'Strength of the Lion ... Arms Like Polished Iron'" 174.
50 | Forret 569.

male slaves turn into perpetrators due to slavery's dehumanizing impact, *The Book of Night Women* challenges static conceptualizations of slave communities as homogenous groups of passive and innocent victims, without justifying acts of intra-black violence and without absolving the black victimizer from guilt and moral responsibility.

In one of the first chapters, James describes how Paris,[51] a black overseer, tries to rape Lilith. Like many other male slaves on Montpelier Estate, Paris is depicted as a ruthless and cruel man, using physical and psychological means to control and humiliate others whenever he can: "He was one of them man who didn't even have to beat and thump and slap, him voice was enough."[52] Subjected to his master's will, in a way similar to Jeptha in *Unconfessed*, Paris attempts to demonstrate and assert his manhood by oppressing and exerting control over black women.[53] He feels free to sexually abuse Lilith because he knows that the white plantation owners and the colonial authorities will not punish him for this crime. Through Paris's hostile treatment of black women, James sheds light on forms of male bonding (across race, class and status) at the expense of black women; he draws attention to what Yvette Christiansë would describe as "the collusion between a slave owner and his male slave:"[54]

---

51 | In James's *The Book of Night Women*, many slaves are named after characters from Greek mythology, such as Circe, Andromeda and Paris. Of course, Paris was the prince of Troy; he triggered the Trojan War by kidnapping Helen from Sparta. In the British West Indies, Barbara Bush explains, many enslaved women and men were "given ludicrous and demeaning classical names—Hercules, Phibia—which stripped them of their African identity." As Ira Berlin argues, similar practices were common in mainland North America: Slaves' "names reflected the contempt in which their owners held them. Most answered to some European diminutive—Jack and Sukey in the English colonies, Pedro and Francisca in places under Spanish rule, and Jean and Marie in the French dominions. As if to emphasize their inferiority, some were tagged with names usually assigned to barnyard animals. Others were designated with the name of some ancient deity or great personage like Hercules or Cato as a kind of cosmic jest: the most insignificant with the greatest of name." Bush, *Slave Women in Caribbean Society* 52; Berlin, *Generations of Captivity* 54; see also Luke Roman and Monica Roman, *Encyclopedia of Greek and Roman Mythology* (New York: Facts on File, 2010) 386.
52 | Marlon James, *The Book of Night Women* (New York: Riverhead Books, 2009) 16. All further references to this novel (BoN) will be cited in the text and will refer to this edition.
53 | For a detailed discussion of black masculinity during slavery, see Brown, "'Strength of the Lion ... Arms Like Polished Iron'" 172-80; see also chapter 4, "'Hertseer:' Re-Imagining Cape Slavery in Yvette Christiansë's *Unconfessed* (2006)," in this study.
54 | Christiansë, "A Freedom Stolen" 109.

Both treat female slaves as inferior beings, mistreating them and reducing them to objects of sexual gratification.

In this scene, and throughout *The Book of Night Women*, however, James refuses to represent his black female characters as passive and submissive. Instead, he highlights the slave women's strong inner determination to offer violent resistance. In an act of self-defense, Lilith seriously injures Paris: "She grab the pot of cerasee tea and don't care that it burnin' her finger. —What de—the man say but before him could even shift, she turn over the pot of tea on him face" (BoN 16). In this phase of the novel, at least for a short moment, James centralizes a Fanonian counter-violence and the liberating effect it has on Lilith: It frees her from her "despair and inaction,"[55] to quote Fanon, and makes her realize that she has the power to resist male dominance on the plantation and beyond: "That was the first time she feel the darkness. True darkness and true womanness that make man scream" (BoN 17). Empowered by her new sense of self, Lilith has the strength to fight against her attacker. In this chapter, ultimately, she manages to escape sexual abuse by killing the would-be rapist Paris with a cutlass. This scene plays a significant role in the novel's plot because it foreshadows the night women's and Lilith's (further) acts of violence against white masters and fellow slaves in the course of the narrative.

In addition to focusing on tensions, conflicts and violence within the slave community, *The Book of Night Women* draws attention to the complex and violent relationship between enslaved subjects and maroon communities in eighteenth-century Jamaica: "What every nigger done know," James's narrator says, "was that after the treaty, the Maroon, the slave sworn friend, become him sworn enemy. The backra pay two pounds for every captured nigger but most time Maroon done hunt and send back niggers even for free" (BoN 78). Signifying on the 1739 peace treaty between the maroon leader Cudjoe and the British, James challenges a clear-cut dichotomy between black victimhood and white suppression, without relativizing the guilt of white colonial authorities, plantation owners and slaveholders. Instead of offering a naïve celebration of black cooperation and solidarity, *The Book of Night Women* explores the brutalizing effect of slavery and white colonial rule on black maroon communities, centralizing the maroons' decision and willingness to turn against and betray other blacks to maintain their own status as free individuals.

---

55 | Frantz Fanon, *The Wretched of the Earth*, trans. Constance Farrington (1961; New York: Grove Press, 1968) 94.

THE SLAVE'S CIRCLE AND THE ETHICS OF REPRESENTING VIOLENCE

"Every negro walk in a circle. Take that and make of it what you will" (BoN 33, 120, 223, 313, 421). Repeated five times throughout James's text to introduce several chapters, these two sentences point to the novel's nihilistic tendency to focus on the captive's desperate and hopeless situation: To be a slave in eighteenth-century Jamaica, *The Book of Night Women* insists, is to be trapped in a vicious circle of oppression, counter-violence and retaliation. While the novel explores different forms of black agency and various acts of defiance against slavery, it ultimately highlights the impossibility to triumph over the white plantation owners and masters and to escape subjugation and exploitation; it demonstrates that the slaves' effort to break out of the vicious circle of violence is doomed to failure: "Every negro walk in a circle. [...] He can't walk like freeman and no matter where he walk, the road take he right back to the chain, the branding iron, the cat-o'-nine or the noose that be the blessing that no niggerwoman can curse" (BoN 120). As the following example illustrates, *The Book of Night Women* particularly dramatizes the white colonizer's immediate and violent response to any attempt to challenge the existing white racist structure. In December 1784, several months before Lilith's birth, the white overseer Jack Wilkins manages to catch a runaway slave called Bacchus; the two men engage in a violent fight in which Bacchus is killed (BoN 260-66). A key scene in *The Book of Night Women*, it evokes the slave's strong yearning for freedom, his desire to overthrow the master's rule and, most importantly, his willingness to risk death rather than endure enslavement. This topic also plays a crucial role in male slave narratives, most notably in the *Narrative of the Life of Frederick Douglass, an American Slave* (1845), in which the fight with the white overseer and slave-breaker Edward Covey is represented as a powerful turning point in Douglass's struggle to regain his manhood and to liberate himself from bondage. As Paul Gilroy has argued, Douglass's *Narrative* shows how "the slave actively prefers the possibility of death to the continuing condition of inhumanity on which plantation slavery depends."[56]

In his neo-slave narrative, James engages in an intertextual dialogue with Douglass's *Narrative* and other male slave narratives by exploring the relationship between counter-violence, black masculinity, freedom, self-worth and self-assertion. In recent years, black feminist scholars such as McDowell and Davis have highlighted "the patriarchal assumptions"[57] in Douglass's 1845 slave

---

56 | Gilroy, *The Black Atlantic* 63; see also Frederick Douglass, *Narrative of the Life of Frederick Douglass, an American Slave*, 1845, *The Classic Slave Narratives*, ed. Henry Louis Gates, Jr. (New York: Signet Classics, 2002) 323-436.
57 | Davis, *Narrative* 24.

narrative: According to McDowell, "Douglass's refusal to be whipped represents, not only an assertion of manhood, but the transcendence of slavery, an option his *Narrative* denies to women."[58] Crucially, unlike Douglass, James is not only concerned with the theme of black male resistance but also, and essentially, investigates the meaning of black female counter-violence in eighteenth-century Jamaica, emphasizing that, as Bush puts it, the slave woman "reacted to slavery with the same intensity and commitment as her menfolk."[59]

Unlike in Douglass's *Narrative*, in *The Book of Night Women*, James's account of the fight between slave (Bacchus) and overseer (Wilkins) ends with the slave's death. Via this episode, James sheds light on the repressive and utterly dehumanizing nature of white rule in eighteenth-century Jamaica; a place that historians like Burnard describe as "a mature and brutal slave society."[60] On Montpelier Estate, like on all the other plantations on the island, whites are heavily outnumbered by blacks; slave revolts are common and feared by white plantation owners and overseers: "White man know that there never be a safe day in the colony," James's narrator remarks. "So they whip we. One hundred, two hundred, three hundred lash and whatever number come after that" (BoN 261).

Like so many other white Jamaicans, Wilkins is a torturer and rapist, firmly determined to preserve white rule, to intimidate slaves on a daily basis and to punish them harshly in order to stifle black resistance and rebellion. After killing Bacchus, Wilkins goes on to commit further acts of horrific violence designed to demoralize the slave community:

Later that night he shove Bacchus' head on a stick and plant the stick right in front of the slave quarters, where Bacchus stay until he rot off. Knowing who Bacchus' sister be, a house slave who not yet fourteen, he drag her from great house to the stable, where he rape her and leave him seed in her. [...] Wilkins say they must teach the negroes a lesson. That Saturday, the negroes get the learning. In the morning when the womens washing before they go to the field, Wilkins ride up and grab Leto, a girl who not be sixteen yet. Leto scream. One hour or so later he summon all the slave to one of the empty fields. —This is what happen to you when you cross with your master! Jack Wilkins say. In the middle of the field was bundles of stick and bush. In the middle of the bundle was a tree trunk. Tied to the tree trunk was Leto who screaming, pleading and crying. (BoN 265-66)

As this excerpt reveals, for Wilkins, violence is a means of control, punishment, domination and oppression as well as a tool to demonstrate the (almost

---

58 | McDowell, *Narrative* xx.
59 | Bush, *Slave Women in Caribbean Society* 164.
60 | Burnard, *Mastery, Tyranny, and Desire* 244.

unlimited) extent of his mastery over blacks. During slavery, Saidiya Hartman explains, "the exercise of power was inseparable from its display because domination depended upon demonstrations of the slaveholder's dominion and the captive's abasement."[61] Seeking to assert and strengthen his position as overseer and to set an example for other blacks, Wilkins forces his slaves to witness Leto's gruesome torture and execution. Knowing that his actions are supported by the state's legal system,[62] he fears no social or legal consequences. As *The Book of Night Women* illustrates, the black women under Wilkins's control are especially vulnerable to abuse since they suffer from both racist and sexist oppression.

For Wilkins, the rape of Bacchus's sister is more than a means of sexual arousal and an act of revenge for Bacchus's insubordination; it is a tool to intimidate the whole slave community: "Rape was a weapon of domination," Angela Davis explains in her influential study *Women, Race and Class* (1981), "a weapon of repression, whose covert goal was to extinguish slave women's will to resist, and in the process, to demoralize their men."[63] As Davis goes on to argue:

If Black women had achieved a sense of their own strength and a strong urge to resist, then violent sexual assaults—so the slaveholders might have reasoned—would remind the women of their essential and inalterable femaleness. In the male supremacist vision of the period, this meant passivity, acquiescence and weakness.[64]

Enslaved men who were forced to witness the rape of black women were painfully reminded of the impossibility of protecting their wives and daughters from abuse. Driven by despair and suffering from powerlessness, many male slaves used violence against black women to regain a sense of self-worth and to reassert their manhood.[65] Detailing Wilkins's divide-and-rule strategy, James shows how the white overseer's use of rape as a weapon eventually results in violent conflicts within the slave community, i.e., in acts of oppression against black women committed by black men. Significantly, in James's novel, the rape

---

61 | Hartman, *Scenes of Subjection* 7.
62 | As Trevor Burnard points out: "White Jamaicans developed a legal system and a social structure in which any brutality exercised by whites towards blacks could be excused by the fundamental necessity of keeping blacks subdued. Only in this way could white fears be assuaged. Such assumptions, of course, were a license for sadism and tyranny among all whites, not just those inclined to psychopathic behavior. Whites knew that they had the full support of the state and white public opinion for whatever they did toward slaves." Burnard, *Mastery, Tyranny, and Desire* 33.
63 | Angela Davis, *Women, Race, and Class* (New York: Random House, 1981) 23-24.
64 | Ibid. 24.
65 | See Forret 568-69.

scene is presented as a flashback, highlighting the constitutive nature of violence in the black protagonist's life: Born as a slave in 1785, Lilith is the daughter of Bacchus's sister and Jack Wilkins; her green eyes are, as Suzanne Marie Hopcroft puts it, "the legacy of her mother's rape by her white overseer father."[66]

Like other contemporary authors who revisit the past of slavery from twenty-first-century perspectives, exploring the nature of white power and rendering "the lives of the nameless and the forgotten,"[67] James must answer the crucial question of how to write about acts of anti-black violence, sexual abuse, annihilation and torture, and to what ends. Depicting Wilkins's atrocities against Bacchus, Bacchus's sister and Leto, the passage quoted above is representative of James's decision to include explicit, and extremely shocking, scenes of violence in *The Book of Night Women*; it illustrates the novel's narrative choice to present the horrors of slavery and, in particular, the black woman's experience of (sexual) abuse in an unsparing, even pornographic, manner.

In cultural studies discourse, the term "pornography" generally refers to "a form of representation that graphically depicts sexuality in order to stimulate its consumer."[68] As Brenda Cossman points out, the last five decades have witnessed heated academic debates about the misogynistic nature and damaging effects of pornography: "Dominance or radical feminism has argued that pornography harms and subordinates women," Cossmann explains. "Beginning in the 1970s, this feminist theory shifted the harm associated with pornography from sexual explicitness to sexism. Some feminists began to identify pornography as a cause of exploitive male sexual practices, and women's subordination."[69] For instance, in her ground-breaking study *Feminism Unmodified: Discourses on Life and Law* (1987), Catharine A. MacKinnon, one of the most prominent anti-pornography feminists, "define[s] pornography as the graphic sexually explicit subordination of women through pictures or words that also includes women dehumanized as sexual objects, things, or commodities."[70]

Since the 1980s, feminists such as Carole Vance have started to challenge this anti-pornography discourse, contending "that pornography has a subversive quality, in representing and advocating sexual pleasure and agency for women."[71] Today, "pornography" remains one of the most controversial topics

---
66 | Hopcroft, "A Heartbreaking History."
67 | Hartman, "Venus in Two Acts" 4.
68 | Brian Longhurst et al., *Introducing Cultural Studies*, 2nd ed. (London: Routledge 2013) 221.
69 | Brenda Cossmann, "Pornography," *Encyclopedia of Feminist Theories*, ed. Lorraine Code (London: Routledge, 2000) 393; emphases deleted.
70 | Catharine A. MacKinnon, *Feminism Unmodified: Discourses on Life and Law* (Cambridge, MA: Harvard UP, 1987) 176.
71 | Cossmann 393.

in cultural and feminist studies as scholars "differ on whether all sexually-explicit material is defamatory to women, or whether pornographic forms can be used to formulate a discourse of female desire."[72]

In a 2014 interview with Kaitlyn Greenidge, James offers the following explanation for his aesthetic choice to depict violence in a pornographic way:

> I have a problem with understated violence. I have a problem with violence that is tasteful. [...] It's nasty, it's bloody, it's painful. There's nothing touching about it. It was very important to me that when I write brutality, it be brutal. And when you say to me, "Well, we can't stomach it, we can't read it," I'm like, "Well, consider the person who had to experience it." [...] The concern a lot of people have with explicit violence, explicit sex, explicit anything, is that it turns into a kind of pornography. And I'm like, "So what?" Risk pornography. [73]

In order to evaluate James's narrative strategy, I will, once again, refer to the theoretical interventions of black feminist critics such as McDowell, Davis and Hartman: In her 1999 introduction to the *Narrative of the Life of Frederick Douglass*, McDowell criticizes Douglass's explicit rendering of violence against the black female body—most notably his detailed description of the beating of Aunt Hester at the beginning of his autobiographical account. "The *Narrative* is literally populated with the whipped bodies of slave women, and in each of these scenes Douglass looks on voyeuristically in a fashion tinged with eroticism,"[74] McDowell contends. "As the *Narrative* progresses, the beatings proliferate, and the women, no longer identified by name, become absolutized as a bloody mass of naked backs."[75] Drawing on McDowell's work, Davis argues that Douglass and other contemporary abolitionist writers do not "apprehend how literary representations of black women's bodies as targets of slavery's most horrific forms of violence might also tend to objectify slave women and discursively deprive them of the capacity to strike out for their own freedom."[76] In *Scenes of Subjection*, Hartman contributes to this discussion about the ethics of narration as she chooses not to incorporate Douglass's Aunt Hester scene into

---

72 | Sarah Gamble, ed., *The Routledge Companion to Feminism and Postfeminism* (London: Routledge, 2006) 276.
73 | Marlon James, "Violently Wrought: Kaitlyn Greenidge Interviews Marlon James," *Guernica* 3 Nov. 2014, 4 June 2015 https://www.guernicamag.com/interviews/violently-wrought/.
74 | McDowell, *Narrative* xxi.
75 | Ibid. xxii.
76 | Davis, *Narrative* 26.

her study in order to draw attention to "the precariousness of empathy and the uncertain line between witness and spectator."[77]

Crucially, James's novel fails to take into account the epistemological insights of black feminist scholars such as McDowell, Davis and Hartman—to reflect on the danger of constructing "women's bodies as objects of slavery's appalling violence:"[78] Whereas Hartman, Morrison and Christiansë are torn between the desire to highlight the female slave's experience of "thingification" and the refusal to narrate it and creatively address that conflict (on a meta-level), *The Book of Night Women* shows no critical awareness of the ethical risks involved in putting the atrocities against slave women into words: James's novel is full of shocking images, gruesome passages and pornographic scenes that "subject the dead to new dangers and to a second order of violence,"[79] to use Hartman's words from "Venus in Two Acts."

In a way similar to Hill in *The Book of Negroes*, James strategically adopts a black female perspective: In doing so, he intends to enter into the commercially successful tradition of female-authored neo-slave narratives that center around black female protagonists. Furthermore, in a self-legitimizing way, he tries to justify his narrative strategy of representing black women's experiences of sexual abuse. Like Hill, James never reflects on the theoretical and ethical implications of "the practice of speaking for others,"[80] on the challenges and difficulties inherent in appropriating the slave woman's voice. While Hill's melodramatic novel fails to acknowledge the true implications of chattel slavery as a dehumanizing system of "thingification," James offers an unsparing account of the utterly destructive and brutalizing nature of slavery, yet refuses to engage in a critical examination of the dangers of writing about scenes of black female subjection and torture. "I didn't want my reader to be at a further degree of remove from the characters," James explains in his interview with Kaitlyn Greenidge. "That was one thing that was very important to me. That you don't get to have a wider view than they do. You don't get to have a bigger sense of perspective than they do."[81] Ultimately, I argue, James's pornographic representations of the (female) slaves' experiences of humiliation satisfy the

---

77 | Hartman, *Scenes of Subjection* 4. See also chapter 4, "'Hertseer:' Re-Imagining Cape Slavery in Yvette Christiansë's *Unconfessed* (2006)," in this study.
78 | Davis, *Narrative* 26.
79 | Hartman, "Venus in Two Acts" 5.
80 | Alcoff 8.
81 | James, "Violently Wrought." In the interview with Kaitlyn Greenidge, James not only refers to *The Book of Night Women* but also to his other two novels *John Crow's Devil* (2005) and *A History of Seven Killings* (2014).

reader's potential voyeuristic desires in that they "reinforce the spectacular character of black suffering."[82]

BLURRING THE LINES BETWEEN VICTIM AND PERPETRATOR: LILITH AS (ANTI-)HEROINE

One of James's central objectives in *The Book of Night Women* is to foreground the utter destructiveness of Caribbean slavery by showing how slavery perverts the slaves' moral values and how Lilith turns into a victimizer. In the course of the novel, James's black protagonist emerges as an incredibly complex character, overwhelmed by conflicting feelings of hate and love, revenge and guilt, fear and decisiveness. Depicted as a rebellious, impetuous and headstrong woman, she struggles to find a way to gain a measure of control over her life, to escape her miserable existence and to set herself apart from the other female slaves on Montpelier Estate.

On an intertextual level, her name refers to a famous character in Jewish mythology and tradition that appears in different incarnations: as a demon and child murderer, as a seducer of men, as Adam's first wife and as a queen of demons.[83] As Geoffrey W. Dennis explains in *The Encyclopedia of Jewish Myth, Magic and Mysticism* (2007), in recent debates, "Lilith has become a rallying point among feminists in critiquing the overwhelmingly male-oriented perspective of traditional Judaism, and she has been adopted as a symbol of feminist resistance to male spiritual hegemony."[84] In *The Book of Night Women*, Lilith is a personification of female vulnerability and resistance: She is both a victim of white brutality and a defiant slave; an oppressed woman and a victimizer who not only resorts to violence to defend herself and to challenge the master's power but who also kills white children and ultimately even attacks fellow female captives to gain influence and power within the slave community.

As the following scene illustrates, James directs our attention to Lilith's willingness to turn against other slaves in order to accentuate the brutalizing effect of slavery on the enslaved: To Lilith's great annoyance, Andromeda and several other female captives are chosen to serve at the Montpelier Estate New Year's Eve ball. Wishing to take over Andromeda's task, Lilith asks the obeah woman Gorgon for help. On the next morning, Andromeda coughs up blood and dies (BoN 98-105). In this passage, *The Book of Night Women* highlights the crucial significance of West African spiritual and religious practices in (eight-

---

82 | Hartman, *Scenes of Subjection* 3.
83 | Geoffrey W. Dennis, *The Encyclopedia of Jewish Myth, Magic and Mysticism* (Woodbury, MN: Llewellyn Publications, 2007) 153-54.
84 | Ibid. 154.

eenth-century) Jamaican culture, focusing particularly on the slaves' strong belief in the magic and subversive power of obeah. As James's novel suggests, obeah practitioners like Gorgon exert enormous (psychological) influence over black women and men; they use obeah to cure illnesses, to prophesy the future, to provoke slave rebellions and, of utmost importance, to intimidate their fellow slaves. In fact, Andromeda's death causes great panic among those who recognize the existence of supernatural forces: "In the kitchen all hell about to break loose. Nobody did like Andromeda, but word spread 'bout how she dead and one woman already run outside the house screaming that Obeah deh'pon di Montpelier Estate" (BoN 110). In other words, in James's novel, obeah is closely connected with "divination, medicine, and protection from malevolent forces,"[85] and it is exploited by some practitioners as an instrument of manipulation and domination within the black community.

In addition to exploring the intricate nature of African (diasporic) spiritualty, the obeah scene serves to characterize Lilith as a multifaceted (anti-)heroine, willing to commit morally unacceptable acts but also capable of expressing empathy with others. In fact, after Andromeda's death, she is plagued by unsettling nightmares:

She hear Andromeda daughter screaming and turn around, lookin' to see where she be. Nothing but darkness. Lilith go over to her mat on the floor and stoop down, her head heavy and not together. Slave death is nothing new and a strong nigger learn to walk past it but Lilith look down on her own hands and keep seeing blood. (BoN 123)

Lilith's owners and her white father Jack Wilkins ruthlessly whip, humiliate, torture and kill blacks on any given day and without any reason; they do not feel any sense of culpability or wrongdoing. In contrast, Lilith is haunted by guilt and shame after acknowledging her responsibility for Andromeda's death and the slave woman's daughter's suffering. In this scene, James shows that Lilith, unlike her white masters, is willing and able to critically reflect on her violent actions and to recognize her moral failures. And yet, in the course of the narrative, as she is confronted with further acts of (sexual) abuse and exploitation, Lilith continues to use violence against both whites and blacks. Like Morrison, Hartman and Christiansë, James participates in a discussion with Afro-pessimism about the crushing power of slavery: Delineating Lilith's transformation into a murderer, *The Book of Night Women* examines how slavery destroys the moral values of the oppressed and dispossessed.

For Lilith, it is Mistress Roget's barbaric killing of Dulcimena at Coulibre that marks a traumatic turning point in her life. Again, James presents the female slave's experience of subjection in an explicit and pornographic way,

---

85 | Rice 477.

without reflecting on what Hartman describes as "the risks posed by reiterating violent speech and depicting again rituals of torture:"[86]

Dulcimena begging for the massa to save her but Massa Roget ride right past her to go to Kingston. The mistress wield the cart whip herself. Lilith always hear she do such a thing but never see for herself before. She flog Dulcimena as hard as she could flog, swinging the whip wide and lashing Dulcimena back till the skin tear into flesh and the flesh tear into blood. [...] Dulcimena get one hundred sixty-six lash that day and the mistress say she would have derby-dose her too if any of the negroes was setting to pass shit. (BoN 203-04)

Highlighting the slave mistress's sadistic practices, James engages in an intertextual dialogue with African American slave narratives, such as Douglass's *Narrative* and Harriet Jacobs's *Incidents in the Life of a Slave Girl* (1861), and with white abolitionist novels, such as Harriet Beecher Stowe's *Uncle Tom's Cabin* (1852):[87] One of the primary goals of anti-slavery writers like Jacobs, Douglass and Stowe was to direct the white American reader's attention to the ways in which, as the historian Dickson D. Bruce, Jr. puts it, "slavery corrupted slaves and slaveholders alike."[88] In order to illustrate the demoralizing effects of the so-called "peculiar institution," they showed how white Southern women, who were represented as innocent, noble, pious, sympathetic and graceful in most nineteenth-century literary texts, were perverted into cruel oppressors, taking pleasure in humiliating and killing black people and in witnessing scenes of torture and abuse[89]—as were their children, yet another paragon of innocence. One reason for describing the destruction of "white innocence" was the inability or unwillingness of contemporary dominant white discourses to attribute qualities like innocence to chattel slaves.

In his *Narrative*, Douglass demonstrates how slavery perverts the mind of Sophia Auld, his mistress in Baltimore: "When I went there, she was a pious, warm, and tender-hearted woman. [...] Slavery soon proved its ability to divest her of these heavenly qualities. Under its influence, the tender heart became

---

86 | Hartman, "Venus in Two Acts" 4.
87 | Harriet Jacobs, *Incidents in the Life of a Slave Girl*, 1861, *The Classic Slave Narratives*, ed. Henry Louis Gates, Jr. (New York: Signet Classics, 2002) 437-667; Douglass, *Narrative of the Life of Frederick Douglass* 323-436; Harriet Beecher Stowe, *Uncle Tom's Cabin*, 1852, ed. Elizabeth Ammons, 2nd ed. (New York: Norton, 2010).
88 | Dickson D. Bruce, Jr., "Politics in the Slave Narrative," *The Cambridge Companion to the African American Slave Narrative*, ed. Audrey A. Fisch (Cambridge: Cambridge UP, 2007) 31.
89 | See Diedrich, *Ausbruch aus der Knechtschaft* 71-74.

stone, and the lamblike disposition gave way to one of tiger-like fierceness."[90] While Douglass initially offers a highly idealized view of his mistress to foreground her inherent virtues of integrity, faith and charity, he uses animal comparisons to describe Auld's development into a ruthless and pitiless slaveholder and to draw attention to the moral decay of white America; for if the country's "true woman" loses her innocence and cleansing power, the entire (white) nation is without a future. Douglass's slave narrative emphasizes the destructive impact of the institution of enslavement on blacks and whites alike and urgently calls for the immediate abolition of slavery in the United States.

In *The Book of Night Women*, James, too, employs the trope of the sadistic and brutal female mistress to shed light on the damaging effects of slavery on black and white society. Moreover, in the passage quoted above (the flogging of Lilith's friend Dulcimena), he explores the meaning of slavery as "thingification" by explicitly describing atrocious acts of violence against black human "flesh,"[91] to use Spillers's term. On the plot level, the torture scene at Coulibre offers a contextualization for Lilith's development into a ruthless victimizer: Her crimes in the second part of the narrative are primarily a result of the dehumanization and degradation she has experienced throughout her life as a slave. After witnessing Dulcimena's execution, Lilith thinks about taking revenge:

Lilith start to imagine what white flesh look like after a whipping. What white neck look like after a hanging and what kinda scar leave on a white body after black punishment. She think of the little Roget boy, Master Henri, of tying and hanging the boy up by him little balls and chopping him head off. She make the thoughts of white blood work into a fever. (BoN 204)

Subjected to intolerable physical pain and psychological torture, Lilith has internalized the white (wo)man's conception of violence as a legitimate tool of punishment and sadistic suppression. Her hatred is directed against all white people, including children like Roget's son; and she hopes that her white oppressors will suffer the same fate as Dulcimena and other brutalized slaves.

The following acts of violence carried out by Lilith could be interpreted as a form of self-liberation, an attempt to express her freedom as a human being: In fact, after killing her master Roget, the novel's protagonist re-experiences a sense of empowerment: "Lilith feel a new thing under skin, something that tingle as her heart jump up and down. It never beat so fast and so loud. True darkness and true womanness that make men scream" (BoN 228). As in the scene of Paris's killing at the novel's beginning, Lilith articulates her willing-

---

90 | Douglass 367.
91 | Spillers, "Mama's Baby, Papa's Maybe: An American Grammar Book" 67.

ness to fight against the (white) patriarchal system. For Lilith, the notion of "true womanhood" is not at all linked with submissiveness and passivity but with resistance and disobedience.[92]

Focusing both on the transformative power of violence for oppressed subjects and the destructive nature of violent acts, James's neo-slave narrative stands in a dynamic intertextual relation to Richard Wright's 1940 *Native Son*, one of the most famous and controversially discussed African American novels of the twentieth century: Concentrating on the pervasiveness of racial oppression and the hardships of black ghetto life in early twenty-century America, Wright unfolds the story of twenty-year-old Bigger Thomas, a black man working as a chauffeur for an affluent white entrepreneur. In a moment of extreme fear and panic, Bigger accidentally suffocates his employer's daughter Mary. Later, while on the run from the police, Bigger rapes his black girlfriend Bessie. Afraid that she will hand him over to the police, he kills Bessie in cold blood. The novel ends with Wright's description of Bigger's time in prison, where the black anti-hero waits to be brought to the electric chair.

The Book of Night Women and *Native Son* are set in different historical periods and explore different cultural, political and social contexts (slavery in Jamaica at the end of the eighteenth century vs. racial segregation in Chicago in the 1930s during the Great Depression). Yet, both novels examine the role and legitimacy of (counter-)violence in the fight for freedom, recognition and self-determination. In *Native Son*, Wright shows how the killing of Mary gives meaning to Bigger's life, at least for a short moment. At this point of the novel, Bigger admits his responsibility for Mary's death and re-conceptualizes his

---

92 | Lilith's concept of "true womanness" could be read as an intertextual reference to and rewriting of the discourse of "true womanhood." In the United States, Hazel V. Carby contends, the prevailing "ideology to define the boundaries of acceptable female behavior from the 1820s until the Civil War was the 'cult of true womanhood.'" As the historian Barbara Welter explains in her famous 1966 "The Cult of True Womanhood: 1820-1860," an essay to which Carby also refers: "Woman, in the Cult of True Womanhood presented by the women's magazines, gifts annuals and religious literature of the nineteenth century, was the hostage in the home. [...] The attributes of True Womanhood, by which a woman judged herself and was judged by her husband, her neighbors and society could be divided into four cardinal virtues—piety, purity, submissiveness and domesticity. Put them all together and they spelled mother, daughter, sister, wife—woman." Hazel V. Carby, *Reconstructing Womanhood: The Emergence of the Afro-American Woman Novelist* (New York: Oxford UP, 1987) 23; Barbara Welter, "The Cult of True Womanhood: 1820-1860," *Locating American Studies: The Evolution of a Discipline*, ed. Lucy Maddox (Baltimore: John Hopkins UP, 1999) 43-44.

crime as a powerful act of defiance against the white oppressive system:[93] "He had murdered and had created a new life for himself. It was something that was all his own, and it was the first time in his life he had had anything that others could not take from him."[94] Even though it ultimately leads to his death sentence, the killing of Mary is constructed as an essential element of Bigger's attempt to (re)gain a sense of self-worth and self-control in a white racist environment. Likewise, in *The Book of Night Women*, Lilith's killing of her slave master Roget is presented as another turning point in the slave woman's life: For Lilith, at least in this part of the novel, "violence is a cleansing force,"[95] to use Fanon's words, a tool to overcome fear and to re-establish her self-esteem.

However, both Wright and James also foreground the utterly disruptive nature of their black protagonists' violent actions: In *Native Son*, Wright emphasizes that, after the killing of Mary, the novel's anti-hero is still overwhelmed and controlled by exclusively negative feelings such as fear and hate. While Bigger's crime against his white employer's daughter has offered him a sense of inner freedom, he is unable to act as a morally responsible being and to recognize and acknowledge the link between individual freedom, on the one hand, and social responsibility and human solidarity, on the other.[96] Addressing the complex subject of intra-black violence, the scene in which Wright's protagonist brutally murders Bessie[97] sheds light on the specific vulnerability of black females in early twenty-century America and Bigger's dehumanizing treatment of women. Equally important, it demonstrates that, as Robert Butler puts it, "Bigger's killing of Mary was not a conversion experience [...] but simply brought to a culmination the pathological tendencies of Bigger's old life."[98] Instead of uncritically glorifying the black man's violent rebellion, *Native Son* ultimately stresses the destructiveness of Bigger's acts in order to focus the

---

93 | See also Markus Nehl, "Richard Wright, *Native Son* (1940)," *The American Novel of the Twentieth and Twenty-First Centuries*, ed. Timo Müller (Berlin: De Gruyter, forthcoming).
94 | Richard Wright, *Native Son*, The Restored Text Established by the Library of America (1940; New York: Harper Perennial, 2005) 105.
95 | Fanon, *The Wretched of the Earth* 94.
96 | Maria I. Diedrich, *Kommunismus im afroamerikanischen Roman: Das Verhältnis afroamerikanischer Schriftsteller zur Kommunistischen Partei der USA zwischen den Weltkriegen* (Stuttgart: Metzler, 1979) 238.
97 | For a critical discussion of Wright's representation of Bessie and the voyeuristic depiction of Bessie's rape, see, for instance, Alan W. France, "Misogyny and Appropriation in Wright's *Native Son*," *Modern Fiction Studies* 34.3 (1988): 413-23; Nehl, "Richard Wright, *Native Son* (1940)."
98 | Robert Butler, *Native Son: The Emergence of a New Black Hero* (Boston: Twayne Publishers, 1991) 46.

reader's attention to violence, deprivation, hopelessness and fear as defining features of black American life in the 1930s.[99]

Entering into a dynamic intertextual discussion with *Native Son*, *The Book of Night Women* powerfully highlights the destructive power of Lilith's vengeful struggle: Like her (in)famous namesake in Jewish mythology, Lilith becomes a child murderer. Equipped with a strong will to survive, she fights against and eventually kills her mistress and, then, decides to set fire to the house with the sleeping children in it. When some of her fellow slaves are accused of the crime, put into prison and stoned by a furious white mob, Lilith does not intervene, primarily because she wants to save her life.

Slavery, *The Book of Night Women* insists, creates abominable conditions of anti-blackness that can lead to morally unacceptable actions on the part of the dispossessed and exploited, blurring, at least on the surface, the allegedly clear-cut distinction between black victim and white perpetrator. However, the novel never allows the reader to forget the one source of these perversions, i.e., chattel slavery and anti-blackness. In a way similar to Wright, James traces his protagonist's development into a murderer, seeking to foreground the centrality of violence to black life and to explore the reasons for violence, tensions and conflicts within the black community: James's novel stresses that many slaves "adapt to the overwhelming cruelty and humiliation of their circumstances in order to survive, often by engaging in behavior that may be deemed reprehensible by outsiders,"[100] to use Caille Millner's words.

Like other contemporary authors of neo-slave narratives,[101] James offers a reflection on the inherent contradictions of violent resistance, emphasizing the impossibility to eradicate violence by using more violence. He invents a protagonist who is haunted by traumatic memories after killing her master, her mistress and their children; a crucial difference, the novel insinuates, to Jamai-

---

99 | See also Butler 46; Diedrich, "Afro-Amerikanische Literatur" 436; Diedrich, *Kommunismus* 222; Nehl, "Richard Wright, *Native Son* (1940)."

100 | Caille Millner, "A Twenty-Year-Old Slave Named Frederick Bailey Slips Away From His Master in Maryland and Makes His Way to the Free State of New York: The Slave Narrative," *A New Literary History of America*, eds. Greil Marcus and Werner Sollors (Cambridge, MA: Harvard UP, 2009) 251.

101 | As Arlene R. Keizer argues in her 2004 study *Black Subjects: Identity Formation in the Contemporary Narrative of Slavery*, "the contemporary narrative of slavery demonstrates how fraught with difficulty resistance is and has been. In fact, one of the signal characteristics of these works is their problematization of resistance. These texts never question the need to struggle against a system that has consistently subjugated people of African descent, but the means through which such resistance can be carried out are closely examined and the contradictions inherent in certain modes of resistance are evaluated." Keizer 9.

ca's white slaveholders who humiliate and murder their slaves without being left with a sense of guilt. In a heated discussion with the slave leader Homer, Lilith vehemently criticizes the night women's plan to start a slave rebellion: "Me get my blood and see me here," Lilith says. "Nothing different. Nothing better. Revenge don't leave me nothing but them burning skin smell that me can't blow out of me nose nor wash out" (BoN 349). Again, in this phase of the novel, Lilith is depicted as a complex, self-critical but also self-confident (anti-) heroine, refusing to fulfil the night women's expectations of unquestioning black female cooperation.

Significantly, while *Native Son* and *The Book of Night Women* focus on different historical locations, they participate in a transnational, cross-generational discussion about the meaning of black (counter-)violence in an anti-black world and, eventually, move beyond an uncritical celebration of the liberating impact of violence for the oppressed. In this regard, on a meta-level, James's novel also challenges reductive interpretations of *The Wretched of the Earth* that exclusively center on Fanon's conceptualization of violence as "a cleansing force:"[102] Noteworthy, as Elizabeth Frazer and Kimberly Hutchings point out in their 2008 essay "On Politics and Violence: Arendt contra Fanon," Fanon's work not only explores "the productive use of violence as a political instrument, providing the momentum motivating the colonized to do what is necessary to overthrow the oppressor, and thereby cleanse both themselves and their world of violence."[103] In the last chapter of *The Wretched of the Earth*, "which deals with mental disorders on both sides of the Algerian war, the idea that using violence may be a way to escape being in violence is countered by case after case in which people remain trapped in the violence they have inflicted and suffered."[104]

Crucially, Lilith's decision not to participate in the slave uprising is strongly influenced by her highly ambivalent experience of having a sexual affair with Robert Quinn, a white immigrant from Ireland. Given Quinn's position as a slave overseer, their relationship cannot be described as consensual. And yet, as Sam Vásquez puts it, James shows how Lilith intentionally "uses her sexual prison to secure a measure of mental and physical freedom, enjoying the material luxuries of the overseer's home—creating a fantasy, albeit a disturbing facsimile of domestic bliss, and protecting herself from other men's sexual assaults."[105] Focusing on the complexity of inter-racial relationships during slav-

---

102 | Fanon, *The Wretched of the Earth* 94.
103 | Elizabeth Frazer and Kimberly Hutchings, "On Politics and Violence: Arendt contra Fanon," *Contemporary Political Theory* 7 (2008): 98.
104 | Ibid.
105 | Sam Vásquez, "Violent Liaisons: Historical Crossings and the Negotiation of Sex, Sexuality, and Race in *The Book of Night Women* and *The True History of Paradise*," *small axe* 16.2 (2012): 51.

ery, James refuses to offer a romantic and idealized view of Lilith's and Quinn's relationship: Even though they begin to forge an emotional bond, ultimately, the novel's female protagonist and the Irish immigrant remain trapped in their roles of slave and overseer. In fact, Lilith's scars are a constant reminder of the white man's cruelties she has been exposed to: "She lie on top of him and let Quinn wrap him arm round her back. But then him skin touch her scars and they both realise what they touching" (BoN 275-76). According to Vásquez, this passage draws attention to "the vicious cycle that sex and violence represent in Lilith's life."[106] As Vásquez goes on to argue, "the physical evidence of the overseer's violence toward her mitigates against any permanent intimacy between these symbolic figures and resituates them as 'slave and master.'"[107]

Unlike Lawrence Hill's *The Book of Negroes*, whose last chapter focuses on Aminata's triumph over slavery and her happy reunion with her daughter May, *The Book of Night Women* charts the failure of black rebellions to challenge existing racist power structures: The night women's revolt is not successful but ends in a bloody massacre, in serious losses on both sides. Lilith's act of charity—she saves her father, the white overseer Jack Wilkins, from being killed by the night women—does not serve to overcome the nihilistic tendencies inherent in James's novel.

The circle of violence, hate and hopeless misery, *The Book of Night Women* insists, cannot be broken; it is passed down from one generation to the next: "But sometimes when a negro die and another negro take him place, even if that negro not be blood, they still fall in step with the same circle. The same circle of living that no nigger can choose and dying that come at any time" (BoN 421). Significantly, this scene highlights one of the novel's central concerns, drawing our attention to the tragic connection between the past of slavery in Jamaica and contemporary forms of anti-blackness, "the link between our age and a previous one in which freedom too was yet to be realized" (LYM 133), to use Hartman's words from *Lose Your Mother*. In this respect, *The Book of Night Women* enters into a fruitful dialogue with Morrison's, Hartman's and Christiansë's neo-slave narratives and Afro-pessimist discourse.

Conclusion

In *The Book of Night Women*, James offers an unsparing account of the slaves' experience of being trapped in a vicious circle of violence, highlighting the utterly destructive nature of slavery as "thingification" as well as the institution's lasting impact on further black generations. Reflecting on the legitimacy and

---

106 | Ibid.
107 | Ibid.

transformative power of violence in the struggle for recognition and freedom, *The Book of Night Women* stands in an intertextual relation to black male literary and theoretical texts, such as Douglass's *Narrative,* Wright's *Native Son* and Fanon's *The Wretched of the Earth.* Emphasizing the impossibility to eradicate violence by using more violence, James's goal is not to justify his slave characters' acts of revenge but to explore the miserable conditions of anti-blackness that trigger their brutal actions. In a way similar to *Native Son* and *The Wretched of the Earth, The Book of Night Women* ultimately moves beyond a reductive celebration of the liberating power of counter-violence and highlights the destructive nature of violent acts.

In several newspaper articles and critical discussions, James's work has been compared to that of Toni Morrison. In his 2009 review for *Time Out Magazine,* Anderson Tepper, for instance, argues that "James has given us an epic novel of late-18th-century West Indian slavery, complete with all its carnage and brutishness, but one that, like a Toni Morrison novel, whispers rather than shouts its horrors."[108] Obviously, Tepper ignores the fact that *The Book of Night Women* presents the horrific violence of slavery in a highly detailed, unsparing and ultimately pornographic manner; he fails to take into account the fundamental differences in Morrison's and James's aesthetic and ethical choices.

Arguably, James's approach to writing slavery is characterized by inconsistencies and contradictions: While James strategically adopts a female perspective and appropriates a black woman's voice, his conceptualization and representation of (female) counter-violence is profoundly influenced by, if not exclusively based on, black male writing traditions. By inventing a female protagonist, James tries to capitalize on the commercial success of female-authored neo-slave narratives and, equally important, to legitimize his narrative strategy of focusing on acts of sexual abuse against women. However, and this is a crucial point, James fails to acknowledge and include the epistemological insights of (black) feminist scholars such as McDowell, Davis, Hartman, Spillers and Alcoff, who have offered thoughtful reflections on "the ethics of historical representation,"[109] the concept of "pornotroping" and the dangers of speaking for, and about, the (gendered) "other." By depicting abominable acts of violence against black human "flesh" in an explicit way, without self-reflexively commenting on the risks of rendering scenes of black female degradation, torture and sexual abuse, *The Book of Night Women* ultimately exposes the enslaved to what Hartman would describe as "a second order of violence."[110]

---

108 | Anderson Tepper, "The Book of Night Women," *Time Out* 25 Feb. 2009, 4 June 2015 http://www.timeout.com/newyork/books/the-book-of-night-women.
109 | Hartman, "Venus in Two Acts" 5.
110 | Ibid.

Epilogue: The Past of Slavery and "the Incomplete Project of Freedom"

In his novella *Every Day Is for the Thief* (2014), which was first published in a different version in Nigeria in 2007, Teju Cole tells the story of a young Nigerian American psychiatrist who leaves New York City to visit his country of birth—for the first time after more than a decade. In a way similar as in his novel *Open City*, Cole adopts the perspective of an urban *flâneur*, a black intellectual who walks through the streets of Lagos. Focusing on the omnipresence of corruption, poverty and violence in present-day Nigeria as well as on the nation's role in the transatlantic slave trade, Cole's unnamed narrator explores the painful connection between the history of Lagos and that of New Orleans:

> The thought is of the chain of corpses stretching across the Atlantic Ocean to connect Lagos with New Orleans. New Orleans was the largest market for human chattel in the New World. There were twenty-five different slave markets in the city in 1850. This is a secret only because no one wants to know about it. [...] The human cargo that ended up in New Orleans originated from many ports, most of them along the West African shore. And here was another secret: none of those ports was busier than Lagos.[1]

In addition to highlighting the historical transnational links between these two cities as sites of the slave trade, Cole's narrator draws attention to disturbing similarities between contemporary Nigerian and (white) American public discourses of remembrance: On both sides of the Atlantic, the history of the slave trade and slavery has been deliberately suppressed or erased from mainstream public memory. Avoiding questions of historical responsibility and guilt, many Nigerians and white Americans try to present a sanitized version of the past, to ignore or downplay the significance of slavery in the history of their countries. Significantly, both *Open City* and *Every Day Is for the Thief* not only explore the meaning of collective acts of "forgetting;" they also reflect on the enduring ef-

---

1 | Teju Cole, *Every Day Is for the Thief* (2014; London: Faber & Faber, 2015) 112.

fects of the slave trade and slavery on contemporary black life. As Cole's narrator in *Every Day Is for the Thief* remarks, quoting William Faulkner: "'The past is never dead. It's not even past.'"[2]

This complex view of the past as unfinished is reflected in the works of Toni Morrison, Saidiya Hartman, Yvette Christiansë and Marlon James: Rather than constructing their texts as narratives of reconciliation and healing, these authors focus on the enduring impact of slavery, examining the ways in which this past still haunts the present. According to a 2010 article in the *Chicago Tribune*, before the publication of *A Mercy*, Morrison had been asked by her editor to change the ending of her novel, i.e., to construct a reconciliatory narrative that closes with the description of Florens's reunion with her mother. "I thought about it," Morrison said, "But then I decided against it because slavery cuts through families. That is what it does, and it is unapologetic and there are no answers for those it affects."[3] Instead of satisfying a reader's desire for a "happy ending" and narrative closure, Morrison vigorously challenges the idea of narration as healing in *A Mercy*. A radical black feminist reflection on the origins of systemic anti-black racism in the United States, her novel self-reflexively elaborates on the impossibility of transforming Florens's story of uprootedness and despair into a narrative of overcoming. Engaging in an Afro-pessimistic re-writing of black history, Morrison presents, as Diedrich puts it, "a discourse on enslavement so fiercely embracing its momentum of negativity that any attempt of escaping into redemption kitsch reception goes up in flames with Florence's writing on the walls."[4] Drawing attention to the persistent and destructive effects of chattel slavery as "thingification," Morrison refuses to conceptualize and celebrate her slave protagonist's creative work in Jacob's house as a triumphant act that could help her cope with her separation from her mother. Focusing on Florens's painful and enduring experiences of loss and fragmentation, *A Mercy* "does not attempt any consoling, recuperative gesture,"[5] to use Christiansë's words.

In *Lose Your Mother* and her insightful essay "Venus in Two Acts," Hartman explicitly reflects on the significance of the past for (understanding) the present, drawing attention to "the link between our age and a previous one in which freedom too was yet to be realized" (LYM 133). In a way similar to Morrison,

---

2 | Ibid. 114. This famous quotation is taken from William Faulkner, *Requiem For a Nun* (1951; London: Vintage, 2015) 85.
3 | Courtney Crowder, "Toni Morrison Discusses Racism and 'A Mercy' during Keynote Speech," *Chicago Tribune* 20 Oct. 2010, 21 Sept. 2015 http://articles.chicagotribune.com/2010-10-20/entertainment/chi-books-morrison-keynote_1_toni-morrison-racism-speech.
4 | Diedrich, "'The Burden of Our Theories' Genealogies'" 269.
5 | Christiansë, *Toni Morrison* 198.

she offers a sophisticated meditation on the ethics of writing and theorizing slavery, arguing against "kitsch" conceptions of fiction based on healing and redemption: "For me," Hartman explains, "narrating counter-histories of slavery has always been inseparable from writing a history of present, by which I mean the incomplete project of freedom, and the precarious life of the ex-slave, a condition defined by the vulnerability to premature death and to gratuitous acts of violence."[6] In her critical (re-)appropriation and radical re-writing of the archive of slavery in "The Dead Book," she resists the temptation to "fill in the gaps and to provide closure where there is none."[7] Her multi-perspective and fragmentary account of the Middle Passage self-reflexively comments on the ultimate impossibility of recovering the voice of the female captive who was murdered on board the *Recovery*. Reading slavery as "thingification" and exploring the destructive nature of anti-black racism in the past and in the present, Hartman refuses to construct the slave woman's story as a triumphant narrative, to provide the reader with a consoling vision of the past.

Christiansë's 2006 novel about Cape slavery cannot be read without taking into account its complex engagement with Morrison's literary and theoretical work. In terms of content and form, *Unconfessed* participates in an intertextual discussion with *Beloved*. Even more significantly, like Morrison's *A Mercy* and Hartman's *Lose Your Mother*, it offers a radical response to reductive reconciliatory interpretations of Morrison's 1987 masterpiece as it deconstructs the naïve idea of the healing power of neo-slave narratives. While Christiansë successfully challenges the racist representation of Sila van den Kaap in the historical record, she employs a fragmentary style and non-chronological structure to reflect on the ethical dangers of depicting the slave woman's experiences of sexual violence and on the ultimate impossibility of recovering her story. "In Sila's case," Christiansë contends, "there can only be the incomplete disappearance that being consigned to the archive ensures. What is dis-appearing then? [...] A boy, dead. A woman consigned to death. A history of living death. The archive is haunted by them all."[8] Drawing attention to South Africa's long history of racial violence, Christiansë presents a powerful black feminist/Afro-pessimist discourse on the hardships of slave motherhood, the crushing power of slavery as "thingification" and the enduring effects of loss.

Unlike Morrison, Hartman and Christiansë, Hill constructs his neo-slave narrative as an ultimately redemptive narrative about the healing power of familial love and a slave mother's triumph over slavery. Whereas Morrison foregrounds the enduring traumatic effects of the destruction of slave families, Hill strategically incorporates melodramatic plot episodes and "fairy-tale" el-

---

6 | Hartman, "Venus in Two Acts" 4.
7 | Ibid. 8.
8 | Christiansë, "'Heartsore': The Melancholy Archive of Cape Colony Slavery" 12.

ements into *The Book of Negroes* (most notably, May's hart-warming reunion with Aminata in London) to celebrate black agency and resistance. One of his primary narrative goals is to present a story that not only bears witness to the incredible cruelty of slavery but also, and paradoxically, offers a consoling view of this history. Taking "recourse to the language of romance,"[9] to employ Hartman's phrase from "Venus in Two Acts," Hill trivializes the painful reality of slave women's experiences in the eighteenth-century transatlantic world. Moreover, he fails to express the true meaning of chattel slavery as a brutalizing system of "thingification." Unlike *A Mercy*, *The Book of Negroes* emphasizes the liberating effects of the slave protagonist's act of writing, without critically engaging with questions about the ethics of narration and about the appropriation of a black female voice. Problematically, Aminata's first-person account suggests that it is possible to work through the past in order to find closure to the trauma of slavery.

In *The Book of Night Women*, James employs the trope of the circle to highlight the utterly dehumanizing and brutal nature of white rule in late eighteenth-century Jamaica, focusing on forms of never-ending violence and the constitutive role of loss in the lives of enslaved women and men. Like Morrison's *A Mercy*, Hartman's *Lose Your Mother* and Christiansë's *Unconfessed*, James's second-generation neo-slave narrative refuses to offer a reconciliatory interpretation of the past. Rather, it enters into an intertextual dialogue with Afro-pessimism about slavery's lasting effects on later generations of blacks. In a way similar to Wright in *Native Son* and Fanon in *The Wretched of the Earth*, James explores the meaning of (counter-)violence for the oppressed, ultimately stressing the destructiveness of his female slave protagonist's acts of violent resistance and revenge in order to draw attention to the captives' hopeless situation. In a self-legitimizing move, James strategically employs a black female protagonist to justify his explicit rendering of scenes of violence against black human "flesh." However, unlike Morrison, Hartman and Christiansë, he fails to take into account the insights of black feminist theory concerning the ethics of representation, thus exposing the enslaved to a second act of victimization[10]—and, like Hill, he never reflects on his use of the female voice/perspective.

Taken together, *A Mercy*, *Lose Your Mother*, *Unconfessed*, *The Book of Negroes* and *The Book of Night Women* engage in a transnational literary re-negotiation of slavery from twenty-first-century perspectives, highlighting the intricate relationship between local and global structures of racial oppression and anti-blackness. Morrison, Hartman, Christiansë and James—unlike Hill—strongly argue against a teleological conception of history as progress

---

9 | Hartman, "Venus in Two Acts" 6.
10 | See ibid. 5.

and powerfully challenge "kitsch" interpretations of slavery. Focusing on loss, dispossession and grief as defining features of the African diaspora in the past and in the present, they not only counter the erasure of slavery from mainstream public memory (in countries such as Ghana, the United States, Canada, Jamaica and South Africa) but also, and essentially, reflect on the enduring effects of slavery on later black generations and "the as-yet-incomplete project of freedom,"[11] as Hartman puts it.

---

11 | Ibid. 14.

Works Cited

PRIMARY SOURCES

Angelou, Maya. *All God's Children Need Travelling Shoes*. 1986. London: Virago, 2012.
Baldwin, James. *Nobody Knows My Name: More Notes of a Native Son*. 1961. New York: Vintage International, 1993.
Christiansë, Yvette. *Unconfessed: A Novel*. New York: Other Press, 2006.
Cole, Teju. *Every Day Is for the Thief*. 2014. London: Faber & Faber, 2015.
---. *Open City*. London: Faber & Faber, 2011.
Douglass, Frederick. *Narrative of the Life of Frederick Douglass, an American Slave*. 1845. *The Classic Slave Narratives*. Ed. Henry Louis Gates, Jr. New York: Signet Classics, 2002. 323-436.
Faulkner, William. *Requiem For a Nun*. 1951. London: Vintage, 2015.
Hartman, Saidiya. *Lose Your Mother: A Journey along the Atlantic Slave Route*. New York: Farrar, Straus and Giroux, 2007.
Hill, Lawrence. *Someone Knows My Name*. New York: Norton, 2007.
Jacobs, Harriet. *Incidents in the Life of a Slave Girl*. 1861. *The Classic Slave Narratives*. Ed. Henry Louis Gates, Jr. New York: Signet Classics, 2002. 437-667.
James, Marlon. *The Book of Night Women*. New York: Riverhead Books, 2009.
Morrison, Toni. *Beloved*. 1987. London: Vintage, 2007.
---. *A Mercy: A Novel*. New York: Random House Large Print, 2008.
Stowe, Harriet Beecher. *Uncle Tom's Cabin*. 1852. Ed. Elizabeth Ammons. 2nd ed. New York: Norton, 2010.
Wright, Richard. *Native Son*. The Restored Text Established by the Library of America. 1940. New York: Harper Perennial, 2005.

SECONDARY LITERATURE

Alcoff, Linda. "The Problem of Speaking for Others." *Cultural Critique* 20 (1991-1992): 5-32.

Alexander, Michelle. *The New Jim Crow: Mass Incarceration in the Age of Colorblindness*. Rev. ed. 2010. New York: The New Press, 2012.

Appadurai, Arjun. *Modernity at Large: Cultural Dimensions of Globalization*. Minneapolis: U of Minnesota P, 1996.

Ashenburg, Katherine. "Seeing Black." *Toronto Life* Dec. 2009. 21. Jan 2015 http://lawrencehill.com/LawrenceHill.pdf. 62-70.

Babb, Valerie. "E Pluribus Unum? The American Origins Narrative in Toni Morrison's *A Mercy*." *MELUS* 36.2 (2011): 147-64.

Baderoon, Gabeba. "'This is Our Speech:' Voice, Body and Poetic Form in Recent South African Writing." *Social Dynamics* 37.2 (2011): 213-27.

Bailey, Katie. "The Book of Negroes Debuts to 1.7M Viewers." *Playback* 8 Jan. 2015. 23 July 2015 http://playbackonline.ca/2015/01/08/book-of-negroes-debuts-to-1-7m-viewers/.

Bak, Hans. "Flights to Canada: Jacob Lawrence, Ishmael Reed, and Lawrence Hill." *Cultural Circulation: Dialogues between Canada and the American South*. Eds. Waldemar Zacharasiewicz and Christoph Irmscher. Wien: Verlag der Österreichischen Akademie der Wissenschaften, 2013. 135-53.

Banerjee, Mita. *Ethnic Ventriloquism: Literary Minstrelsy in Nineteenth-Century American Literature*. Heidelberg: Winter, 2008.

Baumann, Martin. "Diaspora: Genealogies of Semantics and Transcultural Comparison." *Numen* 47.3 (2000): 313-37.

Beaulieu, Elizabeth Ann. *Black Women Writers and the American Neo-Slave Narrative: Femininity Unfettered*. Westport: Greenwood Press, 1999.

Bell, Bernard W. *The Afro-American Novel and Its Tradition*. Amherst: U of Massachusetts P, 1987.

Bennett, Eric. "Alexander Palmer (Alex) Haley, 1921-1992." *Africana: The Encyclopedia of the African and African American Experience*. Vol. 3. Eds. Kwame Anthony Appiah and Henry Louis Gates, Jr. 2nd ed. Oxford: Oxford UP, 2005. 130-31.

Bennett, Lerone, Jr. *The Shaping of Black America: The Struggles and Triumphs of African-Americans, 1619 to the 1990s*. New York: Penguin Books, 1975.

Berlin, Ira. *Generations of Captivity: A History of African-American Slaves*. 2003. Cambridge, MA: Harvard UP, 2004.

---. *The Making of African America: The Four Great Migrations*. New York: Penguin, 2010.

Besson, Jean. "Missionaries, Planters, and Slaves in the Age of Abolition." *The Caribbean: A History of the Region and Its Peoples*. Eds. Stephan Palmié and Francisco A. Scarano. Chicago: U of Chicago P, 2011. 317-29.

Bhabha, Homi K. *The Location of Culture*. London: Routledge, 1994.

Bishop, Ted. "Introduction." *Dear Sir, I Intend to Burn Your Book: An Anatomy of a Book Burning*. By Lawrence Hill. Edmonton: U of Alberta P, 2013. xiii-xviii.

Brah, Avtar. *Cartographies of Diaspora: Contesting Identities*. London: Routledge, 1996.
Broeck, Sabine. "Enslavement as Regime of Western Modernity: Re-reading Gender Studies Epistemology Through Black Feminist Critique." 2008. *Sabine Broeck: Plotting Against Modernity; Critical Interventions in Race and Gender*. Eds. Karin Esders, Insa Härtel and Carsten Junker. Sulzbach: Helmer, 2014. 34-51.
---. "Trauma, Agency, Kitsch and the Excesses of the Real: *Beloved* within the Field of Critical Response." 2006. *Sabine Broeck: Plotting Against Modernity; Critical Interventions in Race and Gender*. Eds. Karin Esders, Insa Härtel and Carsten Junker. Sulzbach: Helmer, 2014. 239-57.
---. *White Amnesia - Black Memory? American Women's Writing and History*. Frankfurt a.M.: Peter Lang, 1999.
Brown, Christopher L. "John Murray, Fourth Earl of Dunmore (1730-1809)." *Slavery in the United States: A Social, Political, and Historical Encyclopedia*. Ed. Junius P. Rodriguez. Vol. 1. Santa Barbara, CA: ABC-CLIO, 2007. 269-70.
Brown, Jacqueline Nassy. "Black Liverpool, Black America, and the Gendering of Diasporic Space." *Cultural Anthropology* 13.3 (1998): 291-325.
---. *Dropping Anchor, Setting Sail: Geographies of Race in Black Liverpool*. Princeton: Princeton UP, 2005.
Brown, Kathleen M. "Bacon's Rebellion." *The Oxford Encyclopedia of American Social History*. Ed. Lynn Dumenil. Vol. 1. Oxford: Oxford UP, 2012. 99-100.
---. "'Strength of the Lion ... Arms Like Polished Iron': Embodying Black Masculinity in an Age of Slavery and Propertied Manhood." *New Men: Manliness in Early America*. Ed. Thomas A. Foster. New York: New York UP, 2011. 172-92.
Brown, Vincent. *The Reaper's Garden: Death and Power in the World of Atlantic Slavery*. Cambridge, MA: Harvard UP, 2008.
---. "Social Death and Political Life in the Study of Slavery." *American Historical Review* 114.5 (2009): 1231-249.
Brubaker, Rogers. "The 'Diaspora' Diaspora." *Ethnic and Racial Studies* 28.1 (2005): 1-19.
Bruce, Dickson D., Jr. "Politics in the Slave Narrative." *The Cambridge Companion to the African American Slave Narrative*. Ed. Audrey A. Fisch. Cambridge: Cambridge UP, 2007. 28-43.
Bruner, Edward M. "Tourism in Ghana: The Representation of Slavery and the Return of the Black Diaspora." *American Anthropologist* 98.2 (1996): 290-304.
Bunch, Lonnie. "The Director of the African-American History and Culture Museum on What Makes '12 Years a Slave' a Powerful Film." *The Smithsonian.com* 5 Nov. 2013. 26 July 2015 http://www.smithsonianmag.com/

ist/?next=/smithsonian-institution/the-director-of-the-african-american-history-and-culture-museum-on-what-makes-12-years-a-slave-a-powerful-film-180947568/.

Burnard, Trevor. "European Migration to Jamaica: 1655-1780." *William and Mary Quarterly* 53.4 (1996): 769-96.

---. *Mastery, Tyranny, and Desire: Thomas Thistlewood and His Slaves in the Anglo-Jamaican World*. Chapel Hill: U of North Carolina P, 2004.

Bush, Barbara. "African Caribbean Slave Mothers and Children: Traumas of Dislocation and Enslavement across the Atlantic World." *Caribbean Quarterly* 56.1/2 (2010): 69-94.

---. *Slave Women in Caribbean Society: 1650-1838*. Bloomington: Indiana UP, 1990.

Butler, Robert. *Native Son: The Emergence of a New Black Hero*. Boston: Twayne Publishers, 1991.

Campbell, Gwyn. "Slavery and Other Forms of Unfree Labour in the Indian Ocean World." *The Structure of Slavery in Indian Ocean Africa and Asia*. Ed. Campbell. London: Frank Cass, 2004. vii-xxxii.

Campt, Tina M., and Deborah A. Thomas. "Diasporic Hegemonies: Slavery, Memory, and Genealogies of Diaspora: Dialogue Participants: Jacqueline Nassy Brown and Bayo Holsey." *Transforming Anthropology* 14.2 (2006): 163-72.

Campt, Tina M., and Saidiya Hartman. "A Future Beyond Empire: An Introduction." *Small Axe* 13.1 (2009): 19-26.

Campt, Tina M., and Deborah A. Thomas. "Gendering Diaspora: Transnational Feminism, Diaspora and Its Hegemonies." *Feminist Review* 90 (2008): 1-8.

Campt, Tina M. *Image Matters: Archive, Photography, and the African Diaspora in Europe*. Durham: Duke UP, 2012.

---. "Imagining Ourselves: What Does It Mean to Be Part of the African Diaspora?" Interview by Jean-Philippe Dedieu. *Think Africa Press* 21 Nov. 2013. 29 Jan. 2014 http://thinkafricapress.com/society/imagining-ourselves-interview-tina-campt-diaspora-photograph.

---. *Other Germans: Black Germans and the Politics of Race, Gender, and Memory in the Third Reich*. Ann Arbor: U of Michigan P, 2004.

Carby, Hazel V. *Reconstructing Womanhood: The Emergence of the Afro-American Woman Novelist*. New York: Oxford UP, 1987.

Carpio, Glenda R. *Laughing Fit to Kill: Black Humor in the Fictions of Slavery*. New York: Oxford UP, 2008.

Césaire, Aimé. *Discourse on Colonialism*. Trans. Joan Pinkham. 1955. New York: Monthly Review Press, 2000.

Chaney, Michael A. *Fugitive Vision: Slave Image and Black Identity in Antebellum Narrative*. Bloomington: Indiana UP, 2008.

Chivallon, Christine. "Beyond Gilroy's Black Atlantic: The Experience of the African Diaspora." Trans. Karen E. Fields. *Diaspora: A Journal of Transnational Studies* 11.3 (2002): 359-82.
Christiansë, Yvette. "Author's Note." *Unconfessed: A Novel*. New York: Other Press, 2006. 349-50.
---. "A Conversation with Yvette Christiansë." *Unconfessed: A Novel*. New York: Other Press, 2006. 351-53.
---. "A Freedom Stolen." *Dialogues Across Diasporas: Women Writers, Scholars, and Activists of Africana and Latina Descent in Conversation*. Eds. Marion Rohrleitner and Sarah E. Ryan. Lanham, MD: Lexington Books, 2013. 101-13.
---. "Glossary." *Unconfessed: A Novel*. New York: Other Press, 2006. 343-47.
---. "'Heartsore': The Melancholy Archive of Cape Colony Slavery." *S&F Online* 7.2 (2009): 1-12.
---. *Toni Morrison: An Ethical Poetics*. New York: Fordham UP, 2013.
Churchwell, Sarah. "Bought and Sold." *Guardian* 24 Jan. 2009. 21 Jan. 2015 http://www.guardian.co.uk/books/2009/jan/24/lawrence-hill-book-ofnegroes.
Clarke, George Elliott. "White Like Canada." *Transition* 73 (1997): 98-109.
Clarke, Kamari Maxine. "Mapping Transnationality: Roots Tourism and the Institutionalization of Ethnic Heritage." *Globalization and Race: Transformations in the Cultural Production of Blackness*. Eds. Kamari Maxine Clarke and Deborah A. Thomas. Durham: Duke UP, 2006. 133-53.
Clifford, James. "Diasporas." *Cultural Anthropology* 9.3 (1994): 302-38.
Cohen, Robin. *Global Diasporas: An Introduction*. 2nd ed. New York: Routledge, 2008.
Cossmann, Brenda. "Pornography." *Encyclopedia of Feminist Theories*. Ed. Lorraine Code. London: Routledge, 2000. 393-94.
Craton, Michael. *Testing the Chains: Resistance to Slavery in the British West Indies*. Ithaca, NY: Cornell UP, 1982.
Crowder, Courtney. "Toni Morrison Discusses Racism and 'A Mercy' during Keynote Speech." *Chicago Tribune* 20 Oct. 2010. 21 Sept. 2015 http://articles.chicagotribune.com/2010-10-20/entertainment/chi-books-morrison-keynote_1_toni-morrison-racism-speech.
Curtis, Isaac. "Masterless People: Maroons, Pirates, and Commoners." *The Caribbean: A History of the Region and Its Peoples*. Eds. Stephan Palmié and Francisco A. Scarano. Chicago: U of Chicago P, 2011. 149-62.
Davey, Monica, and Julie Bosmannov. "Protests Flare After Ferguson Police Officer Is Not Indicted." *New York Times* 24 Nov. 2014. 26 July 2015 http://www.nytimes.com/2014/11/25/us/ferguson-darren-wilson-shooting-michael-brown-grand-jury.html.
Davis, Angela. *Women, Race, and Class*. New York: Random House, 1981.

---, ed. *Narrative of the Life of Frederick Douglass, an American Slave.* By Frederick Douglass. 1845. San Francisco: City Lights, 2010.
Deacon, Harriet. "Remembering Tragedy, Constructing Modernity: Robben Island as a National Monument." *Negotiating the Past: The Making of Memory in South Africa.* Eds. Sarah Nuttall and Carli Coetzee. 2nd ed. Oxford: Oxford UP, 1999. 161-79.
Dennis, Geoffrey W. *The Encyclopedia of Jewish Myth, Magic and Mysticism.* Woodbury, MN: Llewellyn Publications, 2007.
Diedrich, Maria I. "Afro-amerikanische Literatur." *Amerikanische Literaturgeschichte.* Ed. Hubert Zapf. 3rd ed. Stuttgart: Metzler, 2010. 421-47.
---. "'As if Freedom Were a City Waiting for Them in the Distance:' The American Revolution and the Black Hessian Subject." *Transnational American Studies.* Ed. Udo J. Hebel. Heidelberg: Winter, 2012. 97-122.
---. *Ausbruch aus der Knechtschaft: Das Amerikanische Slave Narrative zwischen Unabhängigkeitserklärung und Bürgerkrieg.* Stuttgart: Franz Steiner, 1986.
---. "'The Burden of Our Theories' Genealogies:' Lessons in Decolonization of Gender." *Sabine Broeck: Plotting Against Modernity; Critical Interventions in Race and Gender.* Eds. Karin Esders, Insa Härtel and Carsten Junker. Sulzbach: Helmer, 2014. 266-70.
---. "From American Slaves to Hessian Subjects: Silenced Black Narratives of the American Revolution." *Germany and the Black Diaspora: Points of Contact, 1250-1914.* Eds. Mischa Honeck, Martin Klimke and Anne Kuhlmann. New York: Berghahn Books, 2013. 92-111.
Diedrich, Maria I., and Werner Sollors. "Introduction." *The Black Columbiad: Defining Moments in African American Literature and Culture.* Eds. Diedrich and Sollors. Cambridge, MA: Harvard UP, 1994. 1-8.
Diedrich, Maria I. *Kommunismus im afroamerikanischen Roman: Das Verhältnis afroamerikanischer Schriftsteller zur Kommunistischen Partei der USA zwischen den Weltkriegen.* Stuttgart: Metzler, 1979.
---. "'Things Fall Apart?' The Black Critical Controversy Over Toni Morrison's *Beloved.*" *Amerikastudien/American Studies* 34.2 (1989): 175-86.
Diouf, Sylviane A. "Introduction." *Fighting the Slave Trade: West African Strategies.* Athens: Ohio UP, 2003. ix-xxvii.
Dooling, Wayne. "'The Good Opinions of Others': Law, Slavery & Community in the Cape Colony, c.1760-1830." *Breaking the Chains: Slavery and Its Legacy in the Nineteenth-Century Cape Colony.* Eds. Nigel Worden and Clifton Crais. Johannesburg: Witwatersrand UP, 1994. 25-43.
---. *Slavery, Emancipation and Colonial Rule in South Africa.* Scottsville: U of KwaZulu-Natal P, 2007.
Dubey, Madhu. "Neo-Slave Narratives." *A Companion to African American Literature.* Ed. Gene Andrew Jarrett. Malden, MA: Wiley-Blackwell, 2010. 332-46.

Dubois, Laurent. *Avengers of the New World: The Story of the Haitian Revolution.* Cambridge, MA: Harvard UP, 2004.

---. "The Haitian Revolution." *The Caribbean: A History of the Region and Its Peoples.* Eds. Stephan Palmié and Francisco A. Scarano. Chicago: U of Chicago P, 2011. 273-87.

Dunlap, David W. "Dig Unearths Early Black Burial Ground." *New York Times* 9 Oct. 1991. 7 July 2015 http://www.nytimes.com/1991/10/09/nyregion/dig-unearths-early-black-burial-ground.html.

Edwards, Brent Hayes. "The Uses of Diaspora." *Social Text* 19.1 (2001): 45-73.

Egerton, Douglas R. *Death or Liberty: African Americans and Revolutionary America.* New York: Oxford UP, 2009.

Eggen, Dan. "In Williamsburg, the Painful Reality of Slavery." *Washington Post* 7 July 1991: A1.

Eudell, Demetrius L. *The Political Languages of Emancipation in the British Caribbean and the U.S. South.* Chapel Hill: U of North Carolina P, 2002.

Faherty, Duncan "'It's Happened Here': Slavery on the Hudson." *American Quarterly* 58.2 (2006): 455-66.

Fanon, Frantz. *Black Skin, White Masks.* Trans. Richard Philcox. 1952. New York: Grove Press, 2008.

---. *The Wretched of the Earth.* Trans. Constance Farrington. 1961. New York: Grove Press, 1968.

Fitzsimmons, Emma G. "Video Shows Cleveland Officer Shot Boy in 2 Seconds." *New York Times* 26 Nov. 2015. 26 July 2015 http://www.nytimes.com/2014/11/27/us/video-shows-cleveland-officer-shot-tamir-rice-2-seconds-after-pulling-up-next-to-him.html.

Forret, Jeff. "Conflict and the 'Slave Community:' Violence among Slaves in Upcountry South Carolina." *Journal of Southern History* 74.3 (2008): 551-88.

France, Alan W. "Misogyny and Appropriation in Wright's *Native Son.*" *Modern Fiction Studies* 34.3 (1988): 413-23.

Frazer, Elizabeth, and Kimberly Hutchings. "On Politics and Violence: Arendt contra Fanon." *Contemporary Political Theory* 7 (2008): 90-108.

Gable, Eric, Richard Handler and Anna Lawson. "On the Uses of Relativism: Fact, Conjecture, and Black and White Histories at Colonial Williamsburg." *American Ethnologist* 19.4 (1992): 791-805.

Gaines, Kevin K. *American Africans in Ghana: Black Expatriates and the Civil Rights Era.* Chapel Hill: U of North Carolina P, 2006.

Gallego-Durán, Mar. "'Newness Trembles Me'? Representations of White Masculinity in Toni Morrison's *A Mercy.*" *Toni Morrison: Memory and Meaning.* Eds. Adrienne Lanier Seward and Justine Tally. Jackson: UP of Mississippi, 2014. 243-54.

---. "'Nobody Teaches you to Be a Woman': Female Identity, Community and Motherhood in Toni Morrison's *A Mercy.*" *Toni Morrison's A Mercy: Critical*

Approaches. Eds. Shirley A. Stave and Justine Tally. Newcastle upon Tyne: Cambridge Scholars Publishing, 2011. 103-18.

Gamble, Sarah, ed. *The Routledge Companion to Feminism and Postfeminism*. London: Routledge, 2006.

Gara, Larry. "Underground Railroad." *Slavery in the United States: A Social, Political, and Historical Encyclopedia*. Ed. Junius P. Rodriguez. Vol. 1. Santa Barbara, CA: ABC-CLIO, 2007. 487-89.

Gates, Henry Louis, Jr. "Exactly How 'Black' Is Black America? 100 Amazing Facts About the Negro: Find out the Percentage of African Ancestry in Black Americans." *The Root.com* 11 Feb. 2013. 11 Apr. 2014 http://www.theroot.com/articles/history/2013/02/how_mixed_are_african_americans.html.

---. *In Search of Our Roots: How 19 Extraordinary African Americans Reclaimed Their Past*. New York: Crown Publishers, 2009.

---. "Introduction." *The Classic Slave Narratives*. New York: Signet Classics, 2002. 1-14.

---. "Introduction." *Reading Black, Reading Feminist: A Critical Anthology*. New York: Penguin, 1990. 1-17.

Geusteyn, Maria. "The Art of Looking Sideways: Articulating Silence in Yvette Christiansë's *Unconfessed*." *Postamble: A Multidisciplinary Journal of African Studies* 7.1 (2011): 1-8.

Gilroy, Paul. *The Black Atlantic: Modernity and Double Consciousness*. Cambridge: Harvard UP, 1993.

---. "Living Memory: A Meeting with Toni Morrison." *Small Acts: Thoughts on the Politics of Black Cultures*. London: Serpent's Tail, 1993. 175-82.

Glover, Kaiama L. "Womanchild in the Oppressive Land." *New York Times Book Review* 26 Feb. 2009. 20 Feb. 2015 http://www.nytimes.com/2009/03/01/books/review/Glover-t.html.

Greene, Meg. *Henry Louis Gates, Jr.: A Biography*. Santa Barbara, CA: Greenwood, 2012.

Griffin, Farah Jasmine. "A 'Middle Aged Gray Haired Colored Lady' Appears on the Cover of *Newsweek*: Toni Morrison." *A New Literary History of America*. Eds. Greil Marcus and Werner Sollors. Cambridge, MA: Harvard UP, 2009. 993-97.

Grob, Gerald N. *The Deadly Truth: A History of Disease in America*. Cambridge, MA: Harvard UP, 2002.

Grossberg, Lawrence. "On Postmodernism and Articulation: An Interview with Stuart Hall." *Stuart Hall: Critical Dialogues in Cultural Studies*. Eds. David Morley and Kuan-Hsing Chen. London: Routledge, 1996. 131-50.

Hall, Stuart. "Cultural Identity and Diaspora." *Identity: Community, Culture, Difference*. Ed. Jonathan Rutherford. London: Lawrence and Wishart, 1990. 222-37.

---. "Race, Articulation, and Societies Structured in Dominance." 1980. *Black British Cultural Studies: A Reader.* Eds. Houston A. Baker, Jr., Manthia Diawara and Ruth H. Lindeborg. Chicago: U of Chicago P, 1996. 16-60.

Harmon, Amy. "Blacks Pin Hope on DNA to Fill in Slavery's Gaps in Family Trees." *New York Times* 25 July 2005: A1+.

Harris, Leslie M. *In the Shadow of Slavery: African Americans in New York City, 1626-1863.* Chicago: U of Chicago P, 2003.

Hartman, Saidiya, Eva Hoffman and Daniel Mendelsohn. "Memoirs of Return: Saidiya Hartman, Eva Hoffman, and Daniel Mendelsohn in Conversation with Nancy K. Miller." *Rites of Return: Diaspora Poetics and the Politics of Memory.* Eds. Marianne Hirsch and Nancy K. Miller. New York: Columbia UP, 2011. 107-23.

Hartman, Saidiya V., and Frank B. Wilderson III. "The Position of the Unthought." *Qui Parle* 13.2 (2003): 183-201.

Hartman, Saidiya. *Scenes of Subjection: Terror, Slavery, and Self-Making in Nineteenth-Century America.* Oxford: Oxford UP, 1997.

---. "The Time of Slavery." *South Atlantic Quarterly* 4 (2002): 757-77.

---. "Venus in Two Acts." *Small Axe* 12.2 (2008): 1-14.

Hill, Lawrence. "Adaptation: Rewriting *The Book of Negroes* For the Small Screen." *The Walrus* Jan./ Feb. 2015. 21 Jan. 2015 http://thewalrus.ca/adaptation/.

---. *Dear Sir, I Intend to Burn Your Book: An Anatomy of a Book Burning.* Edmonton: U of Alberta P, 2013.

---. "Freedom Bound." *The Beaver* Feb./Mar. 2007. 21 Jan. 2015 http://www.lawrencehill.com/freedom_bound.pdf. 16-23.

---. "A Word about History." *Someone Knows My Name.* New York: Norton, 2007. 471-74.

Hirsch, Marianne, and Nancy K. Miller. "Introduction." *Rites of Return: Diaspora Poetics and the Politics of Memory.* Eds. Hirsch and Miller. New York: Columbia UP, 2011. 1-20.

Hodges, Graham Russell, ed. *The Black Loyalist Directory: African Americans in Exile after the American Revolution.* New York: Garland, 1996.

---. "Historiography of Early Black Life." *Encyclopedia of African American History, 1619-1895: From the Colonial Period to the Age of Frederick Douglass.* Ed. Paul Finkelman. Vol. 2. Oxford: Oxford UP, 2006. 169-74.

Hofmeyr, Isabel. "The Black Atlantic Meets the Indian Ocean: Forging New Paradigms of Transnationalism for the Global South – Literary and Cultural Perspectives." *Social Dynamics* 33.2 (2007): 3-32.

Holsey, Bayo. *Routes of Remembrance: Refashioning the Slave Trade in Ghana.* Chicago: U of Chicago P, 2008.

Hopcroft, Suzanne Marie. "A Heartbreaking History." *Small Axe Literary Salon* 27 Oct. 2010. 19 Nov. 2011 http://smallaxe.net/wordpress3/reviews/2010/10/27/a-heartbreaking-history/.

Horton, James Oliver. "Presenting Slavery: The Perils of Telling America's Racial Story." *The Public Historian* 21.4 (1999): 19-38.

Huggins, Nathan Irvin. *Black Odyssey: The African-American Ordeal in Slavery.* 1977. New York: Vintage, 1990.

Hutcheon, Linda. *A Poetics of Postmodernism: History, Theory and Fiction.* New York: Routledge, 1988.

James, C.L.R. *The Black Jacobins: Toussaint L'Ouverture and the San Domingo Revolution.* Rev. ed. 1963. New York: Vintage, 1989.

James, Marlon. "Violently Wrought: Kaitlyn Greenidge Interviews Marlon James." *Guernica* 3 Nov. 2014. 4 June 2015 https://www.guernicamag.com/interviews/violently-wrought/.

Janofsky, Michael. "Mock Auction of Slaves: Education or Outrage?" *New York Times* 8 Oct. 1994. 17 Apr. 2014 http://www.nytimes.com/1994/10/08/us/mock-auction-of-slaves-education-or-outrage.html.

Jansen, Ena. "Slavery and Its Literary Afterlife in South Africa and on Curaçao." *Shifting the Compass: Pluricontinental Connections in Dutch Colonial and Postcolonial Literature.* Eds. Jeroen Dewulf, Olf Praamstra and Michiel van Kempen. Newcastle: Cambridge Scholars Publishing, 2013. 166-85.

Jobson, Liesl. "Yvette Christiansë." *Poetry International Rotterdam* 1 Dec. 2009. 28 Aug. 2014 http://www.poetryinternationalweb.net/pi/site/poet/item/15564/10/yvette-christianse.

Jordan, Winthrop D. *The White Man's Burden: Historical Origins of Racism in the United States.* Oxford: Oxford UP, 1974.

Kakutani, Michiko. "Jamaica via a Sea of Voices: Marlon James's 'A Brief History of Seven Killings.'" *New York Times* 21 Sept. 2014. 20 Feb. 2015 http://www.nytimes.com/2014/09/22/books/marlon-jamess-a-brief-history-of-seven-killings.html?_r=0.

Keizer, Arlene R. *Black Subjects: Identity Formation in the Contemporary Narrative of Slavery.* Ithaca: Cornell UP, 2004.

Kläger, Florian, and Klaus Stierstorfer. "Introduction." *Diasporic Constructions of Home and Belonging.* Eds. Kläger and Stierstorfer. Berlin: De Gruyter, 2015. 1-7.

Klein, Herbert S., and Ben Vinson III. *African Slavery in Latin America and the Caribbean.* 2nd ed. New York: Oxford UP, 2007.

Krampe, Christian J. "Inserting Trauma into the Canadian Collective Memory: Lawrence Hill's *The Book of Negroes* and Selected African-Canadian Poetry." *Zeitschrift für Kanada-Studien* 29.1 (2009): 62-83.

---. *The Past is Present: The African-Canadian Experience in Lawrence Hill's Fiction.* Frankfurt a.M.: Peter Lang, 2012.

---. "Visualizing Invisibility, Reversing Anonymity: A Case Study in African-Canadian Literature." *Slavery in Art and Literature: Approaches to Trauma, Memory and Visuality.* Eds. Birgit Haehnel and Melanie Ulz. Berlin: Frank & Timme, 2010. 301-40.

Kristeva, Julia. *Strangers to Ourselves.* Trans. Leon S. Roudiez. 1988. New York: Columbia UP, 1991.

La Roche, Cheryl J., and Michael L. Blakey. "Seizing Intellectual Power: The Dialogue at the New York African Burial Ground." *Historical Archaeology* 31.3 (1997): 84-106.

LeClair, Thomas. "The Language Must Not Sweat: A Conversation with Toni Morrison." *Conversations with Toni Morrison.* Ed. Danille Taylor-Guthrie. Jackson: UP of Mississippi, 1994. 119-28.

Lockett, James D. "The Deportation of the Maroons of Trelawny Town to Nova Scotia, then Back to Africa." *Journal of Black Studies* 30.1 (1999): 5-14.

Longhurst, Brian, et al. *Introducing Cultural Studies.* 2nd ed. London: Routledge 2013.

Lowery, Wesley. "Trayvon Martin Was Shot and Killed Three Years Ago Today." *Washington Post* 26 Feb. 2015. 26 July 2015 http://www.washingtonpost.com/news/post-nation/wp/2015/02/26/trayvon-martin-was-shot-and-killed-three-years-ago-today/.

Lugones, María C., and Elizabeth V. Spelman. "Have We Got a Theory for You! Feminist Theory, Cultural Imperialism and the Demand For 'The Woman's Voice.'" *Women's Studies Int. Forum* 6.6 (1983): 573-81.

MacKinnon, Catharine A. *Feminism Unmodified: Discourses on Life and Law.* Cambridge, MA: Harvard UP, 1987.

Martin, Michel. "Toni Morrison on Human Bondage and a Post-Racial Age." *NPR* 26 Dec. 2008. 1 Sept. 2015 http://m.npr.org/story/98679703.

Mayer, Ruth. *Diaspora: Eine kritische Begriffsbestimmung.* Bielefeld: transcript, 2005.

McDowell, Deborah E., ed. *Narrative of the Life of Frederick Douglass, an American Slave.* By Frederick Douglass. 1845. Oxford: Oxford UP, 1999.

McLeod, John. *Beginning Postcolonialism.* 2nd ed. Manchester: Manchester UP, 2000.

Millner, Caille. "A Twenty-Year-Old Slave Named Frederick Bailey Slips Away From His Master in Maryland and Makes His Way to the Free State of New York: The Slave Narrative." *A New Literary History of America.* Eds. Greil Marcus and Werner Sollors. Cambridge, MA: Harvard UP, 2009. 249-53.

Misrahi-Barak, Judith. "Post-*Beloved* Writing: Review, Revitalize, Recalculate." *Black Studies Papers* 1.1 (2014): 37-55.

---, ed. *Revisiting Slave Narratives/ Les avatars contemporains des récits d'esclaves.* Montpellier: Université Montpellier III, 2005.

Mitchell, Angelyn. *The Freedom to Remember: Narrative, Slavery, and Gender in Contemporary Black Women's Fiction*. New Brunswick: Rutgers UP, 2002.

Morgan, Edmund S. *American Slavery, American Freedom: The Ordeal of Colonial Virginia*. New York: Norton, 1975.

Morrison, Toni. "The Site of Memory." *Inventing the Truth: The Art and Craft of Memoir*. Eds. Russell Baker and William Zinsser. 2nd ed. Boston: Houghton Mifflin, 1995. 83-102.

Murray, Jessica. "Gender and Violence in Cape Slave Narratives and Post-Narratives." *South African Historical Journal* 62.3 (2010): 444-62.

Nash, Gary. "Introduction." *The Negro in the American Revolution*. By Benjamin Quarles. 1961. Chapel Hill: U of North Carolina P, 1996. xiii-xxvi.

Nehl, Markus. "Richard Wright, *Native Son* (1940)." *The American Novel of the Twentieth and Twenty-First Centuries*. Ed. Timo Müller. Berlin: De Gruyter, forthcoming.

Neptune, Harvey. "Loving Through Loss: Reading Saidiya Hartman's History of Black Hurt." *Anthurium: A Caribbean Studies Journal* 6.1 (2008): 1-11.

Newman, Judie. "Round Table: Review of Saidiya Hartman, *Lose Your Mother: A Journey along the Atlantic Slave Route*." *Journal of American Studies* 44.1 (2010): 1-2.

Osagie, Iyunolu F. *The Amistad Revolt: Memory, Slavery and the Politics of Identity in the United States and Sierra Leone*. Athens, GA: U of Georgia P, 2000.

Paton, Diana. "Tacky's Rebellion (1760-1761)." *The Historical Encyclopedia of World Slavery*. Ed. Junius P. Rodriguez. Vol. 2. Santa Barbara, CA: ABC-CLIO, 1997. 625.

Patterson, Orlando. *Slavery and Social Death: A Comparative Study*. Cambridge, MA: Harvard UP, 1982.

Patterson, Tiffany Ruby, and Robin D. G. Kelley. "Unfinished Migrations: Reflections on the African Diaspora and the Making of the Modern World." *African Studies Review* 43.1 (2000): 11-45.

Polgreen, Lydia. "Ghana's Uneasy Embrace of Slavery's Diaspora." *New York Times* 22 Dec. 2005: A1+.

Pride, Felicia "What Does It Take? An Interview with Marlon James (2006)." *To Create: Black Writers, Filmmakers, Storytellers, Artists, and Media-Makers Riff on Art, Careers, Life, and the Beautiful Mess in Between*. Chicago: Agathe Publishing, 2012. E-book.

Quarles, Benjamin. *The Negro in the American Revolution*. 1961. Chapel Hill: U of North Carolina P, 1996.

Rankine, Claudia. "The Condition of Black Life Is One of Mourning." *New York Times Magazine* 22 June 2015. 26 July 2015 http://www.nytimes.com/2015/06/22/magazine/the-condition-of-black-life-is-one-of-mourning.html.

Remnick, David. "Charleston and the Age of Obama." *New Yorker* 19 June 2015. 26 July 2015 http://www.newyorker.com/news/daily-comment/charleston-and-the-age-of-obama.
Rice, James D. "Obeah." *The Historical Encyclopedia of World Slavery*. Ed. Junius P. Rodriguez. Vol. 2. Santa Barbara, CA: ABC-CLIO, 1997. 477.
Rodriguez, Junius P. "Jamaica Rebellion (1831-1832)." *Encyclopedia of Emancipation and Abolition in the Transatlantic World*. Ed. Rodriguez. Vol. 2. 2007. New York: Routledge, 2015. 314-15.
---. "Tacky's Rebellion (1760-1761)." *Encyclopedia of Slave Resistance and Rebellion*. Ed. Rodriguez. Vol 2. Westport, CT: Greenwood, 2007. 497-98.
---. "Trelawney Town Maroons." *Encyclopedia of Slave Resistance and Rebellion*. Ed. Rodriguez. Vol. 2. Westport, CT: Greenwood, 2007. 517-18.
Roman, Luke, and Monica Roman. *Encyclopedia of Greek and Roman Mythology*. New York: Facts on File, 2010.
Rosenblatt, Paul C. "Reading Novels as a Social Science Researcher." *The Impact of Racism on African American Families: Literature as Social Science*. Surrey: Ashgate, 2014. 11-26.
Rushdy, Ashraf H. A. *Neo-Slave Narratives: Studies in the Social Logic of a Literary Form*. New York: Oxford UP, 1999.
---. "The Neo-Slave Narrative." *The Cambridge Companion to the African American Novel*. Ed. Maryemma Graham. Cambridge: Cambridge UP, 2004. 87-104.
Safran, William. "Diasporas in Modern Societies: Myths of Homeland and Return." *Diaspora: A Journal of Transnational Studies* 1 (1991): 83-99.
Sagawa, Jessie. "Projecting History Honestly: An Interview with Lawrence Hill." *Studies in Canadian Literature* 33.1 (2008): 307-22.
Samuelson, Meg. "'Lose Your Mother: Kill Your Child': The Passage of Slavery and Its Afterlife in Narratives by Yvette Christiansë and Saidiya Hartman." *English Studies in Africa* 51.2 (2008): 38-48.
Saunders, Nicholas J. *The Peoples of the Caribbean: An Encyclopedia of Caribbean Archeology and Traditional Culture*. Santa Barbara, CA: ABC-CLIO, 2005.
Saunders, Patricia J. "Fugitive Dreams of Diaspora: Conversations with Saidiya Hartman." *Anthurium: A Caribbean Studies Journal* 6.1 (2008): 1-16.
Scarano, Francisco A. "Slavery and Emancipation in Caribbean History." *General History of the Caribbean: Methodology and Historiography of the Caribbean*. Ed. B. W. Higman. Vol. VI. London: Unesco Publishing, 1999. 233-82.
Schama, Simon. *Rough Crossings: Britain, The Slaves and the American Revolution*. London: BBC Books, 2005.
Schreiber, Evelyn Jaffe. "Personal and Cultural Memory in *A Mercy*." *Toni Morrison: Memory and Meaning*. Eds. Adrienne Lanier Seward and Justine Tally. Jackson: UP of Mississippi, 2014. 80-92.

Sexton, Jared. "'The Curtain of the Sky': An Introduction." *Critical Sociology* 36.1 (2010): 11-24.

---. "The Social Life of Social Death: On Afro-Pessimism and Black Optimism." *InTensions* 5 (2011): 1-47.

Shell, Robert C.-H. *Children of Bondage: A Social History of the Slave Society at the Cape of Good Hope, 1652-1838*. Hanover, NH: Wesleyan UP, 1994.

Shepperson, George. "African Diaspora: Concept and Context." *Global Dimensions of the African* Diaspora. Ed. Joseph E. Harris. 2nd ed. Washington, D.C.: Howard UP, 1993. 41-49.

Sheridan, Richard B. *Sugar and Slavery: An Economic History of the British West Indies*. 1974. Kingston: Canoe Press, 2010.

Shipp, E.R. "Black Cemetery Yields Wealth of History." *New York Times* 9 Aug. 1992. 7 July 2015 http://www.nytimes.com/1992/08/09/nyregion/black-cemetery-yields-wealth-of-history.html.

Siemerling, Winfried. *The Black Atlantic Reconsidered: Black Canadian Writing, Cultural History, and the Presence of the Past*. Montreal: McGill-Queen's UP, 2015.

Spickard, Paul. *Almost All Aliens: Immigration, Race, and Colonialism in American History and Identity*. New York: Routledge, 2007.

Spillers, Hortense J. "Mama's Baby, Papa's Maybe: An American Grammar Book." *Diacritics* 17.2 (1987): 64-81.

Spillers, Hortense, Saidiya Hartman, Farah Jasmine Griffin, Shelly Eversley and Jennifer L. Morgan. "'Watcha Gonna Do?'—Revisiting 'Mama's Baby, Papa's Maybe: An American Grammar Book.'" *Women's Studies Quarterly* 35.1/2 (2007): 299-309.

Spivak, Gayatri Chakravorty. "Can the Subaltern Speak?" *Marxism and the Interpretation of Culture*. Eds. Cary Nelson and Lawrence Grossberg. Urbana: U of Illinois P, 1988. 271-313.

Staples, Brent. "A Convenient Amnesia About Slavery." *New York Times* 15 Dec. 2005. 7 July 2015 http://www.nytimes.com/2005/12/15/opinion/a-convenient-amnesia-about-slavery.html.

Stead, Margaret. "A Better Connection." *Guardian* 29 Oct. 2005. 28 Aug. 2014 http://www.theguardian.com/books/2005/oct/29/featuresreviews.guardianreview27.

Stein, Mark. *Black British Literature: Novels of Transformation*. Columbus: Ohio State UP, 2004.

Straight, Susan. "'The Book of Night Women' by Marlon James." *Los Angeles Times* 8 Mar. 2009. 20 Feb. 2015 http://articles.latimes.com/2009/mar/08/entertainment/ca-marlon-james8.

Taber, Jane. "How *The Book of Negroes*, a Profound Yet Unknown Canadian Story, Became a Miniseries." *Globe and Mail* 2 Jan. 2015. 21 Jan. 2015 http://

www.theglobeandmail.com/arts/television/an-unknown-canadian-story-brings-book-of-negros-to-tv/article22275312/.
Tepper, Anderson. "The Book of Night Women." *Time Out* 25 Feb. 2009. 4 June 2015 http://www.timeout.com/newyork/books/the-book-of-night-women.
Tölölyan, Khachig. "The Contemporary Discourse of Diaspora Studies." *Comparative Studies of South Asia, Africa and the Middle East* 27.3 (2007): 647-55.
---. "Rethinking Diaspora(s): Stateless Power in the Transnational Moment." *Diaspora: A Journal of Transnational Studies* 5.1 (1996): 3-36.
Vasconcellos, Colleen A. "Abolition in Jamaica." *Encyclopedia of Emancipation and Abolition in the Transatlantic World.* Ed. Junius P. Rodriguez. Vol. 2. 2007. New York: Routledge, 2015. 310-12.
---. "Emancipation in Jamaica." *Encyclopedia of Emancipation and Abolition in the Transatlantic World.* Ed. Junius P. Rodriguez. Vol. 2. 2007. New York: Routledge, 2015. 312-14.
Vásquez, Sam. "Violent Liaisons: Historical Crossings and the Negotiation of Sex, Sexuality, and Race in *The Book of Night Women* and *The True History of Paradise.*" *small axe* 16.2 (2012): 43-59.
Ward, Kerry, and Nigel Worden. "Commemorating, Suppressing, and Invoking Cape Slavery." *Negotiating the Past: The Making of Memory in South Africa.* Eds. Sarah Nuttall and Carli Coetzee. 2nd ed. Oxford: Oxford UP, 1999. 201-17.
Wardi, Anissa. "The Politics of 'Home' in *A Mercy.*" *Toni Morrison's A Mercy: Critical Approaches.* Eds. Shirley A. Stave and Justine Tally. Newcastle upon Tyne: Cambridge Scholars Publishing, 2011. 23-41.
Warren, Crystal. "South Africa: Introduction." *The Journal of Commonwealth Literature* 41.4 (2006): 181-214.
Weheliye, Alexander G. "Pornotropes." *Journal of Visual Culture* 7.1 (2008): 65-81.
Weier, Sebastian. "Forum: Consider Afro-Pessimism." *Amerikastudien/American Studies* 59.3 (2014): 419-33.
Welter, Barbara. "The Cult of True Womanhood: 1820-1860." *Locating American Studies: The Evolution of a Discipline.* Ed. Lucy Maddox. Baltimore: John Hopkins UP, 1999. 43-66.
Wenzel, Marita. "Crossing Spatial and Temporal Boundaries: Three Women in Search of a Future." *Literator* 21.3 (2000): 23-36.
White, Hayden. "The Historical Text as Literary Artifact." *The Northern Anthology of Theory and Criticism.* Ed. Vincent B. Leitch. 1978. New York: Norton, 2001. 1709-729.
Wilderson III, Frank B. *Red, White & Black: Cinema and the Structure of U.S. Antagonisms.* Durham: Duke UP, 2010.
Williams, Patricia J. "Emotional Truth." *The Nation* 16 Feb. 2006. 23 Sept. 2014 http://www.thenation.com/article/emotional-truth.

Winks, Robin W. *The Blacks in Canada: A History*. 2nd. Ed. Montreal: McGill-Queen's UP, 1997.

Wood, Marcus. "Round Table: Review of Saidiya Hartman, *Lose Your Mother: A Journey along the Atlantic Slave Route*." *Journal of American Studies* 44.1 (2010): 6-11.

Worden, Nigel, and Clifton Crais. "Introduction." *Breaking the Chains: Slavery and Its Legacy in the Nineteenth-Century Cape Colony*. Eds. Worden and Crais. Johannesburg: Witwatersrand UP, 1994. 1-23.

Worden, Nigel. *Slavery in Dutch South Africa*. 1985. Cambridge: Cambridge UP, 2010.

Wright, Michelle M. *Becoming Black: Creating Identity in the African Diaspora*. Durham: Duke UP, 2004.

Yancy, George. "Lost in Rawlsland: Interview with Charles Mills." *New York Times* 16 Nov. 2014. 26 July 2015 http://opinionator.blogs.nytimes.com/2014/11/16/lost-in-rawlsland/.

Zachary, G. Pascal. "Valiant Battle to Reconstruct Ties to Africa." *San Francisco Chronicle Book Review* 28 Jan. 2007: M1+.

Zeleza, Paul Tiyambe. "Rewriting the African Diaspora: Beyond the Black Atlantic." *African Affairs* 104.414 (2005): 35-68.

Zimmermann, Jutta. "From Roots to Routes: The Dialogic Relation between Alex Haley's *Roots* (1976) and Lawrence Hill's *The Book of Negroes* (2007)." *Cultural Circulation: Dialogues between Canada and the American South*. Eds. Waldemar Zacharasiewicz and Christoph Irmscher. Wien: Verlag der Österreichischen Akademie der Wissenschaften, 2013. 119-34.